The Construction of
Irish Identity in
American Literature

Routledge Transnational Perspectives on American Literature

EDITED BY SUSAN CASTILLO, *King's College London*

The Construction of Irish Identity in American Literature

Christopher Dowd

Routledge
Taylor & Francis Group
New York London

First published 2011
by Routledge
270 Madison Avenue, New York, NY 10016

Simultaneously published in the UK
by Routledge
2 Park Square, Milton Park, Abingdon, Oxon OX14 4RN

Routledge is an imprint of the Taylor & Francis Group, an informa business

© 2011 Taylor & Francis

Typeset in Sabon by IBT Global.
Printed and bound in the United States of America on acid-free paper by IBT Global.

Library of Congress Cataloging-in-Publication Data
Dowd, Christopher, 1975–
    The construction of Irish identity in American literature / by Christopher Dowd.
        p. cm. — (Routledge transnational perspectives on American literature ; v. 13)
    Includes bibliographical references and index.
    1. American literature—History and criticism.   2. Irish Americans in literature.
3. Irish in literature.   4. Irish Americans—Ethnic identity.   5. Irish—Ethnic identity.
I. Title.
    PS173.I75D68 2010
    810.9'35299162

ISBN13: 978-0-415-88043-5 (hbk)
ISBN13: 978-0-203-84196-9 (ebk)

for Adrienne

Contents

Figures

Preface

I was drawn to this project by the gaps I perceived in the current scholarship. While studying the work of American literature scholars, I often noticed a glossing over of Irish ethnicity in discussions of texts with significant Irish characters. Critics would misinterpret or misunderstand the Irish dimensions of the character, sometimes even asserting claims that were factually wrong about Irish Americans. It was obvious to me that taking these works out of an Irish context had often led to bizarre distortions of meaning, as has been the case with interpretations of Huckleberry Finn that cast him as a symbol of Anglo-Protestant normativity. I believed that bringing the insights of Irish Studies to bear on these texts could explain away some of the confusions and cast new light on old topics.

That is not to say that there are not gaps in Irish-American scholarship as well. Though scholars in this field have done an excellent job analyzing the work of American writers of Irish heritage, there has not been nearly enough work that studies the ways in which non-Irish writers influenced, and were influenced by, Irish-American literary production and the ways they participated in the shaping of Irish-American identity. I believed that Irish-American studies could benefit from examining the links between Irish-American texts and the broader canon, and I was interested to see how these linkages might impact conversations about race, ethnicity, and nationalism taking place in other fields of interest.

My goal has been to write a book that falls somewhere in the gap between American and Irish-American scholarship. Although there is some obvious overlap in subject matter between these two areas, they are too often studied in isolation from each other. There has not been as much scholarly interplay between them as there ought to be, and I hope that this book might contribute to resolving that issue.

As colleagues read early drafts of this project, it became clear that writing for these two different scholarly audiences required appealing to readers with different critical contexts. Without a doubt, readers with backgrounds in Irish-American studies will be familiar with writers like Dion Boucicault and James T. Farrell; however, to readers outside the field, these authors might seem more obscure. Similarly, the critical controversy surrounding T. S. Eliot's racism has been thoroughly debated by critics of American modernism, but might be less familiar to those specializing in Irish-American studies. I have endeavored to make each section of this book accessible to readers no matter what their context might be.

For this project, I have focused on nine authors whose Irish characters seemed to revise popular conceptions of Irish identity in America. The selections I have made are by no means exhaustive, and at certain points I considered several alternate choices (which I hope to revisit in the future). What drew me to specific texts were the characters, not the authors. I wanted to explore several variations on Irish identity, and more often than not, I chose a particular text because the characters offered a way to examine some aspect of that identity that I had not yet considered. Sometimes this methodology afforded me the opportunity to revisit favorite works, but other times it took me into areas I never expected to study in depth. It was a joy to read and write about Mark Twain, but I had never been significantly interested in Margaret Mitchell's work until I began writing this book. Yet, both Huckleberry Finn and Scarlet O'Hara offer unique opportunities for studying the way literature participated in the construction of ethnic identity.

Out of necessity, the scope of this study is limited to the period of massive Irish immigration to the U.S. that began with the arrival of the Famine generation in the mid-nineteenth century and ended around the time of the Great Depression. Yet, there is still much work to be done in understanding Irish-American identity prior to this period and afterwards. In addition, I have limited my focus to Irish Catholic identity and have not addressed in any detail the importance of Scots-Irish characters in American literature. These areas will undoubtedly be fruitful subjects for future research.

Acknowledgments

Mary Burke provided substantial guidance and feedback during the years it took to write this book. She was my first and often most critical reader, and every page of this book is the better for her input. Her friendship and enthusiasm contributed substantially to the enjoyment I had in pursuing this project, for which I thank her.

Clare Eby, Brenda Murphy, Tom Shea, and Donna Hollenberg also read my manuscript and provided valuable feedback. I am also grateful to Greg Semenza, Jerry Phillips, and Liz Hart. They were all supportive of my work and helped shape the methodology and discipline with which I approached this project.

I received financial support for the writing of this book from the Timothy F. Moriarty Irish Literature Fund, the University of Connecticut College of Liberal Arts & Sciences, the University of Connecticut Department of English Graduate Program, and the Missouri Southern State University Faculty Research Fund.

For their research assistance, I would like to thank the Homer Babbidge Library (especially Richard Bleiler); the George A. Spiva Library; the University of South Florida Libraries Special Collection; Special Collections, Templeman Library at the University of Kent, Caterbury (http://library.kent.ac.uk/library/special/html/specoll/theatre.htm); and Spencer Scott, Photographic Unit, Templeman Library.

I am in debt to the colleagues, friends, and students who (whether they know it or not) helped me to stay focused and inspired me to write.

There were several moments where my research for this book overlapped with family history, and I have been grateful for the opportunity to know my family better. I would like to thank my family, especially my parents, Bob and Gail Dowd, for their continued support.

Finally, I wish to thank my wife Adrienne, whose impact upon this project is immeasurable.

Introduction

The Irish are a persistent presence in American literature during the period that stretches from the mid-nineteenth century to the mid-twentieth century. They crowd together below decks in Melville and climb the ship's rigging in Cooper; they promote temperance in Whitman, but drink themselves to death in Twain; in James they build shanties along New York's East River and in Crane they work the streets and run frontier hotels; they are among the Southerners in Faulkner, as well as the pioneers in Cather; they entertain high-society crowds in Wharton and privately pray for forgiveness in O'Connor; they go to war in Fitzgerald and plot murder in Eliot; in Steinbeck they lose their fortunes and in O'Neill they lose their sanity. Occasionally, the Irish feature prominently in these works; often, they lurk in the background. Yet, if we are to believe some of the more cursory literary histories, it would appear that, despite this abundance, Irish Americans only exist as two types of character: the lace-curtain social climber and the romantic street tough. This is gross oversimplification. There is more to the Irish in American literature than a mere collection of Teagues and Paddys.

The history of Irish characters in American literature involves much more than a simple parade of stereotypes, and in fact, it complicates the very concept of ethnic stereotype. Though many writers resorted to exploiting the clichés of the drunk thug, the corrupt politician, and the blarney-spouting policeman, there also is a significant heritage of Irish-American characterization that problematizes, defies, or re-appropriates the stereotype for new, often subversive, ends. In order to fully appreciate the dimensions of Irish identity in American literature, we must consider the characters with complex, even problematic, claims to that identity. It is not enough to look for simple patterns that confirm supposed ethnic truisms (either positive or negative); rather, we need to explore the discrepancies within, and the liminality of, Irishness during this pivotal period in U.S. history. Irishness is not and never has been a stable cultural concept in America, despite the supposedly essential and timeless implications of the ethnic stereotype. By studying the literary representations of Irish-American characters, we can witness just how dynamic and responsive Irishness has been to its shifting political and cultural contexts.

The following four chapters put forth an argument for reconsidering the presence of the Irish in the American literary imagination. I hope to lay out a model that will open up scholarly exploration of material that is far more dynamic, diverse, and integral to our understanding of our nation's literature than has been previously thought. I want to revisit familiar territory to uncover the oft overlooked imprint left behind by Irish-American characters, as well as explore new ground where the literary imaginings of ethnic others shifted popular consciousness. By illuminating the imaginative uses that writers found for the Irish-American character, I intend to trace an ethnic narrative from its inception through its maturation and show how it became the prime model for nearly all subsequent ethnic narratives in the U.S.

I am interested in the way that writers of various backgrounds and heritages used Irish-American characters as metaphoric figurations of persistent national anxieties in order to ignite debate on the most immediate social, cultural, political, and religious issues of the day. Often, literary representations of civility, faith, whiteness, patriotism, purity, personal success, family unity, economic prosperity, and moral righteousness all depended on the presence of an Irish-American character who embodied none of these qualities. This character came equipped with ready-made popular associations that made it the ideal shorthand for representations of the unwanted, the outcast, and the vulgar.

During the nineteenth and twentieth centuries, American writers developed a habit of talking about social and cultural deviancy through the metaphorical presence of the Irish. By casting the Irish-American character as perpetually unfit, writers developed a literary device for contemplating destabilizing urges within society and centrifugal pressures toward chaos and savagery. The Irish-American character offered a unique way to personify a whole host of public fears in the body of one person. Through literary constructions of Irishness, writers could discuss political corruption, theories of criminality, threats to public health, challenges to social welfare, the issue of temperance, labor unrest, and the decline of domestic manners and morality. Writers engendered in the character a subtle, but substantial, threat. The Irish existed at the threshold of American identity, and the antidote to this threat required the shoring up of the national identity along ethnic boundaries.

Irishness became a literary figuration of something at once familiar, but at the same time foreign; it became a symbol of essential difference. Ralph Ellison started a line of analysis in 1970 that scholars of African-American literature continue to develop.[1] Ellison wrote that white American authors often "seize upon the presence of black Americans and use them as a marker, a symbol of limits, a metaphor for the 'outsider'" ("What America"). A similar phenomenon can be seen in literature that makes use of an Irish-American presence, with one significant difference. The Irish-American character was never imagined to be the opposite of the white ideal the way the African-American character was; Irishness was not a "shadow" of white Americanness. Instead, the Irish-American character was imagined as a deviation or perversion of the Anglo-American, made all the more monstrous and threatening by its similarities to the mainstream population. It helped define the limits of the American community, not by counterpoint, but by nuance. The Irish-American character showed exactly where an individual crossed the line from white normativity into deviant otherness, from the status of insider into the realm of the outsider. More so than any other ethnic identity in America, the Irish were monstrous doppelgangers for the dominant Anglo-Saxon population because they could almost pass as mainstream Americans despite what was believed to be their fundamental deficiencies.

My project emerges from a need to make literary Irishness less invisible and a desire to understand how it became invisible in the first place. The following pages seek to explain where the Irish-American character came from, how it developed in the nineteenth century, what it became in the twentieth century, and why it remains, even now in the twenty-first century, a profound signifying presence in our popular imaginings.

Literary accounts of the arrival and integration of the Irish into American culture comprise a quintessentially American narrative. These are stories about how ethnic outsiders become cultural insiders. They are stories of transformation in which immigrant loyalty, communal allegiance, poverty, and ethnic bias are not obstacles to success, but rather tools for Americanization. An understanding of the Irish-American character in literature is important because it reveals an evolving understanding of the nature of ethnic identity in an increasingly modern and nationalist American context.

Stories about the Irish in America exemplify some of the earliest and most substantial discussions about ethnic immigrant identity in American culture. Being the first and largest ethnic community to migrate to the U.S. during the immigration boom that began in the nineteenth century, the Irish became touchstones against which the success and failure of future immigrant groups were measured, and similarly, Irish-American stories came to serve as templates for other ethnic narratives. Irish-American writers pioneered methods of ethnic self-representation and stereotype subversion; they learned to write simultaneously for sympathetic and hostile readers; they established rhetorical strategies to subvert social and political expectations; they found ways to criticize their community without undermining it; they demonstrated how to use ethnic identity as an organizing principle for a novel or play; and perhaps most importantly, they revealed how ethnic material could be both artistically and commercially appealing to a broad segment of the population. One of the interesting things about these stories is just how familiar they have become due to their influence on generations of immigrant writing and public discourse about ethnic others. It is hard not to see connections between early Irish-American writers and contemporary Asian-American and Latino-American authors, for instance; or to not recognize very familiar rhetoric in recent debates about illegal immigration, including accusations of biological and socio-logical contamination almost identical to nativist attacks on the Irish over a century ago.

In contemporary American society, Irishness has been largely absorbed into a homogenous white culture, so much so that many Irish Americans would be surprised at the degree to which their ethnicity would have served as a badge of difference a century ago. For many, it is hard to imagine that the Irish were once considered non-white and a threat to the nation's security, health, and economy. Similarly, Irishness has become a largely invisible ethnicity to many modern literary critics due to the almost complete assimilation of the Irish into mainstream American culture in the twentieth century. Too many critics simply do not see Irishness or do not think it relevant. As a result, many Irish-American characters have been de-ethnicized in the critical literature of the past century. Yet, when read within the contexts of their era and conditions of creation, the Irishness of many of these characters emerges as an integral part of the story. Acknowledging the Irishness of such quintessentially American characters as Huckleberry Finn and Scarlett O'Hara challenges some long-held presuppositions and allows for a deeper understanding of the literature and the culture that produced it. I hope to show that such a project is possible and necessary.

This study is not a history of Irish Americans, nor is it a description of the realities of their lives. Instead, I offer an exploration of the dynamic ways in which Irishness was popularly conceived in an American context and show how imagined ethnicity had a direct and immediate impact on the American nation. The process of ethnic identification was—and continues to be—a fundamental aspect of American identity. Examining how writers popularly constructed Irish-American ethnicity through literature reveals the mechanisms by which ethnic groups impact the formation of national communities.

Previous critical work on Irish-American literature has generally fallen into two categories: taxonomies of Irishness or histories of Irish-American writers. I believe the former approach to be minimally useful and even in some cases significantly flawed. Too often these studies function like bird-spotting guides, offering us the opportunity to go out into American literature and identify the various types of Irishmen, but not providing any real understanding of the significance of these types or how they function in a broader cultural context. At best, the taxonomical approach offers some rudimentary framework for understanding ethnic categories, but too often it makes claims to "authentic" ethnicity, which actually reinforces the basis of racial and ethnic stereotyping. The latter approach, which focuses on the lives and works of Irish-American writers, is important, but only provides half of the picture. These studies only show how the Irish perceived themselves, not how others perceived them. To understand the construction of Irish identity in America, we need to consider a broader sampling of authors which includes those who have no Irish heritage.

The most significant study of Irish-American literature remains Charles Fanning's *The Irish Voice in America: 250 Years of Irish-American Fiction* (1990). Fanning's study is by far the most comprehensive and wide-ranging, and is notable for renewing interest in writers like Finley Peter Dunne and James T. Farrell. In his work, Fanning establishes a framework for understanding and appreciating Irish-American fiction in its historical context and marks out those texts that defined certain eras of cultural change. Several literary studies of the past decade have built on Fanning's work, including Ron Ebest's *Private Histories: The Writing of Irish Americans, 1900–1935* (2005), Margaret Hallissy's *Reading Irish-American Fiction: The Hyphenated Self* (2006), and Daniel J. Casey and Robert E. Rhodes' "The Tradition of Irish-American Writers" (2007).

Fanning's work emphasizes what makes Irish-American fiction "uniquely American literature" (1). As he focuses on writers from the eighteenth, nineteenth, and twentieth centuries, he repeatedly shows how issues of alienation and assimilation provided these writers with their subject matter. Irish-American fiction has been fiction about a transplanted people, a struggling minority, an enduring ethnic population, and an assimilative success. In this sense, it has been quintessentially American and predictive of other ethnic literatures. In the following chapters, I extend Fanning's line of inquiry by considering the uniquely American aspects of the Irish-American story as told by a lineage of writers that includes numerous non-Irish writers in addition to well-known Irish-American authors.

Fanning states at the outset of his study that he is only interested in "Irish-American prose fiction" and that Irish-American poetry and drama fall outside the scope of his study (1). Irish-American poetry remains relatively understudied, though Irish-American drama has attracted considerable scholarly interest. John P. Harrington, author of the foundational text *The Irish Play on the New York Stage, 1874–1966* (1997), has edited the most important recent collection on the Irish theatrical diaspora, *Irish Theater in America* (2009). In his introduction, Harrington suggests that the complexity of studying Irish-American drama emerges from "the tension created by performing it—Irishness—before an audience in part identified with Ireland and in part unrelated or actively hostile to it" (xvi). Harrington's comment here seems relevant far beyond the scope of just theatrical work and succinctly points to what I perceive as the dynamic through which Irish identity was constructed in public discourse. Irishness was often just as much a performance off the stage as it was on the stage, and it was constructed in the tension between self-identified Irish Americans and a non-Irish population who frequently displayed hostility to all things Irish. Harrington's studies of Irish drama focus on the theatrical event and the performance, not just on the text written by the Irish-American playwright. As such, his work acknowledges that the (often non-Irish) audience participated in the way Irishness was constructed on the stage. I have attempted to approach the texts discussed in this book (drama, prose, and poetry) in a similar manner. By focusing on the construction and performance of Irish identity and not just on the issues surrounding Irish-American authorship, I try to examine Irishness as a topic emerging from multiple American contexts and across several genres.

This is not a study of Irish-American literature, per se, but rather a study of Irish Americans in literature. Whereas Fanning set out to understand "the fictional self-image of the American Irish," I seek to understand that self-image in relation to the image of Irishness held by others (4). Ethnic group identities are never constructed entirely from within, but always in interaction with other groups. The boundary that defines Irish-American identity has been built by Irish-American writers such as Dion Boucicault, Ned Harrigan, F. Scott Fitzgerald, James T. Farrell, and Margaret Mitchell, as well as by non-Irish writers like Mark Twain, Harold Frederic, Frank Norris, and T. S. Eliot. This study will show how Irish-American identity was produced and perceived across a large segment of American literature by looking at both texts that rarely have been considered in an Irish context before and texts with more obvious Irish-American origins. By placing such works side-by-side, I hope to show the ways in which literature participated in the imagining of an Irish community in America and helped construct an ethnic boundary that redefined the country.

AMERICAN NATIONALISM AND THE IRISH IMMIGRANT

The literary works considered in this study were written during a period in which nationalism obsessed the public. From the end of the Civil War through the turn of the century, America underwent a radical shift in national identity unlike any other period in its history and was host to turbulent public debate regarding the fundamental ideologies and essential qualities of being American. Individuals were no longer sure what united them as a national community or what qualified someone to be an authentic patriot during such an era in which American nationalism displayed mutable, even contradictory, properties. Several significant historic developments led to this anxiety regarding American nationalism, the most important being the Civil War and its fallout.

The Civil War had established a relatively new concept for America: national unity was more important than local loyalties. During the Reconstruction, the government emphasized political, social, and economic cooperation as a tonic to overcome sectional animosity. The passing of the Fourteenth Amendment, which granted due process and equal protection to former slaves, radically changed the concept of American identity by legally eliminating race as a criterion for citizenship. Despite this, race still figured prominently in actual public perceptions of American identity. In

Reforging the White Republic (2005), historian Edward J. Blum argues that Reconstruction was a period more about reconciliation between white Protestants of the North and South than it was about true civic equality, and that nationalism reflected this racial and religious bias. The Civil War and ensuing era of Reconstruction did not truly usher in a new kind of multi-racial/multi-ethnic America, but instead inspired a large segment of the population to equate American nationalism with white Protestantism, a fact that would prove problematic for the Catholic Irish immigrant.

In addition to the Civil War and its aftermath, industrialization proved to be a major factor in the development of American nationalism. The technological transformation of the country broke down outmoded agrarian loyalties and replaced them with new centralized social forms. Workers migrated from rural farms to factory cities, and for the first time, many found themselves living and working within a more diverse population. The proximity of city life and the division of labor created new modes of economic interdependence. Industrial society makes it harder for individuals to ascribe to local loyalties because so much of their lives and livelihoods come to depend on non-local forces. Suddenly the slaughterhouse worker in Chicago depends more on his affiliation and cooperation with the Oklahoman rancher or the New York grocer than he does on his interactions with actual neighbors in Chicago.

The third major element impacting American nationalism at this time was the rise of American imperialism at the turn of the century. The Spanish-American War of 1898 marked the beginning of the U.S.'s imperial projects. To pursue such projects, the country needed to consolidate its sense of national purpose and identity so that it could position itself as a unique and credible global power. America could not go to war as a conglomeration of loosely affiliated communities, but only as a united, centralized nation. In times of war, nationalism tends to be reinforced by the available public media, which at the turn of the century was the newspaper press and popular literature.

In addition, as Walter Benn Michaels argues, it was during this period that American citizens came to believe that an American national identity was something inherited, not something acquired (*Our America* 8). This, in effect, blurred ethnicity and nationality to such a degree that immigrants could not be considered as truly American as those born in the U.S. (even though the native-born population were themselves descendants of immigrants). The acquisition of legal recognition from a state agency did not immediately entitle an immigrant to enter into the American community, as exemplified by the often violent opposition of nativist groups to immigrants (including the Irish) in New York and other East Coast cities in the late nineteenth and early twentieth century.

Racism, classism, and religious discrimination took on a particular kind of national character during the period this study covers. Interestingly, this confluence of anxieties regarding American nationalism coincides with the mass arrival of Irish immigrants to the U.S. At the moment that Americans were struggling to redefine their identity, they were forced to find some way to deal with a growing ethnic group that seemed incompatible with many perceived American principles, but were, perversely, also uniquely compatible with "essential" American characteristics (i.e., nominally white-skinned, English-speaking). Could the Irish ever be American?

During the Famine years (1845–1855), nearly 1.5 million Irish immigrated to the U.S. (K. Miller 291). In the years following the Famine (1846–1921), another 3 million Irish followed. By 1900, there were more Irish living in the U.S. than in Ireland (K. Miller 346). This spike in immigration startled many Americans, some of whom felt the arrival of the Irish was akin to invasion. They had never seen such a disadvantaged and impoverished immigrant group before and were frightened by the potential threat to already unstable American social integrity. Just as America was trying to reformulate its national identity, this new group of immigrants arrived and complicated that goal, putting stress on an already fragile national framework.

Nativist fear led to widespread anti-Irish prejudice and an increase in ethnocentrism. L. Perry Curtis states, "Ethnocentric thinking flourishes in a climate of anxiety, fear, and guilt as these emotions permeate both the individual and the class or group to which he belongs, and it is reinforced by the delusion that the values or physical proximity of the out-group somehow pose a direct threat to his own way of life" (*Anglo-Saxons* 7). These fears were agitated by the Irishman's ability to pass as Anglo-American, since, unlike many other immigrants, he arrived with a knowledge of the English language and also was not visually marked by otherness in the manner of a person of color. Though American identity was still in a formative stage, it seemed inherently at odds with Irish ethnicity. In fact, the Irish became the default out-group, the foil for that identity, representing qualities that were distinctly un-American. Their loyalties to their community, their heritage, and their church became signs of their lack of loyalty to their adopted country. Their support of Irish Republican causes was seen as a rejection of American nationalism. For nativists seeking to protect the interests of native-born peoples from immigrants, the Irish were more than an obstacle to the perceived formation of a national community, they were an immediate and legitimate threat.

Ernest Gellner famously argues that "nationalism is *not* the awakening of an old, latent, dormant force," though that is how it usually presents itself; rather, it is the invention of a nation where it did not previously exist (48). American nationalism presents itself as essential, authentic, and everlasting. Yet, in reality, American nationalism is an invention of the mind—it is an imagined concept—and as such, the real threat of the Irish was that they were a challenge to the American imagination. Many Americans simply could not conceive of a nation in which such poor, dirty, and unusual people could be included. They were incapable of envisaging themselves and the Irish as belonging to the same group. The Irish were too different, and there were limits to the public's imaginative capacities.

IMAGINED ETHNIC COMMUNITIES

In the landmark study *Imagined Communities* (1983), Benedict Anderson proposes a definition of the nation as an "imagined political community":

> It is *imagined* because the members of even the smallest nations will never know most of their fellow-members, meet them, or even hear of them, yet in the minds of each lives the image of their communion . . . all communities larger than primordial villages of face-to-face contact (and perhaps even these) are imagined. (6)

Like Gellner, Anderson rejects the idea of the nation as an essential entity. Nations, unlike dynasties or religious communities, are not believed to be created by a mandate of heaven, nor do they emerge as pre-existing concepts from a Platonic ether; rather, they are the result of communal imagining. What sets Anderson apart from many of his predecessors is that he does not equate imagining with falsity.[2] Imagined ideas (including the nation/community) have significant effects in the real world. Nationalism in particular commands, in Anderson's words, "profound emotional legitimacy" (4). People willingly die for their nation, a fact that indicates just how powerful such concepts can be in the world. We cannot simply dismiss the imagined mechanisms of human society on the basis of their status as creations of the mind. Just because something is imagined does not mean it is bad or untrue. Anderson suggests that we evaluate imagined communities "not by their falsity/genuineness, but by the style in which they are imagined" (6). This approach requires the attention of scholars skilled at analyzing the products of imagination and the circulation of those products throughout a culture; literary scholars appear keenly suited for such work.

Anderson's theory has profound implications for the study of ethnic literature, because an ethnic group is also an imagined community. Like nationalism, ethnicity presents itself as an essential concept. Many people believe in their inherent ethnicity (i.e., that there is something essentially Irish within them); however, there is no manifest reality to ethnicity. It is a product of the imagination and the performance of an identity. Since ethnicity is so closely tied to individual identity and personal pride, some who cling tightly to ethnic identifications might feel such assertions invalidate their identity, but again, the fact that ethnicity is imagined does not imply that it is false. It simply requires that we approach it in a manner suited to imagined concepts. Writing nearly a generation before Gellner and Anderson, Fredrik Barth argues in *Ethnic Groups and Boundaries* (1969) that ethnicities are categories defined by cultural interaction and performative behavior, rather than by any "cultural stuff" such categories inherently contain (15). Barth's work shows his struggle against essentialist thinking, and in his 1998 preface to the new edition of his book, he makes use of the vocabulary popularized by modern critics to clarify his point, noting that ethnicity is a matter of "social organization" and "self-ascription" rather than "empirical cultural difference" (6). Barth's work is a call-to-action for scholars to study the "mechanisms" of ethnicity, not its "manifest forms" (5). And in the decades since Barth first published his work, such approaches have gained traction and proven their efficacy.

Some scholars have approached ethnic literature with a goal toward confirming a text's authenticity. Their analyses function as attempts at validation by linking the ethnicity of the text to claims of exclusive hereditary truth. Werner Sollors describes this kind of flawed approach as "biological insiderism" because, by resorting to an essentialist argument, it suggests that people from different ethnic backgrounds cannot truly understand each other's ethnicity, nor can they share a common human history, and this would seem to undermine the point of studying ethnic literature in the first place (*Beyond* 13). Sollors (like Gellner, Anderson, and Barth) does not believe that ethnicities are "natural, real, eternal, stable, and static units," arguing instead that ethnicity is a process ("Invention" xiii–xv). By shifting his focus in this way, Sollors is able to explore ethnicities as "collective fictions" using the tools available to him as a literary scholar ("Invention" xi). Near the end of *Beyond Ethnicity* (1986), Sollors offers a new definition of ethnic literature: "works written by, about, or for persons who perceived themselves, or were perceived by others, as members of ethnic groups, including even nationally and internationally popular writings by 'major' authors and formally intricate and modernist texts" (243).

This redefinition of ethnic literature proves useful because it acknowledges the importance of perception and imagination in the construction of such texts, and it allows us to move away from essentialist analysis toward the more valuable work of process analysis—the understanding of how ethnicity functions in literature and what it reveals about human culture and history. This study builds on Sollors' work by considering Irishness as a "process" and a "collective fiction." The following chapters do not seek to validate authenticity, but instead explore the ways in which Irish ethnicity has been imagined.

Contemporary Americans tend to view ethnicity as a positive thing, as something that helps them resist homogenization. They proudly display badges of their ethnicity and embrace their hyphenated identities in order to distinguish themselves from the crowd while also legitimizing and stabilizing their sense of self. In particular, Irish-American identity has become a much-celebrated ethnic identification. Diane Negra suggests that this is because Irishness functions as "the ideal guilt-free white ethnicity of choice" (11). She calls Irishness a form of "enriched whiteness," which might make it sound like some kind of wholesome bread, but actually points to the way that Irishness has become a claim to authentic cultural difference, similar to the differences claimed by Hispanic Americans or Asian Americans, while also affirming that the Irish are also essentially a white people (1). In the twenty-first century, Irishness is a mark of cultural (and sometimes racial) legitimacy and quality, but this marks a radical shift from the past.

In a study of this significant change in the function of ethnic identifications in America, Richard Alba observes that "ethnic identities have become ways of claiming to be American . . . Ethnic identity can be a means of locating oneself and one's family against the panorama of American history" (318–9). Yet, this is not how ethnicity functioned in the past. Ethnic identifications used to be markers of profound illegitimacy in America. The word "ethnic" originally meant "pagan" or "heathen," and in nineteenth-century America it was used in a more secularized sense to indicate "non-standard" people who were considered "not fully American" (Sollors, *Beyond* 25).[3] Studies of ethnicity need to consider how and why such change took place in America, which means that they must give more attention to the manner in which ethnic groups form and maintain their identities.

One of the best ways to study ethnicity is by studying literature because the written word functions as a primary mechanism of social organization for ethnic groups. Anderson describes the written word as the most important technology of the imagined community and argues that, since the eighteenth century, it has been the novel and the newspaper that have allowed for widely dispersed communities to imagine themselves as unified. He says that by reading and embracing the same books and news reports, individuals confirm the solidity of their community (25–7). It is only technology that limits the size and scope of the imagined community. Huckleberry Finn seems to intuit the power of the written word in creating communities; in the often ignored sequel *Tom Sawyer Abroad* (1894), Huck equates his dislike of civilization with a dislike of newspapers:

> Now, one of the worst things about civilization is that anybody that gits a letter with trouble in it comes and tells you about it and makes you feel bad, and the newspapers fetches you the troubles of everybody all over the world and keeps you downhearted and dismal 'most all the time, and it's such a heavy load for a person. I hate them newspapers, and I hate letters, and if I had my way I wouldn't allow nobody to load his troubles onto other folks he ain't acquainted with on t'other side of the world that way. (Twain 91–2)

What Huck protests here is his forced participation in a community to which he does not want to belong (a theme consistent with protests he makes in earlier books). The act of reading makes him "acquainted" with people he has never actually met and forces him to empathize with them. They are no longer just "other folks" or strangers, they are part of a community that shares its "heavy load" among its members. Being part of an imagined community is tough on Huck (an issue explored in Chapter 2), but for most people it allows for a satisfying sense of belonging. Imagined communities (including imagined ethnic communities) help orient individuals and give them a sense of continuity with the past and a better-defined sense of purpose in the present.

The novels, poems, and dramas that this study considers indeed functioned as technologies of the imagination by engaging Americans in a process of self-definition. By picking up a book or entering a theater, Americans participated in the most visceral and immediate method of communal identification. Though they read their Twain novels alone in their home, they knew that there was an entire national community out there doing likewise. Such thoughts allowed individuals to imagine themselves as part of that wider community—that enormous nation—which shared certain experiences, likes, dislikes, anxieties, and prejudices.

ANTI-IRISH SENTIMENT IN THE U.S.

For much of the nineteenth-century, the Irish were a uniquely undesirable ethnic minority in America—the hated immigrant group *du jour*. They relinquished this title only after more "exotic" immigrants (i.e., Eastern Europeans and Jews) who wore "seemingly strange clothes" and spoke "unfamiliar, odd languages" began pouring into American cities at the turn of the century (Meagher, *Inventing* 65). Anti-Irish sentiment peaked in the period 1850–1880, the decades that saw both the arrival of the Famine immigrants and the previously mentioned anxiety over American national identity. Historian Kevin Kenny also believes that developments in the field of natural science (especially the publication of Charles Darwin's *On the Origin of Species* in 1859) and the rise of Irish physical force nationalism shaped the features of anti-Irish sentiment in America ("Race" 366). Racialized caricatures of the Irish as violent ape-men bent on political anarchy clearly owe much to theories of the evolution of species and public discomfort with Fenian politics (see Figure I.1).

Despite the way it was characterized, the threat the Irish posed had very little to do with actual biological difference and much more to do with perceived difference. The Irish did not look so unlike mainstream Protestant Americans; however, they were imagined to be inherently incompatible with the native-born population. There was so much to fear: the Irish were poor, unskilled, and believed to be incapable of self-discipline; they were Catholic, which led to a belief that their loyalty to the Pope might interfere with their loyalty to their country; they were racially ambiguous; they tended to live, work, and vote as a mass rather than as individuals; they were willing to work low-wage jobs and work as strikebreakers (Kenny, "Race" 372); they were thought to be violent and prone to criminality and alcoholism; they appeared antediluvian, which seemed at odds with American progressivism; they could be antagonistic to strangers and seemed opposed to bourgeois

Figure I.1   "An Irish Jig" by James A. Wales, published in *Puck* 8.191, 3 November 1880: 150.

ideals and leadership (K. Miller 327); and many believed that the Irish reproduced at a rate that would overwhelm the Anglo majority of the country. Though most of these fears appear to originate from class and social contexts, they were invariably attributed to the biological inferiority of the Irish. Kenny observes that, though there were "many reasons why people disliked the Irish," these reasons were expressed "in the language of race" ("Race" 365). Such expressions locate undesirable social traits as inherent deficiencies and hereditary predispositions, and by doing so ignore the social, political, and economic forces that also define ethnic identity. In *Imagined Communities*, Anderson argues that such racialized language seeks to erase nationness by "reducing the adversary to his biological physiognomy" (148). By describing the Irish as fundamentally flawed organisms (and sometimes even as contagious diseases infecting the country), popular racial discourse presented the Irish as a physical contamination of America, rather than as a part of it. Anti-Irish sentiment can then be understood as, in part, an attempt to deny the Irish an American national identity and an attempt to expose those who claim such an identity as impostors.

Anti-Irish sentiment in America grew out of English origins. Much of the racialized rhetoric used to describe the Irish in the press and literature, as well as many of the distinguishing features of the Irish-American stereotype, can be traced to Old World animosities; however, studies of American and British attitudes toward the Irish have been slow to meld. British studies tend to approach anti-Irish sentiment as primarily a function of nationalism, whereas American studies tend to approach it as a function of race. Kenny tries to bridge the gap by looking at the various flavors of anti-Irish sentiment as "specific variations on common themes" ("Race" 364). He suggests several reasons for the difference in attitudes, but most importantly observes that in England, the Irish primarily threatened political sovereignty, whereas in America, they primarily threatened social order ("Race" 364–70). This distinction reveals interesting aspects of the issue. In America, the Irish never really tried to undermine the authority of the government in the way that they did in Great Britain, and as such they were never conceived in American popular culture as an overtly political threat. Instead, the Irish challenged the stability of communities and were thus characterized as cultural dangers. Simply put, the Irish did not see themselves as the opponents of America; they saw themselves as a new type of American. In the Irish imagination, America did not occupy the same kind of adversarial position as did England. The Irish wanted citizenship and inclusion in an American national identity—two fundamental desires that they never really craved from Great Britain. Of course, such radical shifts in perception and context led to anti-Irish sentiment in America taking on significantly different features from British precedent. Despite its Old World origins, anti-Irish sentiment in America functioned as an expression of uniquely New World concerns.

The literary stereotypes of the Irish reflect many of the transformed concerns of Americanized anti-Irish sentiment. Such stereotypes allowed writers to cast the Irish as cultural boogey-men, societal villains, and ethnic clowns. The Irish became stock characters, easily and quickly recognized by American audiences. A bit of Irish brogue or a shillelagh signified an immediate otherness that resonated with the public. All that it took to conjure up a whole range of anti-Irish sentiment was a surname that began with an "O'" or a "Mc." In one of the earliest American frontier novels, *Modern Chivalry* (1792), Hugh Henry Brackenridge achieved this effect on the very first page, thereby establishing a framework for his book built on lampooning the Irish. The novel describes the adventures of Captain John Farrago and his "bog-trotter" sidekick: "The servant that [Farrago] had at this time, was an Irish-man, whose name was Teague O'Regan. I shall say nothing of the character of this man, because the very name imports what he was" (29). Many other American writers played on similar, existent shorthand to create their Irish types, and as such, characters with stereotypically Irish names and traits populate numerous texts in the American literary canon. This is not to say that the stereotypes were the only Irish characters in American literature; however, the stereotypes were so pervasive and popular that writers who wished to include an Irish character in their work had to respond to the ste-reotypes in some way, either by writing against them or by re-appropriating them for new, possibly subversive, purposes.

The following chapters approach Irish stereotypes, not as *a priori* contain-ers of shared ethnic characteristics, but rather as discursive sites that reveal the process of how ethnic identity is popularly constructed. I reject the more classical theory of stereotypes as binary systems in which an individual must fall either inside or outside the category, since such an approach ignores the overlapping, fuzzy boundaries of such categories and the possibility for individuals to have degrees of relationship to the stereotype.[4] I believe liter-ary representations of Irishness function as part of a radial system in which individual Irish characters do not just adhere to or refute the stereotype, but instead demonstrate dynamic degrees of similarity with other Irish characters (including "stereotypical" characters like the stage Irishman). This approach allows us to explore how concepts of Irishness changed in different periods and contexts and further allows us to move beyond monolithic concepts of Irish identity to study individual instances of Irishness in literature.

This study explores the manner in which Irish-American identity has been discursively constructed in literature and the significance that this constructed identity had on American culture during the formative period between the Civil War and the Great Depression. It examines not only *how* the Irish were popularly conceived of in literature, but also *why* such char-acterizations appealed to writers and their readers. It considers in detail how a sense of Irishness was imagined by both Irish-American writers con-scious of the process of self-definition and by non-Irish writers responsive to shifting cultural currents. By surveying significant works that represent the changing attitudes toward the Irish, it reveals not only how a process of Americanization influenced generations of immigrants, but also how the Irish radically influenced emerging American nationalism. In short, a his-tory of Irishness is a history of Americanness, and of the development of ethnic identity in the U.S.

1 Staging Ireland in America

Dion Boucicault was the most prolific and popular dramatist of the nineteenth century, but most of his plays are long out-of-print, are rarely performed, and garner scant interest compared to the works of his contemporaries. He greatly influenced the most notable names in Irish drama—Shaw, Synge, O'Casey, Wilde—yet, his name rarely is considered alongside theirs. During his own life, audiences, critics, and colleagues thought very highly of him, but by the turn of the century, he fell out of fashion as popular tastes turned away from melodrama toward the more realistic styles of Ibsen and Strindberg.

Similarly, Edward "Ned" Harrigan, the most dominating presence in nineteenth-century American musical theater and the oft-credited inventor of both the modern musical and the situational comedy, has become an increasingly obscure figure over the past century. As a celebrated actor, songwriter, and playwright, he became one of the "original men who owned Broadway" (Moloney 1). After his death in 1911, some of his most notable songs endured as marching band and glee club favorites, but his plays have almost entirely vanished from American awareness.

If the popular image of the Irish in the nineteenth century was created primarily on the stage, as critics like Peter Bischoff and Peter Noçon have argued, then it makes sense to begin a study of the Irish character in America with a consideration of the most popular and influential Irish-themed plays of the era (61). Both Boucicault and Harrigan wrote dramas that deeply resonated with their audiences and profoundly affected the ways in which Irish identity was popularly conceived. They both succeeded in finding ways to commercialize Irishness in a city (New York) that still associated the Irish with the recent violence and bloodshed of the Draft Riots (1863) and the Orange Riots (1870–1871). The early success of their works attests to their ability to engage with the public's anxiety regarding growing American nationalism and the shifting ethnic composition of American culture. The audiences who filled the seats of Boucicault's and Harrigan's shows thought of the theater as an arena in which they could vent frustrations; it was a place where class prejudices, ethnic antagonisms, and nationalist struggles could be explored and (possibly) satisfied. For Irish immigrants, the theater was, as Gwen Orel puts it, a kind of "ethnic press" that "provided a place where Irish people otherwise separated by class, gender, and religion could gather to celebrate the home they had in common" (67). For the non-Irish in the audience, it was a place where spectacle and humor could allay a host of social and cultural fears.

Throughout the nineteenth century, nativist fears were given form on the American stage in the stereotype of the stage Irishman. This stock character, what Joep Leerssen calls a "labour-saving device" of the playwright, was initially created centuries earlier in British theaters to satisfy national concerns regarding England's rowdy neighbors (78). Leerssen notes that the stage Irishman was intended to evoke "apprehension" and "reassurance" by emphasizing the Irishman's innate "viciousness" while also establishing his "utter inferiority" (102). Early stage Irishmen were wild drunks who dressed like savages and were prone to mutilating the English language with Gaelic exclamations and curses. Despite their anger and villainy, they were little more than dumb animals who, when handled properly, really posed no threat to civilized man.

In the eighteenth century, the stage Irishman came to display more comedic dimensions, and, instead of hissing at Irish monsters, audiences took to laughing at Irish clowns. The earlier villainous ethnic caricature did not vanish entirely, but it proved less popular than the new, more positive characterization: the smiling Irish rogue whose simplicity, pugnacity, and blustering allowed him to overcome any obstacle. This stage Irishman was still a blatant fool who often retained a menacing disposition and subhuman physical features, but he also displayed new qualities with which audiences could sympathize. He was less overtly threatening than the earlier type, though imagined no less ethnically inferior.

The Irishness embodied in the comedic stage Irishman was a neutered Irishness. It reaffirmed English cultural superiority and eased concerns about current events in Ireland (political unrest, economic disaster, starvation, violence) by portraying the Irish as inherently loyal and grateful to English authority. English audiences sympathized with this new stage Irishman in a way that they did not sympathize with actual Irishmen, and this discrepancy reveals significant cultural disconnect within Anglo–Irish relations. Declan Kiberd sees the immense popularity of Irish characters in English theaters during the years of the Great Famine and the converse disdain for real Irishmen seeking refuge in English cities at the same time as an example of a repressive regime sentimentalizing its victims, "an attitude compounded of guilt, fear, affection and racial superiority" (22). Leerssen similarly remarks that the more positive characterization of the Irish during this time did not necessarily imply English sympathy for Ireland, but rather a need for the English to believe that Ireland was sympathetic to them (132). While this stage Irishman was still very much a stock character of limited dramatic depth, he functioned within popular imagination in a more complex way than previous iterations of the type. He still had to satisfy the traditional functions of the stereotype, but now he also had to ease the guilt and fear of a new historical context.

What emerged from English theaters of this period was an image of the Irish so enduring that echoes of it can still be found in British and American popular culture. Many critics point to Maurice Bourgeois' description from 1913 as the principal definition of the type, and it certainly envisions the kind of stage Irishman that both Boucicault and Harrigan were familiar with and obligated to respond to in their own plays:

> The stage Irishman habitually bears the general name of Pat, Paddy or Teague. He has an atrocious Irish brogue, perpetual jokes, blunders and bulls in speaking and never fails to utter, by way of Hibernian season-ing, some wild screech or oath of Gaelic origin at every third word: he has an unsurpassable gift of blarney and cadges for tips and free drinks. His hair is of a fiery red: he is rosy-cheeked, massive, and whis-key loving. His face is one of simian bestiality with an expression of diabolical archness written all over it. He wears a tall felt hat (billicock or wideawake), with a cutty-clay pipe stuck in front, an open shirt col-lar, a three-caped coat, knee breeches, worsted stockings, and cockaded brogue shoes. In his right hand he brandishes a stout blackthorn, or a spring of shillelagh, and threatens to belabour therewith the daring per-son who will tread on the tails of his coat. For his main characteristics (if there is any such thing as psychology in the stage Irishman) are his swagger, his boisterousness and his pugnacity. (qtd. in Duggan 288–9)

This comical, but still somewhat menacing, character traveled across the Atlantic Ocean and found new popularity on a new continent. By the time Famine emigrants arrived in the U.S., the stage Irish stereotype was already firmly ensconced in American minds.

American audiences became acquainted with the stage Irishman through early British dramas, and thus comic fools named MacBuffle, O'Balderdash, O'Blunder, MacBrogue, Mactawdry, O'Trigger, and O'Whack formed some of the earliest conceptions of Irishness in the U.S.[1] Much of the humor in these plays stems from the Irishman's inappropriate presence in a civi-lized context. He might first appear to be an upright, restrained gentleman, but minor provocations can bring out his "true" Irish nature and incite his characteristic fury and logorrhea. The common element running through many of these early plays was an insinuation that the Irish resort to vio-lence and "Irish bull" to solve all problems. Though the threatened violence was largely farcical and the torrent of nonsensical gibberish quite funny, it nonetheless reinforced a certain perception of the Irish in America, namely, that they could appear civilized, but were really violent, illogical savages at their core.

It was not long before American playwrights put their own spin on the stereotype. An Americanized version of the stage Irishman appeared as early as 1767 in Andrew Barton's *The Disappointment or the Force of Credulity*. In his history of the stage Irishman, G. C. Duggan claims that America had fully appropriated the character by the late eighteenth century and was "already beginning to create for itself the illusion of a fanciful type of Irishman and a mythical Ireland" that would characterize so much of the Irish-themed drama of the next century (142). While early British representations of the character tend to focus on national difference, verbal awkwardness, and a proclivity for violence, American portrayals of the stage Irishman often emphasize class difference, communalism, and general naiveté. Bischoff and Noçon suggest that "the indigenous American plays . . . tended to give a more sympathetic portrayal of the Irishman" than their British equivalents (62). The Americanized stage Irishman is not as explicitly menacing as the British version—the trouble he causes is more often the result of ignorance than criminality—but he is equally threatening in his own way. His mere presence disrupts social equilibrium. He blunders through delicate political and social situations, in effect spoiling the cultural harmony of America and undercutting any opportunity for national prosperity. In addition, Bischoff and Noçon suggest that one important difference between the English and American versions of the character was that, in America, Irishness was dramatized as a condition of "being torn between two countries and cultures" (63). These split loyalties led to new dramatic dynamics not commonly found in English plays. America's Paddy, while not breaking completely away from his British origins, more closely resembled the kind of Irish that Americans saw flooding into the country in the wake of the Famine: he was an impoverished peasant, eager but ill-equipped for life in the New World, and of ambiguous national and social loyalties.

Anglo Americans enjoyed ethnic humor and found pleasure in seeing performances that created a spectacle out of a marginalized culture while at the same time asserting the primacy of a white, Protestant majority. The contrast between cultures formed the basis of many entertainments in early American stage history, most notably in the blackface minstrel show. In fact, the Americanized stage Irishman owes much to the minstrel tradition. The Irish reputation for song and dance fit in well with established vaudeville routines; as minstrel performances lost their appeal, it seemed simple enough to remove the blackface make-up, switch from negro dialect to an Irish brogue, and keep the show going. Berndt Ostendorf describes minstrelsy as the staging of negrophobia as negrophilia because it defuses the threat of black bodies by transforming them into amusing clowns (81). The Irish characters that emerged in the wake of the minstrel tradition similarly can be thought of as the staging of celtophobia as celtophilia. By portraying the Irish as ineffectual buffoons, American writers eased concerns regarding the immigrant threat. How dangerous could the Irish be, logic would suggest, if they were all like the singing and dancing Paddys in the vaudeville theaters?

Notably, both of the authors I consider in this chapter began their careers by performing in these early types of ethnic comedies. Boucicault made his 1854 acting debut in the U.S. as Patrick O'Plenipo, a typical stage Irishman, in English dramatist James Kenney's *The Irish Ambassador.* Harrigan got his start and made his early reputation by performing in blackface vaudeville sketches. Yet, by the 1870s, both of these dramatists achieved something different with their ethnic comedies, and in particular with their representations of Irish character. Both Boucicault and Harrigan found a way to re-appropriate and re-imagine the stage Irishman as a character with both Irish and American dimensions.

Scholarship of the stage Irishman often focuses so intently on how unrealistic the stereotype is that it forgets to consider the contexts in which the stereotype circulated. Dale T. Knobel criticizes this kind of approach as seeking "the uniformities in the portrayal of the character across time and place rather than the peculiarities of a particular stage Irishman occupying a specific historical niche" (50). What is too often ignored is that the stereotype—real or not—impacted ethnic discourse in significant ways. The imagined Irishman of the stage might never actually be found on the street, but theatergoers carried him in their minds, and such concepts necessarily influenced real-world ethnic relations. Knobel argues,

> We can regard the stage Irishman as both reflective and prescriptive; the ethnic vocabulary of the stage was adapted from the ethnic vocabulary of the streets, but once established, the stage Irishman was such a pervasive element of popular culture that it no doubt served as a mechanism of diffusion itself. (68)

The stage Irish character itself was a site of ethnic engagement, often for the slandering of the Irish, but also, as I hope to show, for a subversive reformulating of Irish identity in an American context. In this chapter, I consider two playwrights who occupied "a specific historical niche" and created new variations on the old stereotype. The clarity of Boucicault's and Harrigan's visions of Ireland and Irish-American identity allow for a unique opportunity to explore the imaginings of a generation. I am interested in examining how the American stage—and these two playwrights in particular—helped to facilitate new ethnic imagery and a vocabulary that would allow the Irish to be thought of as being entitled to an American identity.

AMERICANS "ASTRAY ON AN IRISH BOG": DION BOUCICAULT'S *THE SHAUGHRAUN*

When Dion Boucicault's *The Shaughraun* completed its wildly successful 1874–1875 premiere run at Wallack's Theater in New York, a group of Irish Americans presented the playwright with a testimonial plaque "in recognition of the services his literary and artistic work have been to Ireland and the Irish people." Such an accolade set the play apart from Boucicault's earlier work, the hundred plus melodramas that had earned him a reputation as an amusing entertainer. *The Shaughraun* was the latest of his "Irish plays," and the attention that it received marked it as something more substantial, more literary, than anything the author previously had produced.[2] The plaque, presented to Boucicault on behalf of Irish Americans "from Boston to Savannah and from New York to San Francisco," prompted the playwright to respond, "This sir, is the greatest honor of my life except one, and that was conferred upon me once, fifty years ago, when, upon entering the world, I found myself to be an Irishman" ("Shaughraun" 5). Though he places emphasis here on the importance of circumstance and nativity in defining his ethnicity, the presentation of this award to Boucicault was in fact a celebration of the way he helped redefine and reconstruct Irish ethnicity for a whole generation who only vaguely remembered Ireland or who (more often) never had seen it for themselves.

Surprising many of his detractors who thought him a quaint showman past his prime, Boucicault achieved both popular and financial success with *The Shaughraun*. The play even received a degree of critical acclaim. *The New York Times* proclaims it "one of the most original and brilliant plays which the present generation has had the opportunity of seeing" and further describes Boucicault as a "true genius" ("Amusements," 16 November 1874: 5). Henry James, who seems to try hard not to like the play in his review, admits a begrudging admiration for Boucicault and calls *The Shaughraun* "the theatrical event of the season" ("Some" 123). This was certainly how Edith Wharton remembered the play as well, as she describes in *The Age of Innocence* (1920):

> It was a crowded night at Wallack's theatre.
>
> The play was "The Shaughraun," with Dion Boucicault in the title role and Harry Montague and Ada Dyas as the lovers. The popularity of the admirable English company was at its height, and the Shaughraun always packed the house. In the galleries the enthusiasm was unreserved; in the stalls and boxes, people smiled a little at the hackneyed sentiments and clap-trap situations, and enjoyed the play as much as the galleries did. (113)

The glowing reviews and enthusiasm of New Yorkers drove box office sales to impressive levels; during its initial four-month run, *The Shaughraun* grossed nearly a quarter of a million dollars and gave Boucicault the biggest payday of his career (Fawkes 194–5).

Yet, *The Shaughraun* epitomizes Victorian melodrama and sensation and makes liberal use of Irish stereotypes. In particular, the play's titular hero descends from a literary heritage that had been defaming the Irish for hundreds of years. Boucicault had built a reputation, as both an actor and playwright, for exploiting the stage Irishman for commercial success. Many of his contemporaries saw no difference between his Irish rogues and the blustering drunks who had been the comic relief in so much drama of the previous two centuries. Throughout his life, Boucicault came under numerous attacks. A Catholic priest from New York decried *The Shaughraun* as "a disgrace to the Irish people" ("Criticising" 5). The *Irish World*, the most popular Irish-American newspaper of the time, published numerous letters attacking Boucicault, including some that accused him of being a "willing slave" of the British and a "cancer" eating away at Irish nationalism (McFeely 63). The Abbey Theater criticized him for perpetuating the stage Irish stereotype, and co-founder W. B. Yeats accused Boucicault of having "no relation with literature" (O'Brien 137).[3] One notable theater producer accused Boucicault of "merely re-vamping age-old clichés" and "making a mockery of [Ireland]" (Cave, "Staging" 163). The *Freeman's Journal*, Ireland's oldest nationalist newspaper, went as far as to call Boucicault's work "gross trumpery" (Potter 611).

Boucicault's contemporaries are not his only critics. Many modern scholars express bafflement at his success and popularity in America during the late nineteenth century. In particular, scholars of Irish and Irish-American literature seem unsure how to handle such a polarizing figure, who at times has been hailed as a national hero, but who also has been accused of making a profit from insulting iconography. Though he is often studied and even acknowledged as a pioneer by theater scholars, he is frequently "dismissed as a compromised figure" by literary critics (Meer 149).[4] John P. Harrington observes that, despite recent renewed interest in Boucicault as a political playwright, he "has been increasingly a troubling presence, at once admirable and deplorable" (*Irish Play* 29–31). Though he is without a doubt the major dramatist of his era, both America and Ireland have been hesitant to claim him as part of their literary heritage because he does not fit neatly into either national identity, and as a result his works have been largely ignored. Yet, many of us are drawn back to his plays because we sense that their literary merits have been overlooked. They exhibit deceptive simplicities that mask rich cultural complexities. The seeming anomalies in the work invite us to examine more carefully the apparent puzzle of *The Shaughraun*—namely, that, despite expectations, many Irish Americans of the nineteenth century approved of the play and considered Boucicault's characters to be "realistic depictions of the native race" (Graves 29).

Dionysus Lardner Boucicault was born in Dublin in 1820.[5] His mother, Anna Maria Darley, belonged to a prominent Irish Protestant family, but his father's identity remains a bit of a mystery. Nominally, he is the son of Samuel Smith Boursiquot, a merchant of Huguenot extraction, though many historians believe it more likely that he was fathered by his mother's lover, Dr. Dionysus Lardner, a prominent Irish scientist. He was educated at a variety of schools in England and, though he was discouraged by his family from doing so, he started a career as an actor in provincial repertory groups outside London when he was seventeen. As a young actor, he achieved success playing Irish characters, many critics not realizing that his accent was genuine (Fawkes 21–3). His first real success as a playwright came in 1841 with *London Assurance*. Over the next decade he wrote and produced nearly forty additional plays (many of which were adaptations and translations) and began to establish his reputation as a cunning businessman, a bold (even immodest) showman, and a popular commercial performer.

The love affair between Boucicault and the U.S. began in 1853 when he moved to New York in search of better opportunities to pursue his progressive business ideas and artistic ambitions. What he found exceeded his expectations. Not only did he discover the business opportunities and freedoms he had been craving for his work, but he also happened on a community that seemed inherently dramatic and receptive of theatrical spectacle. He writes that "[New York] was not a city. It was a theatre," and he then praises the quality of the city's dramatic foundations: "[I] was surprised to find the American theatres superior in every respect to the theatres in England. The New York audiences were keener and more sincere; their taste was of a finer kind; their appreciation was quicker" ("Leaves" 229–30). Boucicault fell in love with America and American audiences, who were receptive to a man of such impressive skill and ambition. The Irish immigrants adored him because he was an Irish superstar and a powerful link to their heritage, and the Anglo-American crowds loved him because of his dynamic, Barnum-like showmanship and his presentation of never-before-seen stage spectacles. In this new land, Boucicault saw the opportunity to escape from the confines of English and French drama and do something new—as a writer, as an actor, and as a businessman.

Though Dublin was his birthplace and London was where he worked for so much of his career, Boucicault came to think of New York as his home. He became a naturalized citizen of the U.S. in 1873 and began to identify himself thereafter as Irish American (Meer 149; "Serious").[6] Many of his most notable works were written in his adopted country and premiered here. He did not consider Irish topics as limiting his appeal, but rather as enhancing his stage profile, especially among Americans. His use of Irish themes found much sympathy particularly in the city of New York, which had a population that was more than one-quarter Irish. Boucicault believed there to be a special synergy between Ireland and America, and he sincerely imagined that "the American heart is strung with chords torn from the Irish harp" ("Shaughraun" 5). Though his audience was not exclusively Irish American, Irish Americans were, as the *New York Times* reported, "the class most likely to be interested" in his work ("Amusements," 7 April 1860: 5).

Harrington observes that Boucicault "came to the Irish drama as a novelty and a stage innovation late in his career" and did so out of a kind of desperation for material (*Irish Play* 15). When the first of Boucicault's Irish dramas, *The Colleen Bawn*, opened in New York in 1860, the playwright made a curtain speech during which he proudly declared, "I have written an Irish drama for the first time in my life" (Fawkes 118). The play marks a turning point in his career. Audiences witnessed something fundamentally different from Boucicault's previous efforts, something novel and more dynamic, achieved by turning to Ireland for his inspiration. *The Colleen Bawn* proved more popular than any of Boucicault's previous works and paved the way for similar efforts to dramatize Ireland and Irish culture, including *The Shaughraun*. Boucicault himself was aware of the shift in his writing. Regarding *The Colleen Bawn*, he writes (with characteristic immodesty) in an autobiographical fragment,

> It may be said to have created the Irish Drama. It threw so new and brilliant a light on the Irish Character that it swept away all precedent . . . It exhibited that a great fund of pathos underlies and elevates the Irish nature . . . It was a gleam of sunshine through a shower, nothing like it had ever been seen before.[7] ("A bit of autobiography" 8–9)

Bruce McConachie describes Boucicault's claim to have created the Irish drama at this moment in his career as "premeditated blarney," noting that the playwright had written Irish characters before (213). This, of course, is true; Boucicault had both written and performed Irish characters on numerous earlier occasions; however, the inclusion of an Irish character does not transform his previous melodramas into Irish dramas. It takes more than a bit of brogue to achieve that. Boucicault was correct in realizing that *The Colleen Bawn* was something new for him, a truly Irish-themed theatrical spectacle. It was the first time he tried to stage Ireland and Irish identity, and the first time he grappled with Irish politics and legends. *The Colleen Bawn* gave him a taste of what was possible; he would achieve the fulfillment of his new dramatic direction in *The Shaughraun*.

The Shaughraun is remarkable because it achieved what no other play had achieved before and what few other plays have achieved since: it presented a concept of Irishness that transcended national loyalties. Despite its reliance on stereotypes, spectacle, and melodrama, *The Shaughraun* was celebrated as authentically Irish wherever it was performed in the world. Audiences accepted Boucicault's representation of Irish identity, which is initially surprising given that they would riot against J. M. Synge's similar portrayal of Irishness in *The Playboy of the Western World* (1907) just a few decades later.[8]

The Shaughraun tells the story of Robert Ffolliott, a Fenian prisoner recently escaped from Australia and returned to his ancestral land in Sligo. In his absence, the villainous Cory Kinchella has driven the Ffolliott family into financial disaster and is positioned to take their land away from them. Robert must seek to right this wrong while avoiding capture by English authorities and also while pursuing the love of his lady, Arte O'Neal.

Complicating the action of the play, the man charged with apprehending Robert, Captain Molineux, has fallen in love with Claire Ffolliott, Robert's sister, and finds his loyalties divided between his duty and his heart. Added into this mix is Conn the Shaughraun, a free-spirited Irish rogue and faithful friend to the Ffolliott family who functions, in David Krause's terms, as a "clown ex-machina" who perpetually swoops in to save the day (193).

Boucicault borrows heavily from precedent for this play. Almost all of the individual plot elements of *The Shaughraun* have origins in previous literary works, and many were in fact clichés: the beautiful and lonely Irish girl working the farm, the villainous land-thief oppressing Irish families, the Englishman who falls in love with the Irish girl, the stage Irishman who sings and dances his way to victory. Boucicault also evokes many familiar images (the rocky coastline, the dairy farm, the crumbling castle, the dangerous bog) and scenarios (the Irish wake, the English fox hunt). By offering so many familiar tropes, Boucicault draws his audience in and makes them comfortable, which then allows him to do something unprecedented and startling. *The Shaughraun* appears on the surface to be a simple collection of familiar dramatic devices, but Boucicault repurposes these devices to evoke a different kind of sympathy for the Irish character.

Boucicault's play makes it possible to reassemble a model of Irish-American culture from the end of the nineteenth century. By focusing on the appeal of *The Shaughraun*, I hope to deduce the ways in which Ireland and Irishness were popularly imagined in the U.S. and show how certain triggers within the play engendered a powerful feeling of identification within the Irish-American population. Historian J. J. Lee argues that, unlike other immigrants, "the Irish had to succeed as a people, not just as individuals. They would have to construct an image of themselves as Irish *and* as Americans that would gain acceptance in the broad mainstream of American culture" (16). This project of complex cultural imagining required an artist like Boucicault in order to succeed. Irish Americans needed help navigating an evolving cultural dynamic; they needed help formulating their own Irish identity as something compatible with their American identity, and Boucicault offered the help they needed. If it was not clear to his audiences what it meant to be Irish anymore, he would make it clear. He would present a vision, familiar but new, that would have particular appeal both for the Irish in America, and for the broader population that sometimes saw the Irish as a threat.

Many believed Boucicault's vision of Ireland was accurate. In its initial review, *The New York Times* claims that Boucicault depicts "Ireland and Irishman as they are" ("Amusements," 15 November 1874: 7). Similarly, *The New York Herald* trots out an old cliché and praises him for holding "the mirror up to nature" ("Shaughraun" 5). Of course, these reviews overestimate the play's representation of workaday Irish life. Even a cursory glance at the play reveals numerous inaccuracies and exaggerations. Some more level-headed critics spoke up during *The Shaughraun*'s run to temper earlier overestimations. Chief among them was Henry James, who in discussing the play states:

> The public . . . does not go with the expectation of seeing the mirror held up to nature as it knows nature—of seeing a reflection of its actual, local, immediate physiognomy. The mirror, as the theatres show it, has the image already stamped upon it—an Irish image . . . true to an original or not; the public doesn't care. ("Some" 122–3)

James indicates that the play is largely a pre-fabricated imagining of Irishness that builds on the audience's desires, rather than reality. In later years, George Bernard Shaw similarly reflected that Boucicault "was not holding the mirror up to nature, but blarneying the British public precisely as the Irish car-driver, when he is 'cute' enough, blarneys the English tourist" (qtd. in Graves 29). James and Shaw are correct. In *The Shaughraun*, Boucicault appeals to sentimentalized Irish patriotism and nostalgia in order to present a mythical Ireland populated by romanticized Irish characters; however, this does not mean we should dismiss these representations. Quite the contrary, Boucicault's play gives us a unique insight into how Ireland was imagined. Whether factually accurate or not, this imagining shows what audiences wanted Irish identity to be, what they aspired to as Irish Americans, and what they thought was a fair measuring stick for their Irish nationalism and pride.

Before offering his re-imagining, Boucicault had to disabuse his audience of certain ideas about Ireland and Irishness. Due to the fact that so many Irish Americans in his audience were born in America or only faintly remembered their native land, Boucicault makes sure to include a character in the play who also has a limited knowledge of Ireland—Captain Molineux. As an Englishman, Molineux, of course, has little understanding of the Irish people or the Irish landscape.[9] The play begins with admissions of his ignorance. In the first scene, he becomes lost in the Irish countryside, complains about his inability to pronounce Irish names, fails to understand the basic workings of Irish farm equipment, misunderstands Irish domestic manners, and has his beliefs about Irish behavior thoroughly refuted by (what he assumes to be) two simple country girls. All of this causes him to remark, "I am astray on an Irish bog here, and every step I take gets me deeper in the mire" (262).[10] His confusion and disorientation throughout this scene and the rest of the play result from the disconnect between what he believes about Ireland and what he actually sees before him. Notably, he is not in the bogland, but his understanding of Ireland formed through reading English accounts of the country (especially military accounts) has predisposed him to conceive of Ireland as an intractable morass, and so he uses the stereotype of the bog to make sense of his current dilemma. Generations of writers had described Ireland as one giant bog that swallowed up English travelers and soldiers, and Molineux struggles to reconcile this idea with his current experience. His faltering reliance on old clichés demonstrates his struggle to form his own conception of the country; as the play unfolds, Molineux is forced beyond the comfortable boundaries of stereotype and must develop his own understanding of the Irish. Richard Allen Cave believes that the challenges to Molineux's preconceptions are there to show "how false and patronizing his assumptions about the Irish are" ("Staging" 121). That is certainly part of the effect, but Molineux's ignorance also functions as a gateway for audience members who might be equally ignorant. How many people sitting in the seats of Wallack's Theatre could pronounce "Suil-a-Beg" any better than Molineux does? Who could work a butter churn better than he? Most of the audience, including those of Irish descent, would feel just as awkward if dropped down in the middle of Arte O'Neal's backyard; they would be just as much "astray on an Irish bog." Boucicault cleverly positions Molineux as the audience's surrogate; as he learns how to navigate Ireland, the audience will too. The fact that Boucicault makes this gateway character English prepares the audience for the cultural reconciliation he proposes later in the play. When the Irish-American audience identifies with the Englishman, they are primed for the somewhat manipulative political maneuvering Boucicault requires in the end. Through Molineux, the audience is allowed to make similar concessions of ignorance regarding Ireland. Once this is achieved, Boucicault can present a new, more satisfying vision to fill the void.

The Irish in America yearned for artistic images of the old country because such works allowed for an imagined journey back to a better time and place. In *How the Irish Became Americans* (1973), Joseph P. O'Grady argues that this romantic craving among Irish Americans was the result of the deplorable conditions in the ghettos. It seems logical, he suggests, that Irish Americans living in squalor would create "a romantic picture of the Emerald Isle that soon possessed no resemblance to the land they had left" (38). The Ireland that these immigrants imagined was already a fictional landscape. What Boucicault does, then, is not a whole cloth fabrication of a new imagined Ireland—for Famine generation immigrants had been imagining it in folk narrative and songs for nearly three decades before *The Shaughraun*'s premiere—but rather a more studied revision of what was already in the minds of his audience. This required that he play on the familiarity and appeal that four specific Irish story elements (mythology, religion, culture, politics) had for his audience.

The Shaughraun creates a portrait of Ireland soaked in the romanticized myth that Irish immigrants had brought with them to America. Boucicault does not evoke the realities of post-Famine Ireland, but instead seems to reach back to pluck an image from the epic past. Though the play is set in the modern world, it uses more ancient and romantic imagery as sentimentalized scaffolding to frame its action. Boucicault's Ireland is one in which curses still have power, songs unite the people, and heroes triumph because they are connected to the spirit of the land—a land that has memory and agency. Father Dolan, the paternal guardian of the Ffolliott family, reminds us that this is a land that "many a strange family have tried to hold possession of," but "the land seemed to swallow them up one by one" (265). The land itself conspires against the play's villains (disorienting them, starving them, draining away their fortunes) and assists the heroes (providing food and shelter, enabling escapes). In this sense, what audiences experienced was a dramatic staging of the popular poetic figure Erin/Hibernia, the personified spirit of Ireland.

Notably, Boucicault's romanticized Ireland is also thoroughly Catholic, even though he himself was raised in a Protestant household. He knew that his New York audience understood Catholicism as a defining element of Irish life, and so he emphasized that idea in his drama by making the moral center of the play a parish priest. Father Dolan embodies such an idealized sense of Catholic Ireland that even non-Catholics in Boucicault's audience found themselves moved by his honesty, piousness, and essential goodness; the *New York Times* went as far as to suggest that Roman Catholicism would gain many more converts if it was like what *The Shaughraun* depicted ("Amusements," 16 November 1874: 5).

Just as important to the play's appeal were allusions to Gaelic culture, most notably in the play's use of the Irish language. The play is peppered with a smattering of basic Irish vocabulary (rendered phonetically), but the most notable Irishism is the title itself. *The Shaughraun*, which in very early drafts was known as *Boyne Water*, was a title that Lester Wallack of Wallack's Theater was not comfortable with, believing it to be an unpronounceable word that held no meaning for American audiences. Boucicault insisted, though, and Wallack came to agree that the title had an "estranging novelty" that was part of the romantic attraction Boucicault was creating (Grene 15). It did not matter if anyone knew what the word meant, or if they could pronounce it. Even Irish Americans would have had some difficulty with it, since the Irish language was already in decline. The telling reality was that Boucicault's Irish was a bastardized Irish that resonated with audiences because it sounded authentic and easily evoked nostalgia for the old country.

The last of the four elements that Boucicault knew would be familiar and appealing to Irish audiences in New York was nationalist politics. The play features a Fenian hero being hunted by British authorities, a contentious land struggle, allusions to the treachery of informers, and several direct references to recent actual attacks on the police in both Ireland and England. Boucicault clearly means to evoke nationalist sympathy as part of his imagined reconstruction of Ireland. Yet some critics express frustration at his overly romantic brand of Irish nationalism. Biographer Robert Hogan laments what he considers the playwright's dishonest use of Irish political themes and states that Boucicault "Walt-Disneyed it up for public consumption" (87). Of course, given the period, Boucicault's political angle actually seems provocative. Krause reminds us that "if any playwright had dared to treat this incendiary subject seriously in 1874, he and his play would certainly have been suppressed as an incitement to riot" (193). Many of the American east coast elite (including the "lace curtain" middle-class Irish) supported Home Rule and land reform, but were less inclined toward revolution or violent republicanism (Kenny, "American-Irish" 291–2). Kerby A. Miller states that a major problem facing those with nationalist sympathies in America was "how to promote Irish revolution while residing in a nation whose government was at peace with Ireland's oppressor and whose Protestant citizens generally regarded Irish-American agitation as foolish or criminal" (337). Boucicault's skill as a playwright shines through in his ability to rally for Irish nationalism while appealing to both sympathetic and antipathetic audiences alike. He achieves this by promoting reconciliation as an alternative to physical force nationalism. *The Shaughraun* repeatedly emphasizes the deep admiration that Molineux, the English authority, and Robert, the Irish rebel, have for each other and suggests that there is hope for them to overcome their circumstances and find peace. In fact, the end of the play implies that they will become family through Molineux's marriage to Robert's sister. Such a relationship must have been surprising to those who considered the Irish and English to be fundamentally incompatible, yet it must also have been satisfying to Irish Americans, weary of the racism of American cities, to see on stage an Irish triumph over biased ideology, cultural stereotype, and artificial class boundary. While Boucicault seems to oversimplify and idealize many aspects of Irish politics, he nonetheless finds a way to incorporate a kind of Irish patriotism that could be embraced by many Americans.[11]

Despite aiming to reconstruct a vision of Ireland built on romanticized myth, religion, culture, and politics, Boucicault also aspired (perhaps paradoxically) to a new kind of realism. He saw photography, still a relatively new art, as competition since it offered people a vivid way to imaginatively travel back to Ireland. Though photographers of nineteenth-century Ireland who marketed their work in the U.S. did not always aspire to realistic topics, often favoring staged nostalgia instead, they employed the most directly representational method available at that time. Boucicault admired the vividness of these early photographs, no doubt recognized their popularity among his target audience, and soon suggested that "the stage might be employed in a similar [photographic] manner to embody and illustrate the moving events of the period" ("Leaves" 230). What he produced was a composite vision of Ireland that, like early photography of the country, blended the picturesque, the nostalgic, and the spectacular while presenting itself as authentic representation. Boucicault's visuals aimed to evoke a sentimental portrait of Ireland, not a realistic one, though that was how he frequently described them:

> I have endeavored to tell the truth about my country. I mean about what is beautiful and good and innocent in that land. I have drawn a

portrait of one you love, and I know right well how much of the feeling you exhibit here to-night is due to the artist who stands before you, and how much more is due to the tender interest you take in the subject he has chosen to illustrate. ("Shaughraun" 5)

Boucicault admits here that in his attempt "to tell the truth" about Ireland he has selected the "beautiful," the "good," and the "innocent" elements for emphasis. For him, the truth of Ireland does not require documentary realism, but rather a kind of artistic realism that, like early photography of the time, presented a vision of the country with exacting—even "realistic"—detail. The most immediate tool for Boucicault to use in presenting his vivid portrait of Ireland was the set design itself.

The *New York Times* lavishes praise on the Wallack's Theater set of the 1874 premiere of *The Shaughraun*, proclaiming that "the scenery would alone be well worth going to see" ("Amusements," 16 November 1874: 5). In particular, the paper commends scene painter Matt Morgan for his visually stunning backdrops ("Amusements," 15 November 1874: 7). Though the original backdrops are gone, watercolor reproductions of the set and backdrops were made by artist Joe Clare; the watercolors themselves were then photographed at the behest of Queen Victoria, an avid Boucicault fan (see Figures 1.1–1.6).

Figure 1.1 Backdrop for Act 1, Scene 1: the ruins of Suil-a-more Castle. (Special Collections, Templeman Library, University of Kent, Canterbury).

Figure 1.2 Backdrop for Act 1, Scene 2 and Act 2, Scene 6: the Devil's Jowl. (Special Collections, Templeman Library, University of Kent, Canterbury).

Figure 1.3 Backdrop for Act 1, Scene 3: exterior of Father Dolan's Cottage. (Special Collections, Templeman Library, University of Kent, Canterbury).

Figure 1.4   Sketch of the set for Act 1, Scene 4: interior of Father Dolan's Cottage. (Special Collections, Templeman Library, University of Kent, Canterbury).

Figure 1.5   Backdrop for Act 2, Scene 7: Rathgarron Head. (Special Collections, Templeman Library, University of Kent, Canterbury).

Figure 1.6 Sketch of the set for Act 3, Scene 2: Mrs. O'Kelly's Cabin. (Special Collections, Templeman Library, University of Kent, Canterbury).

Throughout *The Shaughraun*, Boucicault evokes imagery familiar to his audience from popular illustrations and travel books about Ireland. Included are rugged, rocky seascapes, looming castle ruins, quaint cottages, a dairy barn, a Catholic sanctuary, the ruins of an abbey, and an English jail. Many of the sets depict picturesque visions of the "ould sod"—images that Harrington describes as the kind of "generic Celtic scene[s] of moonlight and shimmering waters" deplored by later writers (*Irish Play* 21). Yet, audiences were dazzled by Boucicault's portraits of Ireland because, in conjunction with numerous clever stage effects, each set was like "a painting that moved" (Booth 160). Audiences were transported to a place that was at once familiar but also startlingly more vivid than any they had ever experienced. Boucicault permits the audience to recognize Ireland before cleverly manipulating the images to use them as frames for unfamiliar and unusual dramatic moments.

One such moment takes place in Act 1, Scene 2 at an imposing cleft in the rocky coastline called "the Devil's Jowl." It is here, concealed in the cliffs, that Robert hides from the British authorities and here that he first meets his pursuer, Molineux. At first, Molineux does not realize that Robert is his man and spends time relaxing with him on the rocks. In such an environment beyond either Irish or British civilization, the two men can enjoy each other's company as equals, not adversaries. Boucicault plants the seeds of political reconciliation in a setting that is imposing and potentially dangerous (especially for Molineux who does not understand the Irish landscape), but one that, nonetheless, frames a path (the cleft) to tranquility. On the rocky shore of Ireland, looking west across the Atlantic and drinking American whiskey together, these two men imagine a place where the Irish and English can coexist peacefully. On his arrival at the Devil's Jowl, Molineux describes Ireland as an "infernal country," but by the end of the scene he seems amused by its "extraordinary" qualities as he walks arm-in-arm with an Irishman up the cliff path (269–70).

Another repurposing of familiar Irish iconography with radical new intent takes place at the end of Act 2 when Molineux follows Claire up to Rathgarron Head and learns that she has been keeping him occupied while her brother makes his escape from prison. Claire has led Molineux up there, not for a romantic interlude, but in order to light a signal fire that will tell Robert's accomplices offshore to bring in their boat and whisk him away to safety. At this moment, Molineux must choose between doing his duty of recapturing Robert or following his heart by helping the Fenian to escape. Claire leaves him alone to make his choice, and so Molineux stands alone on stage, isolated against the generically Celtic backdrop of the abbey ruins, the Irish coast, the moonlight, and the shimmering waters. The familiar Irish setting hosts an unusual character: a sympathetic and forlorn Englishman. Against such a majestic and good country, Molineux's loyalty to flawed ideology stands no chance. He is overwhelmed by Ireland and its people, and his previous beliefs about the country are finally destroyed. At last, he realizes that Ireland is not just an intractable bog and the Irish not just backward savages, and so he chooses to do what his heart tells him is right. Boucicault is not subtle in visually staging this scene of internal struggle; he positions Molineux on a precipice on the western shore of Sligo on a moonlit night with a literal beacon for Irish freedom looming behind him waiting to be ignited if the Englishman makes the right choice. Boucicault presents Ireland at this moment as a place of enlightenment and transformation for foreigners, and he also has the signal fire on Rathgarron Head lit by an Englishman, visually connecting Irish freedom with English cooperation.

An even more significant example of Boucicault's manipulation of familiar Irish imagery occurs during the wake for Conn, who had been supposedly killed while helping Robert escape from jail, but actually is still alive and feigning death for his own amusement. The Irish wake remains to this day one of the most cliché tropes of stories about the Irish and would have been a very familiar setting to even the non-Irish audience members at Wallack's Theater. Yet, Boucicault plays with this familiar spectacle and achieves something new. The audience is invited inside to participate in the Irish wake, to join with the keening, singing, drinking, and carousing around the body of Conn the Shaughraun, the fallen spirit of Irishness. Even Molineux, an outsider, is welcomed in to pay his respects at the "festive solemnity" (317). Yet, within a very short scene, intimate pain is transformed into hope; Conn's wake transforms into a wedding, news arrives that the Queen has pardoned the Fenian prisoners, and the Shaughraun comes back to life. Boucicault's craft allows him to construct such a scene that forces the audience to participate in a kind of Irish communion. By utilizing established Irish elements, Boucicault is able to re-blend common imagery into a new portrait that combines Irish grief, political freedom, and hope for the future.

Though none of the individual elements of the play were new, their effect was unprecedented. *The Shaughraun* proved successful in 1874 because, despite the playwright's reliance on familiar iconography and stereotype, nothing like it had ever been seen in a New York theater. This was not just another occasion to laugh at the Irish, but instead it was an opportunity to laugh with the Irish—an apparently slight, but ideologically important distinction. The visual spectacle of *The Shaughraun* appealed to Irish Americans who often thought of their exile as painful separation but also desired to believe that the Irish spirit could be reborn in America. Such stage sets reaffirmed for them that they were not cut off from Ireland and that they still had access to their homeland. *The Shaughraun* also appealed to Anglo Americans who were apprehensive about the ethnic otherness of Irish immigrants, but who were given a kind of permission by the play to abandon old prejudices and appreciate the Irish in their immediate context. Though Boucicault's sets partook of common Irish clichés, he recast those clichés as symbols of cross-cultural reconciliation and harmony rather than as symbols of essential difference. His cleverness as a dramatist allowed him to re-appropriate familiar images for subversive new ends.

Boucicault's process of re-imagining Ireland in America goes hand-in-hand with his project of re-imagining the Irishman in this new context. As much as he creates a vivid portrait of Ireland in *The Shaughraun*, he goes to even greater lengths to describe an idealized sense of Irish identity. The play rejects the more common stereotypes of Irishness and offers something different in their place. It not only challenges the prejudicial beliefs of the non-Irish audience members, but also attempts to instruct Irish-American audience members in how to be properly Irish. Cave suggests that during a Boucicault performance "an audience is being educated skillfully about a complex of Irish responses" ("Staging" 109). He elaborates the point elsewhere by explaining that Boucicault specifically wished to educate his American audiences "into a proper appreciation of the Irish sensibility and of Irish values" ("Presentation" 115). Such a project would have had obvious appeal to the Irish in America, as it helped them make sense of their too often ambiguous and conflicted identity.

Boucicault openly despised the stage Irishman and those who exploited it for theatrical and financial gain. He condemned other playwrights who used the character as "low down, good for nothing blatherers" and described the generation of "Irish plays" that preceeded his as "remarkable for [their] stupidity" (Fawkes 117; "Amusements," 31 March 1860: 8). He never considered himself guilty of exploiting the same Irish stereotype or of engaging in the kind of drama that he thought of as unfashionably like "negro minstrelsy," a comparison he made that perhaps expresses an underlying racial unease regarding the similarities between stage Irishmen and stage Negroes and a desire to put more distance between dramatic representations of the two groups in America ("Amusements," 31 March 1860: 8). In newspapers, letters, public speeches, and theater programs, he repeatedly claimed that his personal project was to abolish the stage Irishman from theaters forever, or, as he once put it, he would "[knock] the stuffing out of that old libel 'Ragged Pat'" (Hogan 81). With the production of *The Shaughraun*, some critics thought he finally had succeeded. *The New York Times* claimed that the play had "almost driven the old-fashioned rough-and-tumble Irishman from the stage. The caricature has gone. The portrait from nature has been substituted in its steed" ("Amusements," 15 November 1874: 7). Of course, as noted earlier, not everyone agreed with the sentiment that Boucicault had destroyed the stage Irishman; many, in fact, believed he reinvigorated it.

The truth seems to be a compromise between the two positions; Boucicault's Irishman is not quite the same as what came before, but he does not completely escape from the stereotype either. Boucicault's Irishman is something in between an "out-and-out caricature and reasonable archetype" and is transformed primarily by the new context the playwright creates (Graves 35). Just as Boucicault repurposes common Irish imagery for his set designs, he similarly repurposes the stock Irish character for a new agenda. He offers the audience just enough familiarity to draw them in and then he once again subverts dominant ideology.

Conn the Shaughraun, the role that Boucicault himself performed in the New York premiere, has just enough of the expected characteristics to be recognizable, but several new qualities that violate precedent. *The New York Herald* describes Conn in terms that clearly cast him as nothing like previous stage Irishmen. Their review notes that the Shaughraun is

> a true type of a class of the Irish peasantry, in disposition cheerful, buoyant, generous, enthusiastic, sympathetic and compassionate, and who, though in rags, possesses a nature at once patriotic, chivalrous and loving, eager to battle for the right and ready in wit and strategy for fun or for emergency, with his heart full of faith, yet open to joy or sorrow as the sunshine or shadow may fall on his own path or that of his friends. ("Shaughraun" 5)

This description seems a startling counterpoint to the stage Irishmen who came before. Conn is not a blustering idiot, an ineffectual buffoon, or an ape-like monster. As Maureen Waters argues, there is nothing inherently threatening or brutal about Boucicault's Irish rogues (55). Maureen Murphy similarly notes that Conn is distinguished from earlier Irish rogues by his "kindness and loyalty" as well as his "courtesy and nobility" (29). In the end, what we get is an honorable scamp, more mischievous than malicious.

Though Conn at first appears to be (superficially) yet another stage Irishman, he actually subverts the stereotype. In the beginning, he seems to be an amoral vagabond; even his own mother testifies that "Conn nivir did an honest day's work in his life—but dhrinkin', and fishin', an' shootin', an' sportin', and lovemakin'" (271). Yet it is pointed out that all of these activities, which are associated with being a good-for-nothing rogue, are also the activities associated with being a wealthy gentleman. Conn's mother reflects that "a poor man that sports the sowl of a gentleman is called a blackguard" (271). Hinted at in these lines is the notion that the only difference between the stereotypical Irishman and the stereotypical gentleman is money. This theme deflates the space between the peasant Irish and the aristocracy and further challenges dominant class boundaries. As much as the Irish in America faced racial obstacles, they also confronted class barriers. In America, the "Irish Race" was, to a large degree, defined as much by their poverty and employment status as anything else. They were often considered socially inferior, even "non-white," simply because of the kind of work they engaged in (a concept explored in Chapters 2 and 4). It must have been tremendously satisfying to have it pointed out that there was little difference between an Irishman like Conn and an aristocratic gentleman. It reaffirmed that poverty did not truly define ethnicity. In other circumstances, Conn's amusements could be described as the prerogative of the wealthy. His "sowl" was as good as any man's, even if his wardrobe was not. By proxy, all Irish witnessing Conn's adventures could claim a kind of spiritual equality that trumped economic circumstance. The Shaughraun, after all, would not be ashamed of being poor.

Neither does Conn embody the cowardice so commonly ascribed to the stage Irishman. He does not just lie and cheat to save his own skin, but instead he does so "to save the entire Irish way of life from encroaching English culture" (Graves 34). Conn's humor is integral to his heroism, and unlike earlier stage Irish heroes of compromised loyalties, Conn emerges from and remains true to the Irish community. He openly and willingly opposes British authority and stands as a hero, not just another ineffectual comedic fool. He evokes laughter, but is also the primary heroic agent of Boucicault's drama. He spends the entirety of the play in action to save others: he travels across oceans to rescue Robert from a penal colony; he poaches game so that Arte and Claire will not starve when their land is stolen from them; he breaks Robert out of prison a second time and risks his life providing a decoy during the escape; and he protects Moya, his damsel in distress, from murderous villains looking for revenge. Conn's clownishness and his predilection for alcohol do not render him incompetent, as such traits usually do the stage Irishman. Instead, Conn's wit and compassion reveal him to be the most capable hero of the play.

The presence of Conn on stage as a metonymical model for Irishness certainly had broad appeal to many audiences. *The Shaughraun* was warmly received by theatergoers in England, Ireland, and Australia; yet, there are certain aspects of Conn's character that had particular appeal for Irish Americans. *The Shaughraun* has a deep affinity for American ideals. Certainly, Conn's status as an underdog mirrored the social status of Irish Americans. Like them, Conn faced social adversity, economic hardship, attempts to deny his freedom, and mounting pressures to reform his supposedly vulgar ways. In addition, Conn is a transient in the play, not only ranging across the scope of Ireland, but also literally traveling around the world. He not only survives this rootlessness, but also thrives on it. A population of immigrants struggling in a new world would find comfort in seeing a hero who could so remarkably succeed while in the same situation they themselves faced. Waters suggests that "[t]he appeal of such rascals was undoubtedly related to the very serious business of social and economic survival . . . The appeal of the rogue was the appeal of the forbidden, the daring and romantic choice" (51). Conn's triumph over the opposition blazes a trail for Irish Americans to follow. He shows how the socially disadvantaged can respond with "laughing generosity" instead of "angry rebellion" or "servile submission" (Kosok 27). Suggested in Conn's triumph, then, is that Irish Americans could find success through similar means. Their laughter and tolerance would succeed where anger and violence had failed. Irish Americans could embrace the idea of their roguishness as a kind of defense mechanism. Boucicault implies that the Irish in America, like Conn, can be rascals whose virtues outweigh their faults. And importantly, the Irishness represented by Conn is not isolating or anti-British, but quite the opposite. Conn's idealized Irish identity posits an alternative to dominant Anglo-centric behavior while still being compatible with it. Conn is thoroughly Irish but is just as at home among foreign sailors and British soldiers as he is among Irish peasants, justifying Harrington's description of him as the play's "agent of reconciliation" (*Irish Play* 11).

The Shaughraun notably ends with Conn's direct appeal for acceptance from the audience. He needs someone to testify that he is, at heart, a good and decent person. So he turns to the crowd in the theater and addresses them: "You are the only friend I have. Long life t'ye!—Many a time have you looked over my faults—will you be blind to them now, and hould out your hands once more to a poor Shaughraun?" (326). The play ends with cheering and shouts of approval from the audience. Though Boucicault was not above begging for applause, we can witness something subtler here. When the audience shouts out in favor of Conn, they voice their support for this new kind of Irish character and identity. Boucicault cleverly draws his audience in to participate in the final action of the play, and in doing so, he requires their active engagement with his vision of Ireland. He invites them to join the community on stage and, in effect, makes them part of a re-imagined Ireland that lingers even after the curtain drops.

Throughout the play, many of the characters express anxiety regarding their love of Conn. Their moral, civilized selves know they should scorn such a vagabond, but their romantic selves (their truly Irish selves,

Boucicault might even suggest) love the Shaughraun. Robert sums up the feelings of everyone in the play, as well as everyone in the audience who felt conflicted about enjoying the performance of a stage Irishman: "I ought to be ashamed of my love for the Shaughraun" (268).

But of course, he is not. And neither is the audience.

Boucicault describes Conn in the Dramatis Personae as more of a soul or spirit than a person. He simply is "the Shaughraun" and nothing else. He ends the play as exactly the same character that he started as; no growth is necessary for him. When Father Dolan asks him in the last lines of the play if he will reform, Conn responds, "I don't know what that is, but I will!" (326). The audience admires Conn's simplicity, which allows him access to greater depths of love and freedom. Krause describes Conn as Ireland's Huckleberry Finn who, like "the unreconstructed Huck," is "a better man in his primitive freedom" (194).[12] For the audience, Conn becomes a promise that a more reconciled Irish identity is possible. He is the ideal to which Boucicault's Irish-American audience could aspire. Despite cultural stereotypes, social ostracism, financial ruin, and political agendas, Conn triumphs. He achieves the good life by his own efforts. As Boucicault's Irish fans presented him with that testimonial plaque in 1874, they must have believed they could triumph as well.

CRAVING CONDESCENSION: EDWARD HARRIGAN'S *THE MULLIGAN GUARD BALL*

In May of 1873, the vaudeville comedy team of Ned Harrigan and Tony Hart premiered a new act in Chicago that they called "The Mulligan Guard." It satirized the "ridiculous pseudomilitary target companies" that were being formed by immigrants not allowed to join the regular militia (Moody, *Ned* 47). The duo appeared on stage as a pair of bumbling Irishmen in ragged military outfits, complete with over-sized medals and awkwardly large weapons (Figure 1.7). During the short sketch, the two made a mess of trying to master military maneuvers from a manual, and then they sang a marching song, lyrics by Harrigan and music by David Braham, that combined American patriotism with Irish ethnic pride, all the while gently mocking both:

> We crave your condescension, / We'll tell you what we know
> Of marching in the Mulligan Guard / from Sligo ward below.
> Our Captain's name was Hussey, / a Tipperary man,
> He carried his sword like a Russian duke, / whenever he took
>   command.
>
> (Chorus) We shoulder'd guns, and march'd, and march'd away
> From Baxter street, we march'd to Avenue A.

With drums and fife, how sweetly they did play,
As we march'd, march'd, march'd in the Mulligan Guard

When the band play'd Garry Owen, / Or the Connamara Pet;
With a rub a dub, dub, we'd march / In the mud, to the military step.
With the green above the red boys, / To show where we come from,
Our guns we'd lift with the right shoulder shift, / As we'd march to
    the bate of the drum.
—*Chorus.*

Whin we got home at night, boys, / The divil a bite we'd ate,
We'd all set up and drink a sup / Of whiskey strong and nate.
Thin we'd all march home together, / As slippery as lard,
The solid min would all fall in, / And march with the Mulligan Guard.
—*Chorus*

This song proved to be the most famous musical number of Harrigan's career, and despite its origins as a send-up of military pomp, it remained a standard of military bands around the world for several decades, even proving popular in India, where Rudyard Kipling describes a regimental band playing the song in *Kim*. The overblown pride of the two singing guardsmen contrasted with their incompetence at handling their weapons and evoked the general annoyance the public had for local ethnic militias. So, when the two guardsmen misspoke in the first line of the song—asking for "condescension" instead of "attention"—the audience was only too willing to oblige. No one could take these men seriously as either American patriots or honorable Irishmen since, in both respects, they were grotesque parodies. The humor of this vaudeville sketch derived not only from the comical staging of ethnic stereotype, but also from the lampooning of a certain kind of American nationalism. Indeed, amused condescension seemed the only possible response to Harrigan and Hart's performance.

It has been over a century since the Mulligan Guards paraded on the stage, and looking back it might be easy for us to condescend to them too. They seem to be stock melodramatic characters, Irish minstrels, without the complexity of character found in Irish dramas from after the turn of the century. Yet, despite the malapropism in their theme song, they do crave our attention and deserve to be heard even now. Though "The Mulligan Guard" is a relatively short comedic sketch of limited dramatic depth, it essentially tells the story of two ethnic minorities trying to become American. Is it enough to dress the part, carry a flag, pledge allegiance, and follow the rules of an etiquette manual? The guardsmen do just that, but if anything, seem less American for their efforts. Though their antics invite laughter, they also indicate the real dilemma of the immigrant: how to assimilate without losing cultural heritage. The Mulligan Guards represent

Figure 1.7   Ned Harrigan and Tony Hart as the Mulligan Guards.

an attempt to make simultaneous claims to Irish and American identities, and though they do not appear initially successful, this was only Harrigan's opening salvo in what would be a career-long project of depicting the way ethnic minorities help to shape national identity. The Mulligan Guard routine immediately became the highlight of the Harrigan and Hart repertoire and formed the precedent for nearly every other play that Harrigan wrote in his lifetime.

Harrigan reworked "The Mulligan Guard" vaudeville sketch into a longer play, *The Mulligan Guard Ball*, which premiered in New York at the Theatre Comique in 1879 and ran 153 performances (a stunning achievement for the time) before it moved on to engagements in Brooklyn and Boston. Harrigan charged low admission prices (fifteen cents in the gallery to seventy-five cents for an orchestra chair), which allowed him to draw in a diverse segment of the population, including regular uptown theatergoers as well as working-class fans from Lower East Side neighborhoods (Moody, *Ned* 91). The play proved so popular that it spawned seven sequels over the next five years, all of which featured the same cast in the same roles and all of which proved very successful, though the first play was generally considered the best of the series.[13]

Harrigan himself performed the lead role of Dan Mulligan, a character who in many ways resembles the classic stage Irishman (Figure 1.8). Yet, Harrigan did not see his Irish hero as belonging to that defamatory type. In an article he wrote for *Pearson's Magazine*, Harrigan describes Dan as a much nobler and flattering figure than previous stage Paddys: "I trust that in him I have given a true and adequate portrayal of the honest, thrifty, home-loving, genial Irish-American citizen. In him I sought to incarnate the jolly, big-hearted, thoroughly wholesome Irish type . . . He stands for Irish manhood in its strength" (504). Though Dan Mulligan's stereotypically Irish traits (i.e., drinking, fighting, blarneying) cannot be ignored, we should acknowledge that he also breaks from precedent. In *The Mulligan Guard Ball*, Harrigan presents a new type of stage Irishman that is as significantly different from Boucicault's as Boucicault's had been from his predecessors. Harrigan's Irishman did not live in the fields of Ireland, but rather in an American ghetto. His major dilemmas in life are not British oppression or the hard life of peasantry. Instead, Harrigan's Irishman confronts new problems: an uncomfortable proximity to other ethnic groups, overcrowding in the tenements, political exploitation, working-class stagnation, generational strife, and the challenge of asserting both American and Irish pride at the same time. Harrigan imagines an Irish identity far more specific to an American context than any previous writer, and in the character of Dan Mulligan he recreated the Irishman for end-of-century America.

Many of Harrigan's fans assumed that he was an Irish-born Catholic; however, he actually was born in the Lower East Side of New York to non-Catholic parents of mixed Irish/English heritage. In his entire life, he only made one brief visit to Ireland (Moody, *Ned* 7). Nonetheless, many Americans considered him to be "no less Celtic" than the popular Irish-born playwrights of the time (i.e., Boucicault, Brougham), and despite Harrigan's agnosticism and false brogue, he popularly was thought of as "the very image of an orthodox Hibernian" (Kahn 68). Harrigan gained his familiarity with Irish culture by growing up in what was a predominately Irish neighborhood. During his youth he lived in Cork Row (now Corlear's Hook), a place considered "the toughest portion of the toughest ward in the city" (Moody, *Ned* 11). As a young man, he also worked alongside numerous Irishmen in the local shipyards and fire companies. Immersed in New York's urban life, he came to strongly identify with an Irish identity, and many of his later plays, including *The Mulligan Guard Ball*, drew on his first-hand knowledge and experience of Irish life in New York's "Bloody Sixth Ward."[14]

Figure 1.8 Harrigan as Dan Mulligan in *The Mulligan Guard Ball* (Kahn).

Harrigan made a career out of crafting ethnic caricatures for the stage and made his acting debut at age sixteen by performing a minstrel routine of his own composition at an amateur theater show in New York (Moody, *Ned* 13). At eighteen, he ran away from home and began performing with his banjo and burnt cork make-up in San Francisco's melodeon theaters

(Moody, *Ned* 17–8). As his career progressed, he wrote and performed a broad range of "lowlife" types, including Italians, Germans, and Chinese, but he was most famous for his Irish characters. He created his Irish with more care and sympathy, emphasizing their wit and humor. His skill at portraying such characters, and at writing amusing "Irish" songs, popularly linked his name—which itself was recognizably Irish—with Irish performance. Harrigan played to his strengths, and to audience expectations, by focusing on Irish characters and themes throughout the rest of his career, using other ethnic characters mostly as foils for his Irish heroes.

Harrigan's frequent portrayal of the Irish in his work and his growing reputation as both an actor and writer led to comparisons with other notable Irish dramatists and performers of the time, most often Boucicault. Critics eagerly linked the two playwrights' names in reviews, usually in an effort to tout Harrigan's authenticity. For instance, *The New York Herald* proclaimed Harrigan's work to be just as purely Irish as *The Shaughraun* (Moody, *Dramas* 543). Such comparisons would have been warmly welcomed by Harrigan, since Boucicault was the gold standard not only for theatrical Irishness, but also for box office success. Harrigan was undoubtedly influenced by the elder playwright's work, and, initially, Boucicault thought very highly of Harrigan, once telling him, "You have done for the Irish in New York what I have done for the Irish in Ireland" (Kahn 67). However, Harrigan and Boucicault's relationship later soured when Harrigan performed in *The Skibbeah*, a blatant plagiarization of *The Shaughraun*. Harrigan sided against Boucicault in the ensuing legal controversy and even wrote a song mocking the playwright:

> We'll find out who wrote Shakespeare
> If we don't it isn't our fault
> Twas wrote by Poole and Buffalo Bill
> And claimed by Boucicault. (Moody, *Ned* 53)

Like Boucicault, Harrigan drew heavily on Irish stereotypes and clichés but still received praise for his realism and authenticity. *The New York Times* called the ethnic characters of *The Mulligan Guard Ball* "exactly true to life" ("Mulligan Guards Again" 4). Though the accolades given to Harrigan and Boucicault appear similar, there is a fundamental difference in their "realism" that indicates their divergent approaches to representing Irishness in America. In relation to Boucicault, such praise proves surprising because his work was so clearly sensationalistic and his characters so explicitly modeled on preexisting types. Boucicault believed the realism of his work was in his portrayal of an authentic Irish spirit, a kind of essential Irishness with which his immigrant audience craved to be filled. Boucicault never claimed to be presenting the facts of Irish life—but Harrigan did. Harrigan described his plays as accurate representations of life in the slums and in *Pearson's Magazine* stated that his characters were "genuine human types" drawn from "actual life" (505). Elsewhere, he once joked that immigrants would not come to his shows because what they would see on stage would be indistinguishable from what they saw at home (Kahn 13). Compare this rhetoric to Boucicault's claim that his descriptions of the "beautiful and good and innocent" were descriptions of "the truth" of Ireland ("Shaughraun" 5). Harrigan would never accept such selective nostalgia as "the truth."

Whereas Boucicault tried to instruct his audience how to be Irish in America, Harrigan aimed to show his audience how to be Irish American. The distinction is significant because the former required the playwright to present an ethnic identity believed to be lost, diminishing, or foreign, but the later required the playwright to simply represent an ethnic identity extant. Boucicault's was a project of reclamation and recovery; Harrigan's was one of reaffirmation, and as such, he could position his work as a study of a unique ethnic population, interesting not for their ties to an ancient land and its history, but for their vibrant tenacity and success in a modern American context.

As Harrigan's career developed, his plays were increasingly viewed as akin to anthropological explorations of the lower classes of American life. Audiences came to believe that he offered a unique kind of voyeuristic opportunity to observe the mean streets of New York and the wild Irish who inhabited them. Mick Moloney, the noted Irish folk musician and ethnomusicologist, describes Harrigan's work as "the ultimate theater of realism" that makes earlier depictions of lower class life look "generic and superficial" (8–9). The papers described Harrigan as "a Bowery Dickens," who, like the celebrated English author, took his audiences to places they normally might not venture (Dormon 35). Harrigan emphasized this quasi-anthropological approach of his by suggesting that he had found something pure and true in staging the mundane, violent, dirty, and unromantic lives of New York's Irish and once said,

> [Human nature] thins out and loses all strength and flavor under the pressures of riches and luxury. It is most virile and aggressive among those who know only poverty and ignorance. It is also then the most humorous and odd. (Moody, *Dramas* 547)

Audiences came away from a Harrigan performance believing that they had witnessed a faithful representation of human nature as it existed in the ghetto. Of course, Moloney points out, Harrigan's realism was selective and steered clear of the most brutal aspects of urban life, such as infant mortality, disease, and violent crime (11). Nonetheless, the plays offered theatergoers a chance to visit the Five Points without leaving the safety of their balcony seats. In the theater, they could safely meet characters who were virile and humorous, but too odd or aggressive for polite society.

Notably, Harrigan was influenced by the popular trend of literary realism in a way that Boucicault never was. In an 1886 article in *Harper's Monthly*, William Dean Howells, the noted author, critic, and pioneer of American literary realism, proclaimed Harrigan "part of the great tendency toward the faithful representation of life which is now animating fiction" (316). Such a claim urges us to consider Harrigan in the context of American writers like Jack London, Frank Norris, Theodore Dreiser, and Stephen Crane, or in the context of dramatists like August Strindberg, Henrik Ibsen, and Anton Chekov—an idea that might seem initially preposterous, but appears less so when you realize that his artistic agenda for the representation of ethnicity had more in common with the literary realists than it did with a melodramatist like Boucicault. Howells further defended his claim that Harrigan was a realist writer:

> Mr. Harrigan accurately realizes in his scenes what he realizes in his persons; that is, the actual life of this city . . . Mr. Harrigan shows us the street cleaners and contractors, the grocery men, the shysters, the politicians, the washer-women, the servant girls, the truckmen, the policemen, the risen Irishman and Irish woman, of contemporary New York . . . the illusion is so perfect that you lose the sense of being in the theatre; you are out of that world of conventions and traditions, and in the presences of facts. (315–6)

Howells' list of realistic persons conflates occupational types and ethnic types, as if it was as easy to recognize an Irishman by his appearance and behavior as it was to recognize a policemen by his uniform or a street cleaner by his broom. He easily accepts these portrayals of Irishness as facts, though he later argues that Harrigan sometimes "forgets his realism" when it comes to representing "colored" characters (316). Howells never considers that Harrigan's Irish are just as much caricatures as his more comically exaggerated blacks.

Even though Dan Mulligan is no more of a real Irishman than Conn the Shaughraun, he was imagined as a true definition of an ethnic type. James H. Dormon criticizes Harrigan and his audience for "failing to fathom the vital distinction between ascriptive and descriptive reality" (22). Though many people believed that the Mulligans and their neighbors were exactly like the kind of Irish found on the street, they were (like Boucicault's Irish characters) an artistic re-imagining of Irish identity. They emerged from the same history of stage Irish stereotypes and exhibited the same kind of comic exaggerations. What distinguishes Harrigan's Irish from Boucicault's (or any other writer of the time, for that matter) is the manner in which Irishness is imagined. Unlike any other dramatist, Harrigan celebrates Irishness first and foremost as an aspect of American culture. His Irish are not just an insular minority; they are vanguards at the intersection of ethnicity and nationality who consistently prove themselves to be more adept at navigating turbulent cultural forces than any other group. The appeal of *The Mulligan Guard Ball* was that it translated Irishness into something compatible with Americanness.

Harrigan tapped into the prevalent need to define national identity that obsessed late nineteenth-century Americans (see Introduction). His plays depicted the frontlines where such redefinition was taking place and showed how the economic, political, and social transformations occurring in the ghetto had implications throughout the country. Harrigan's vision was generally a positive one, which appealed to multiple audiences: American nativists who wanted relief from their immigrant fears and Irish Americans who wanted reassurance that they fit into the larger culture. Dormon suggests that Harrigan's audiences had "a social-psychological *need*" (36) to believe in the reality of *The Mulligan Guard Ball's* "cartoon ethnic world" (27). Though, in hindsight, Harrigan's depictions do not appear realistic, at the time they resonated within the public imagination and so show us how the Irish were popularly imagined as part of American identity. For this reason, Harrigan's work deserves more scrutiny. Boucicault may have transformed the stage Irishman into something reconcilable with American ideals, but Harrigan furthered the process by depicting the stage Irishman as an American ideal itself.

A close examination of *The Mulligan Guard Ball* proves challenging due to the style of Harrigan's working methods: he never printed his plays, nor did he make any attempt to preserve them for posterity (Moody, *Dramas* 544).[15] Unlike Boucicault, who formed touring companies for his plays, offered print editions, and seemed to have larger literary ambitions, Harrigan appeared content to let his works be entertainments confined to their time. For him, The Mulligan Guards could only be performed by his acting company; thoughts of other people in other times playing the parts did not occur to him. His surviving manuscripts and typescripts clearly display his indifference to a literary legacy: there are multiple versions of plays with little indication of which version(s) saw production; there is little record of the frequent improvisations or added topical materials he routinely incorporated into his shows; and large portions of significant stage direction were omitted from his scripts, often covering what would be up to five minutes in performance with the notation "business at rehearsal." As one critic observes, his plays "were built in the theatre, not in the study" (Moody, *Dramas* 541). Despite these textual obstacles, *The Mulligan Guard Ball* proves worthy of study precisely for its fragmentary nature. It was a play firmly rooted and responsive to the moment in which it was initially produced, and it demonstrates a concern with continuity rather than legacy. It does not attempt to define essential Irish characteristics for all time, but rather it attempts to show how the Irish of one generation achieved their success. It is important to remember that Harrigan chose to emphasize the continuity of his dramatic vision by creating a series of sequels that followed the Mulligan family throughout their lives, rather than re-staging the original play season after season, as Boucicault did with *The Shaugh-raun*. Harrigan once remarked that his goal was to "let the Mulligan family work out its own history naturally" (Moody, *Ned* 97). Though we can never hope to study the full spectacle of *The Mulligan Guard Ball* as it appeared under Harrigan's direction, the surviving text offers sufficient material from which to draw some important conclusions.

Like many of Harrigan's plays, *The Mulligan Guard Ball* is set in Manhattan's Lower East Side, among the shipyards, saloons, and tenements that were home to immigrants and freed blacks. The Mulligans live in the notorious Five Points neighborhood, which was razed over a century ago, but is still remembered for its poverty, vice, and crime. The squalor and violence of the Lower East Side neighborhoods gained an international reputation during this time. Charles Dickens described the Five Points in his *American Notes* (1842):

> This is the place: these narrow ways diverging to the right and left, and reeking every where with dirt and filth. Such lives as are led here, bear the same fruit here as elsewhere. The coarse and bloated faces at the doors have counterparts at home and all the wide world over. Debauchery has made the very houses prematurely old. See how the rotten beams are tumbling down, and how the patched and broken windows seem to scowl dimly, like eyes that have been hurt in drunken frays. Many of these pigs live here. Do they ever wonder why their masters walk upright in lieu of going on all-fours? and why they talk instead of grunting?

Henry James visited Manhattan's Lower East Side half a century later and described the tenements in similar terms, noting that the latticework of fire escapes was like a "spaciously organized cage for the nimbler class of animals in some great zoological garden . . . a little world of bars and perches and swings for human squirrels and monkeys" (*American* 102). Yet, despite the negative physical conditions of the area and its reputation for being the vilest place in New York (if not America), it was also one of the first neighborhoods in the country where racial integration occurred and where immigrant minorities gained a foothold in American politics.

Harrigan had affection for the area and saw it as the perfect setting for his plays. He described the Lower East Side as a place "where vice in rags held carnival all night long" (Moody, *Dramas* 535). This carnival-like neighborhood was dirty and violent, but in Harrigan's work, it was also a place of excitement, energy, and life. To help capture the sense of the place, Harrigan frequently obtained his costumes and props directly from the inhabitants of the Sixth Ward, even going as far as to purchase clothes from people he would meet on the street. He also based the specific locations in his dramas on actual locales; most notably, "Mulligan's Alley" stood in for the notorious "Murderer's Alley" (Moody, *Dramas* 541). Scenic artist

Charles W. Witham, who had previously worked for both Edwin Booth and Boucicault, provided the backdrops and set designs for many of Harrigan's shows and embraced the realistic style demanded of this later work.

Living in such a spot, Dan Mulligan struggles to find a way to assert an American identity compatible with his Irish heritage. Though he often appears to be a character with allegiances to two worlds, he strives to bring those two halves of his identity into unison. He marches with an Irish militia, but they march for an American cause. He proudly displays a row of American flags, but makes sure to have a row of Irish flags mixed in (28). Similarly, he takes great pride in American history, but insists that the Marquis de Lafayette, the Revolutionary War hero, was really an Irishman named Lafferty (32). Dan rewrites the American narrative with an Irish subtext in an effort to place the Irish within an American continuity and legitimize his own position in a new country. He wants to show that his Irish pride does not stand in opposition to his American aspirations, but rather in confluence with them, and so he tries to establish Irishness as, what Timothy Meagher calls, an "alternative Americanism."

The appeal of Harrigan's Irish, as I have already suggested, was that they appeared more capable of success in an American context than any other ethnic minority. *The Mulligan Guard Ball* dramatizes a difficult, yet successful, integration of the Irish character into American society and shows how the Mulligans assert an American identity, not in spite of their Irishness, but through it. They distinguish themselves as qualified for, and entitled to, full citizenship in the American community and express desires for what all American families want: opportunity, freedom, prosperity, security, and political privilege. Yet, they face three significant obstacles: ethnic conflict, class antagonism, and generational strife. Harrigan shows this Irish family to be adept at navigating these issues, and in the process shows the Irish to be exemplars of American ideals.

The Mulligan Guard Ball tells the story of Dan Mulligan, an Irishman who immigrated to the U.S. in 1848, fought in the Civil War, and subsequently settled in New York's Lower East Side to raise a family. He and his wife Cordelia have raised one son, Tommy, who has ambitions for work and family that would take him out of the ghetto. As the play opens, the family prepares for a ball to support the Mulligan Guard, the local Irish militia of which Dan was a founding member. The ball is being organized by Tommy and the rest of the Young Mulligans, who have largely taken over from the prior generation of guardsmen. Also revealed early on is Tommy's intent to elope with Kitty Lochmuller, the daughter of a German "bologna butcher." The play divides into two plotlines that are only tangentially related. The first follows the conflict between the Mulligan Guard and the Skidmore Guard (a rival, all-black neighborhood militia) and culminates in a showdown at the local pub when it is discovered that the two groups have booked the same location for their festivities on the same night. The second plotline borrows heavily from the *Romeo and Juliet* formula and details Tommy and Kitty's plans to go against their parent's wishes and secretly marry.

The plot of the play is thin and many of the scenes do seem to be excuses for the "slambang" antics and general melee for which Harrigan was known, traits that led one critic to accuse him of writing "prolongations of sketches" (Moody, *Dramas* 546). Notably, Howells disagreed with this appraisal of Harrigan's work and saw in his apparent plotlessness the beginnings of a new realistic conception of dramatic action and characterization. In 1889, he wrote in *Harper's Monthly*,

> We believe that the American drama, like the American novel, will be more and more a series of sketches, of anecdotes, of suggestions, with less and less allegiance to any hard and fast intrigue . . . Because the drama has been in times past and in other conditions the creature, the prisoner, of plot, it by no means follows that it must continue so; on the contrary, it seems to us that its liberation follows; and of this we see signs in the very home of the highly intrigued drama, where construction has been carried to the last point, and where it appears to have broken down at last under its own inflexibility. ("Editor's Study" 315)

In comparison to the works of a playwright like Boucicault whose melodramatic sensibilities dictated plot-driven dramas, Harrigan's plays do appear fragmentary and unfocused. Yet, I am inclined to agree with Howells that Harrigan was engaged in a new, even progressive, type of drama and was not simply bastardizing conventions. Harrigan achieves his dramatic effects through saturation, especially when it comes to delineating ethnic characters. We discover his concept of Irishness not through overt plot devices and blunt characterizations, but through repeated exposure to individual characters and a piecemeal assemblage of their traits. Ultimately, his characters prove more multi-faceted and complex than it might be imagined that such characters with vaudeville roots could be.

Harrigan builds the fragmented actions of his play around a kernel of ethnic and racial conflict and depicts the Irish as part of a competitive milieu that includes blacks, Germans, Italians, and Chinese. Though they are forced to live and work together, these various peoples cling to racist beliefs and antagonisms. Moloney suggests that the play "acted as a catharsis for audiences experiencing the day to day stress of adjusting to new neighbors in unfamiliar surroundings" (9). Of course, much of the ethnic friction is intended by Harrigan for cathartic comedy, but it also serves to establish a kind of hierarchy among the various ethnicities of the slums, with the Irish shown to be safer, more civilized, more progressive, and (by inference) more American than any other group. In the play, the Irish assert their privilege by marginalizing other minorities, a phenomenon that several historians observe was common in urban America in the nineteenth century. Though Irish Americans would have had much in common with other immigrant ethnic groups and would have stood to benefit from cooperation, they by and large did not do so. Meagher observes that though the "merger into a class-conscious working class was always a potential alternative" for the Irish, they instead often engaged in "competition for power and resources" with other ethnic groups (*Columbia* 7–11). Noel Ignatiev specifically studies the relations between the Irish immigrants and the freed blacks who often found themselves living in the same neighborhoods and competing for the same jobs and says that "while Afro-American and Irish-American workers often, and quite militantly, opposed established authority, they rarely collaborated to do so" (47). Instead, Irish Americans embraced ethnic antagonism and racism as paths to assimilation.

In *The Mulligan Guard Ball*, one of Dan's two main rivals is the German butcher, Lochmuller, who in the first scene of the play overhears Dan disparaging the German people and challenges him to make good on his words by engaging in a fistfight. Cordelia and Tommy defuse the situation, but the conflict between the patriarchs never truly goes away. Though they are neighbors and (supposedly) friends, Dan repeatedly insults Lochmuller, his profession, and his heritage, considering him nothing more than a degenerate maker of "bow wow puddings" (18). Throughout the rest of Acts 1 and 2, Dan plots to corner Lochmuller and give him a beating for his impudence, thinking it will teach the German to respect the Irish. Even getting a shave at the barber shop in preparation for the Mulligan Guard Ball becomes an inter-ethnic competition for the two men when the barber has to agree to shave half of "Germany's" face and then half of "Ireland's" because neither man will allow the other the privilege of going first (53). Though both men have a variety of grievances with the other, Harrigan couches all of their disputes in ethnic terms; Dan's insults of Lochmuller become insults of all "Dutchmen," and Lochmuller's responses become attacks on the Irish.

Of course, the main issue between Dan and Lochmuller is that their children wish to marry. The co-mingling of German and Irish blood disgusts both men. Dan would prefer his son to marry a nice Irish girl like Mary O'Brien, even though Tommy does not find her "stylish" enough (15). Similarly, Lochmuller tries to set his daughter up with Mr. Kline, the "Swiss warbler," a man he regards as better than any Irishman, which is hypocritical since he himself married an Irishwoman. When Tommy announces his intentions to his parents, Dan responds, "The name of Mulligan will never be varnished wid the name of Lochmuller. The divil a drop of Dutch blood will ever enter the family" (15). He then threatens to tie a stone around his feet and throw himself off the Battery if Tommy goes through with it (16). The prospect of intermarriage frightens Dan because he believes it would dilute the purity of his Irish family at a time when the Irish are trying to establish themselves as the ideal immigrant minority. Though he never uses terms like miscegenation or mongrelization, his fear of "mixed blood" likely resonated with audiences who were familiar with these concepts and had misgivings about intermarriages themselves. Of course, Harrigan borrows his plot from *Romeo and Juliet*, but by giving it an ethnic American context he achieves something unique. Tommy and Kitty are not just children of politically opposed families (the Mulligans and Lochmullers share many political and economic sympathies); rather, we are to understand that they are children of two different breeds. Though historically the Irish often were thought of as a threat to American racial integrity, Harrigan depicts them in this play as defenders of racial purity. Harrigan imagines New York as a place where upward mobility is linked with ethnic competition, and the Irish are most deserving of the prize.

Dan's other adversary is Simpson Primrose, the leader of both the Skidmore Guard and an anti-Irish society known as the Full Moons. Harrigan casts these black organizations as persistent ideological and physical threats to the Irish of the Five Points and attributes to them the most vitriolic anti-Irish prejudice in the play. The black characters are the ones who seek to reduce the Irish to stereotypes and accuse them of being a dirty, alcoholic, violent people in need of quarantine and fumigation (26). They further describe the Irish as socially and culturally inferior, and often question the patriotism and professionalism of the Mulligan Guard in comparison to the Skidmores. In one scene, Primrose admits a hatred for the Chinese, but insinuates that the Irish are even worse, saying he prefers "Mongolians" to "Milesians" (42). Harrigan's audience would have been very familiar with such slanders, but not necessarily from the mouth of a black man, and such a change in speaker radically repositions anti-Irish sentiment as a sign of social (even racial) inferiority. For example, in Boucicault's *The Shaughraun*, Captain Molineux shows himself to be prejudiced and slanders the Irish, but his actions and words are part of a dramatic arc to enlightenment and he comes to realize how wrong his original impressions of the Irish were. Yet, in *The Mulligan Guard Ball*, Primrose never embarks on an arc of enlightenment, and it is implied that none is required since his anti-Irish prejudice is a function of his black identity. A white man slandering the Irish was considered ignorant and could be shown the error of his ways; a black man doing so was considered too socially ambitious and needed to be reminded of his position. Boucicault tries to elevate impressions of the Irish by showing them to be on an equal level with the English, a dramatic move that allows the audience to come to the same conclusions (potentially) as Molineux; however, Harrigan tries to elevate impressions of the Irish by showing them to be better than blacks, which forces the audience to defend Irishness as a means to defend their own whiteness.

Harrigan's black characters also pose a physical threat to the Irish as they always come on stage armed with razors and knives, no matter the occasion or setting. The threat of black violence lingers throughout the first half of the play and seems unavoidable when the Skidmores confront the Mulligans at the Harp and Shamrock Pub. Through an error, the pub owner has double-booked the room for both groups' celebrations, and neither militia is willing to back down. The Mulligans shout "kill the niggers," and the Skidmores draw their weapons, before the owner intervenes and arranges a truce that sends the Skidmores to a room upstairs, a compromise that Primrose accepts since it implies that the blacks are (literally) above the Irish (97–8). Yet the peace is short-lived: the Skidmores fall through the ceiling in the middle of the dance, and the promised melee finally breaks out at the close of Act 2.

By showing the Irish and blacks to be enemies, Harrigan primed his audience to accept the Irish as part of a white American community. In comparison to the razor-wielding blacks (who would have been portrayed by actors in blackface), the Irish appeared quite acceptable, safe, and civilized. The worst that Harrigan's Irish were capable of was comedic violence (i.e., exploding cigars, bungled military maneuvers), but the black characters in the play commit real violence—they actually draw blood with their razors and start what is essentially a race riot. The Mulligans are poor and silly, but they do not threaten the establishment in the same way that the Skidmores do.

Dormon claims that Harrigan's African-American characters signify "a potential threat not only to the Irish but to white society at large" (30). If this is true, then Irishness becomes a metonymical model, at least within Harrigan's theater, for a white hegemony, and the conflict between the Mulligans and the Skidmores comes to represent the racial strife between whites and blacks in post-war America. In addition, Harrigan associates anti-Irish prejudice with black identity and, by such an association, made it less appealing for his predominately white audience to hold similar views. Such a move also unfairly placed the burden of a white sin (since anti-Irish prejudice had origins in Anglo culture) on black shoulders so that a path to reconciliation and assimilation could be opened between the Irish-American and Anglo-American populations.

Though Harrigan's ethnic humor and racial biases often seem distasteful, his portrayal of inter-ethnic relations in the slums proves worthy of attention because he gives expression to the complex relationship between race, ethnicity, and class. In an odd way, while still clinging to certain racist beliefs, Harrigan expresses a kind of hope for ethnic reconciliation through economics. He envisions the various peoples of the Lower East Side as what Ignatiev calls a "common culture of the lowly" (2). Though the Mulligans, Lochmullers, and Skidmores are suggested to be genetically and temperamentally incompatible, they also are shown to be economically and socially reliant on each other. In *The Mulligan Guard Ball*, ethnic outrage gets pacified by financial interdependence.

Despite their various grievances, Dan and Lochmuller find their social and financial well-being intricately entwined. They come to realize that they both belong to the same political lodge when they clasp hands and recognize the secret handshake. They are then forced to give their word, "Dimocrat to Dimocrat," that they will not quarrel in the house (18).

They also find common ground in their mutual hatred of Italians and their condescension toward blacks. Most significantly, though, Dan and Lochmuller know that they financially depend on each other. The Lochmullers rent their apartment from the Mulligans, who in turn buy their meat from the Lochmullers. In fact, the reason that the two men continually put off their promised fisticuffs is because they both owe each other money and do not want to do anything to jeopardize payment of their respective bills.

Similarly, the Irish and blacks depend on each other's patronage and economic cooperation. Circumstances require the Mulligans and Skidmores to live and work together. They buy their groceries from the same store, pay bills to the same collectors, and even use the same washerwoman (who mixes up Dan and Primrose's shirts, so that the Irishman actually wears a black man's clothes in Act 3). The economy of the neighborhood depends on inter-racial cooperation. Primrose, a professional barber, serves all ethnicities in his shop. Similarly, the Harp & Shamrock pub willingly plays host to both the Mulligan Guard Ball and the Skidmore Fancy Ball. Circumstances have placed the Irish and blacks together, and Harrigan shows the relationship to be functional, if not equal. Despite their anger toward each other, Dan and Primrose try to be accommodating. When they learn of the double-booking at the pub, they eventually accept the compromise and shake hands, with Simpson remarking, "We've allus been on speaking terms wid de Mulligan Guards and as we are gwine upstairs to have our pleasure, we want to be friendly" (99). The Mulligan Guard then gives their usual adversaries three cheers of support. Of course, a fight eventually does break out, but the issue is resolved enough to allow Primrose and another member of the Skidmores to work as servers at Dan's wedding anniversary the very next night. This reconciliation, while enforcing the subservience of blacks to Irish, also attempts to diffuse the threat of racial violence and show the Irish as adept at resolving such conflict.

In regards to racial relations, Lauren Onkey suggests that *The Mulligan Guard Ball* dramatizes a "constant slippage between identification and anger" ("Melee"). Though Harrigan's Irish display clearly racist ideologies and even use racism as a means to get a leg up in society, they at times also show an ability to recognize the other in themselves. The Irish in the play are not at all secure in their racial or cultural position in America, and Harrigan represents this by dramatizing the conflicting forces at work in their lives. In order to be accepted as American, they believe they must appeal to the white Protestant hegemony, but day-to-day circumstances require cooperation with other minority groups. Harrigan seems to acknowledge the pressures for (and advantages of) assimilation, but also suggests that it is an impractical and flawed process.

His characters ironically strive to achieve broad social acceptance by dividing themselves into rigid ethnic factions, and so their long-term aspirations stand in opposition to their immediate need for practical cooperation. While I do not think it accurate to ascribe to Harrigan an anti-assimilationist agenda, I do think he saw fractures in the system and perhaps felt obliged due to his artistic sensibilities to represent them in realistic fashion. The racism of his characters is more complex and conflicted than might be imagined; he does not posit the Irish and black populations of the Lower East Side as congenial neighbors, nor does he present them as stalwart enemies. Though Dan is quick to shout "kill the niggers" when the Skidmore Guard arrives at the Harp & Shamrock, he also chastises Lochmuller at the barbershop for using the same word and pronounces that "a man has no right to insult a colored man to his face" (56).

In considering the ethnic and racial aspects of Harrigan's plays, Moloney argues that the playwright's work "always promoted the kind of accommodation that is the essence of true tolerance in any multicultural society" (18). While I do not think that *The Mulligan Guard Ball* goes quite as far as promoting accommodation and tolerance, it certainly challenged audience assumptions about ethnic relations. Harrigan does not offer any solution for reconciling ethnic and racial conflicts, but by acknowledging and representing the complexity of these conflicts, he likely pushed more than some of his audience members to question their understanding of how such groups fit into the American community.

Harrigan shows the Irish of the Lower East Side to be responding to diverse pressures, their identity shifting based on time and circumstance. By acknowledging the confusion and instability of Irish identity, Harrigan presents an Irish character unlike any that had come before. Dan is not a pure spirit of Ireland like Conn the Shaughraun; rather, he is a simple workingman, trying to make sense of conflicting ideologies and nationalisms in a rapidly modernizing city. Whereas Boucicault's vision of the Irish is unchanging and nearly sacred, Harrigan's vision shows them to be flawed, but generally good, people willing to adapt to new circumstances. Boucicault's stage Irishman largely inverts the stereotype by showing previously derided characteristics to be fundamental strengths; Harrigan's stage Irishman breaks with precedent, not because it inverts the stereotype, but because it struggles against the stereotype to become something new, modern, and American.

Harrigan tries to establish Dan Mulligan as an idealized urban man and agent of modernity who thrives in his environment by proving adaptable. Dan navigates the turbulent social dynamics of the city and perseveres with good humor despite overwhelming obstacles to his success, and in doing so, he establishes a new image of the Irish in America that Maureen Murphy describes as "high-spirited but also responsible and trustworthy" (30). Harrigan gives him a job in the city gasworks, which means that he literally powers the city with his sweat and strength, lighting the streets of New York and providing warmth for all its residents. As Cordelia observes,

"If it wasn't for Daniel Mulligan, the divil a light we'd have in the city" (6). Harrigan attempts to set his Irishman up as a modern everyman, which is perhaps his most subversive achievement in *The Mulligan Guard Ball*. In dominant cultural imaginings, Irishness was a blatant sign of otherness, filth, violence, drunkenness, and general social backwardness, but in Harrigan's world, the Irishman embodied the decency and respectability of the growing urban working class. He subtly and smartly works the stereotype around so as to present in Dan—a beer-drinking, meat-eating, family-loving, God-fearing, manual laborer—the nobility of the hardworking immigrant. Meagher argues that the Irishman would eventually become the symbol for such characteristics in later years, "the archetype of the 'regular guy,' the 'average joe,' who rejected aristocratic pretension, snobbery, and the blandishments of society and stood with his own, his boys" ("Fireman" 625). Dan Mulligan seems to be one of the first steps in this direction. Harrigan once again entwines ethnic and class issues so that when audiences cheer a hero of the common man, they also are cheering for a hero of the Irish people.

However, the most significant challenge Dan faces in *The Mulligan Guard Ball* is not ethnic, racial, or class related at all—it is generational. Things are changing for the Irish in the Lower East Side, and the next generation has different ambitions than their parents and no interest in maintaining the status quo. Tommy is not, and cannot be, the same kind of Irishman as his father. He is more ambitious and rebellious; he wants better food, nicer clothes, and better entertainments; he identifies more directly with an American identity; and though he is a member of the Young Mulligan Guard, he sees the group as more of an opportunity for socializing than for affirming his ethnic loyalty. Tommy criticizes the original Mulligan Guard of his father's generation, referring to them as "old timers" and "millers" who constantly interfere in the affairs of the "young fellows" and he will not even wear the Mulligan Guard uniform to the ball, opting instead for a stylish new suit (12). At home, he distances himself from the insular Irishness of his parents and the more stereotypical signs of their ethnicity: he corrects their pronunciation when their brogue mutilates the occasional word; he teases his father about his past as a saloon owner; he condemns his father's pipe smoking as a dirty habit; and he commits the ultimate taboo by marrying a non-Irish girl. In addition, Tommy is the only one in his family who does not speak Irish in the play, but instead utilizes popular slang terminology that confuses and alienates his parents.[16]

As radically different as Tommy is from his father, there is appeal in his character too, since he gives voice to second generation concerns and allows Harrigan to show yet another facet of Irish-American identity. There often were significant cultural differences between Irish immigrants and their American-born children that resulted in a different kind of Irish-American identity coming into maturity near the turn of the century. Meagher observes that second-generation Irish Americans were often more eager to participate in American popular culture and sports, more ambitious to climb the economic ladder, and more interested in the new Catholic revival than their parents' generation (*Columbia* 131–2). In literature, this divide between the generations became what Werner Sollors calls "the metaphor of the declining second generation," because it symbolized a falling away from "authentic" ethnicity and served as a warning to future generations not to make the same mistake (*Beyond* 222). Tommy's actions in the play do agitate such fears since his breaking with tradition and marriage to a German girl signal the end of what had been (until his generation) a purely Irish family. Dan views Tommy's choices as a betrayal of family and heritage, and cannot conceive of why anyone would want a life beyond the Five Points, since his own greatest ambition is to garner more power and prestige in the neighborhood and, perhaps, become "Boss Mulligan" (68).[17] Yet, Harrigan also humorously points out Dan's hypocrisy, since Dan is just as critical of the generation before his as Tommy is of Dan's. Dan has moved beyond the strife of the old land and has little patience for hearing about the woes of Ireland. When Mrs. Dublin launches into another one of her stories about the old country, Dan tries to shut her up by handing her a drink and telling her to "put that down your Irish Channel" (71).

Harrigan espouses hope for Tommy, too, and shows that there is something admirable, even American, in his desire to break free and be his own man. Tommy loves and respects his father, but he also complains that "he tries to queer everything I put my hand to" (80). Tommy must break with his family and transform himself in order to succeed in America—ideas that play directly into audience affection for the self-made man. After marrying Kitty, Tommy plans to move out west because he believes that "new countries make new men" (22). He embraces Horace Greeley's suggestion to "go west, young man" and seems determined to carve out a piece of America for himself and his new, multi-ethnic family. In this aspect of the play, Harrigan appears to hint at the possibility for a different kind of assimilation available on the frontier, but not available in east coast cities (see Chapter 2 for more on this concept).

Though Boucicault may have been the more famous playwright and *The Shaughraun* the more enduring play, I suspect that Harrigan likely impacted Irish-American discourse in a more direct and significant way. Few writers ever quote him or credit him as an influence, but his approach to Irish representation seems to be the one that gained traction over the years. It is hard not to see echoes of Dan Mulligan in Eugene O'Neill's Con Melody or Edwin O'Connor's Frank Skeffington, or reflections of Tommy Mulligan in James T. Farrell's Studs Lonigan or J. P. Donleavy's Sebastian Dangerfield. Harrigan's play, while not as celebratory of Irish identity as Boucicault's, resonated with a public who recognized that Irishness was more complex than any single stage Irishman could ever present. *The Mulligan Guard*

Ball re-imagined Irishness as something dynamic and changing, and while it built on very old stereotypes, it acknowledged that being Irish American was different than being an Irishman in America. At times, Harrigan's characters appear confused and conflicted, but this is part of their appeal since we can see in their struggle to define their ethnic and national identities a sincere portrait of the trials that formed modern American society.

2 "Sivilizing" Irish America

At the end of Mark Twain's *The Adventures of Huckleberry Finn* (1884), the boy protagonist realizes he can never fit into civilized society and famously proclaims, "I got to light out for the Territory ahead of the rest" (296). Unable and unwilling to assimilate to the standards of his community, Huck opts instead to travel into the western wilderness, beyond the reach of those who would change him. This ending is mirrored in the final pages of Harold Frederic's *The Damnation of Theron Ware* (1896), in which the young Protestant minister, having gone native living among the Irish of upstate New York, similarly chooses to head west, to "the other end of the world," in order to escape the community that no longer will accept him (313). Attracted by the "impalpable outlines" and "undefined dimensions" of the Western Territory, Theron hopes to find a community that will value his new, Irish-influenced identity and exclaims, "Stranger things have happened than that, out West!" (314–5). A similar ending is found again in Frank Norris' *McTeague* (1899). Once more, a community exiles the undesirable and uncivilized Irishman into the wilderness. Like Huck Finn and Theron Ware before him, McTeague is forced to slip past the boundaries of his community and live on the western margins of America. In the concluding chapters of the novel, motivated by an instinctual knowledge that he does not belong in the company of other men, McTeague retreats to a series of increasingly remote locales and finally finds refuge in the very antithesis of civilization: Death Valley.

All three of these novels posit exile as the alternative to assimilation. Those who fail to achieve at least the semblance of conservative, Anglo-Saxon gentility, manners, and thinking are denied the rights of full citizenship. Huck Finn, Theron Ware, and McTeague attempt to fit in, but are rejected by mainstream society because they prove to be destabilizing elements in their communities. Their Irish natures and sympathies mark them as socially rebellious, unequivocally dangerous, and uniquely unsuited for an American way of life. They go west to that region of America that Frederick Jackson Turner described in 1893 as "the meeting point between savagery and civilization," a place where real democracy existed and where an immigrant could experience "effective Americanization" (200–1). But do these characters experience the transformation that Turner promises, or are they simply exiled to the borders as a kind of cordon sanitaire? This chapter explores how three American realists not of Irish descent tried to answer the question at the heart of nativist anxieties about Irish assimilation: can the Irish be civilized?

In the decades after the Famine, the Irish in America came to be seen more and more as a unique threat to the social order. The Irish had a reputation (popularized by English writings) for being disturbers of the peace, lawless rebels, and ignorant criminals whom the English had been unable to civilize over the past several centuries (Potter 167). Some despaired that the U.S. would fare no better. Aggravating the situation was the perception that Irish Catholics were uniquely unsuited to life in a country that was "spiritually, intellectually, culturally and emotionally" the child of Protestant Reformation ideology (Potter 245). As historian Kerby Miller observes, what upset many Americans more than stereotypical Irish drunkenness, violence, or superstition was the Irish's obliviousness toward "bourgeois ideals and leadership," their antagonism toward strangers, and their resentment of employers and other wealthy citizens (327). These were people who apparently could not, or did not want to, assimilate into a society that espoused individualism, moral restraint, and personal ambition. In addition, some argued that the Irish placed a disproportionate strain on city services (i.e., police, hospitals, jails, poor houses) and they resented that tax money was being siphoned off to support an ethnic group who could not support themselves. Such beliefs gave rise to a perception that the Irish were a cultural and economic burden unfairly inflicted on the social body of America.

In the late nineteenth century, several prominent scholars advocated social reform as a way to deal with these immigrant problems and the perceived health and safety threats brought by ethnic minorities into American communities. Native-born Americans were terrified by the spikes in crime and pauperism, the rise in mortality rates, and the proliferation of contagious diseases, all attributed to the growing population of foreign-born residents. The immigrant horde (of which the Irish comprised the largest percentage) was thought of as an immediate threat to public safety and welfare, but social reformers urged the public to think of immigrants as reformable; they could be made safe, it was believed, if only America undertook a project of civilizing and remaking their characters. Such suggestions differed significantly from the proposals of the previous century that advocated confinement and deportation of dangerous aliens and that led to the passing of the Alien and Sedition Acts and thereby legalized the unconstitutional persecution of immigrants in the name of national security. More importantly, the concept of social reform implied that ethnic otherness could be transformed into something safe and compatible with domestic Americanness. While social reformers did not necessarily deny a link between ethnicity and bad behavior, they vigorously advocated for programs that could overcome even the most stubborn or inherent qualities of troublesome groups like the Irish.

Charles Loring Brace pioneered numerous programs of social reform (including foster care) and detailed his general approach to rehabilitating ethnic minorities in *The Dangerous Classes of New York* (1872), in which he stated a belief that "the worst evil in the world is not poverty or hunger, but the want of manhood or character" (389). He viewed the problems of immigrant ghettos as primarily moral dilemmas, and so sought to implement programs that would address moral privation among that population. His goal was not to punish poor immigrant communities, but "to prevent their growth" (ii). Brace's major suggestion was an explicitly religious program that proposed taking poor children, who if left in their current environment would succumb to evil, and sending them to live out in the country with Protestant farming families. By removing the influence and temptations of their urban communities (including the influence of their native religious officials and ethnic nationalist groups), Brace believed such children could be transformed into productive, upright American citizens.

Brace addressed the unique problem of the Irish in America, specifically singling them out as more in need of social reform than other groups. He believed that the Irish were more virtuous in their home country than in the U.S. and that their transplantation to a new land and the "breaking of the ties" with the native country had a "bad moral effect" on them (34–6). Brace also blamed a lack of positive social structure among Irish families and the "chilling formalism of the ignorant Roman Catholic" mindset for their decline. He even hinted at a biological explanation for Irish incivility, writing,

> It is well known to those familiar with the criminal classes, that certain appetites or habits, if indulged abnormally and excessively through two or more generations, come to have an almost irresistible force, and, no doubt, modify the brain so as to constitute almost an insane condition. (43)

Brace's formulation here falls just short of implying hereditary or genetic deficiency in the Irish, but does point to a biological transmission of undesirable social traits. While avoiding the accusation that social evils were inherent in the Irish character, it does suggest that badness is in the blood. Brace even blamed the bad behavior of other ethnic groups, especially the Italians, on the supposed "ancient Celtic blood" they must have had in them (194). In the end, Brace's brand of social rehabilitation considered the Irish reformable, but required a near total break with all things Irish-American in order to subdue (if not purge) the wickedness in their character.

Jacob A. Riis addressed the same problems as Brace, but came to different conclusions. In *How the Other Half Lives* (1890), he refuted Brace's project because it placed all of the blame on the ethnic minority rather than on the social majority that created the abhorrent conditions of the ghettos and that exploited the immigrant population. Riis wrote,

> The "dangerous classes" of New York long ago compelled recognition. They are dangerous less because of their own crimes than because of the criminal ignorance of those who are not of their kind. The danger to society comes not from the poverty of the tenements, but from the ill-spent wealth that reared them, that it might earn a usurious interest from a class from which "nothing else was expected." (197)

Riis' formulation shifted away from the individual to focus on the environment, and his program for reform reflected this by advocating for better sanitation, fresh air, and light in the ghettos, as well as a complete redesign of tenement buildings to improve comfort and hygiene. He believed that the physical darkness of tenement life created the moral darkness witnessed by the rest of the city (18). Like Brace, he believed that the foreign classes of the city could be reformed to a new way of life and could come to embrace wholesome American values, but he thought such change was achieved by attacking the root of the problem: the social and economic greed of landlords and politicians.

Again like Brace, Riis considered the Irish a special case in immediate need of such reform. He described the Irish as "hereditary beggars" who were harder to lift up out of their depressing conditions because, unlike mere criminals who wanted more from their lives, paupers were content to wallow in filth and misfortune (187). Riis also argued that the Irishman was ill-suited for domesticity, being more inclined to spend his free time in saloons than at home building stable family structures (25). Finally, he suggested that the Irish, having been abused by native-born Americans for decades and become "apt pupils" at such abuse, were now cruelly antagonizing newer immigrant groups and instigating conflict and violence in the ghettos (22). The Irish could be reformed, Riis thought, but he held out less hope for them than other minority groups since they were more entrenched in a fundamentally un-American social pathology.

Riis' project for social reform was more liberal and sympathetic than Brace's, and despite its numerous faults, it urged Americans to start thinking of assimilation as a challenge, not just for ethnic minorities, but for the whole of American society. Unlike Brace, who suggested breaking up the "fever nests" of the ghettos and scattering children around the country so that their "moral disease" could be wiped out by diffusion (26), Riis indicated the possibility for transforming ethnic others by transforming their environment. Despite these differences, both men emphatically clung to the belief that immigrants could be made American and that such transformation was necessary if the country was to survive its evolution into a modern nation.

The implications of these projects of social reform on literature of the nineteenth century are significant because they mark a moment in American history when the country started to imagine that immigrant others could become, under certain circumstances, part of the national community. By no means did everyone believe such reform was possible or likely, but as such ideas gained popular currency, more and more novelists explored the various methods and outcomes in their books. Late-century novelists reflected the anxieties of a population unsure what to do about the aliens in their midst, and like the social reformers, the novelists seem intent to determine what was to blame for the problematic immigrant group's behavior (environment or heredity) and what was the best way to reconcile the ethnic individual with the broader society.

The novels considered in this chapter partook of an unsettled debate regarding Irishness in America and reflect the ambitions of those who endorsed the reformation of the Irishman and those who thought such change was impossible. In the fictional portrayals of society's attempts to civilize Huckleberry Finn, enlighten Theron Ware, and domesticate McTeague, we can see a dynamic range of approaches to dealing with powerful assimilationist forces, ranging from a voluntary exile, to an inversion of the ethnic transformation paradigm, to a brutal sterilization of the foreign element; and though all three novels present radically different degrees of optimism for Irish reform, they all connect the future of Irish America with the Western Frontier and its promise of transformation. In American literature, it would seem, it is only in the borderlands that the Irish can succeed or fail to earn a place in a democratic, national community.

A MANUAL FOR RESISTING ASSIMILATION: MARK TWAIN'S *THE ADVENTURES OF HUCKLEBERRY FINN*

In what seems almost a throwaway comment in *How the Irish Became White* (1995), Noel Ignatiev describes *The Adventures of Huckleberry Finn* as "a very Irish story" (58). This comment, which Ignatiev does not fully explain, provokes us to give a new kind of attention to Mark Twain's novel because what makes *Huck Finn* significant as an Irish-American artifact is the Irishness of the story itself. The novel describes society's repeated attempts to reform and civilize a delinquent Irish boy, but Twain criticizes such a project of social reform by showing Huck to be a better person in his unreconstructed existence than in an assimilated status quo. The qualities that Twain celebrates in Huck (his rebelliousness, his simplicity, his emotionality, his connection with the earth, his affinity with black people, his dramatic flair, his lyrical wit) are the very same qualities that many Americans felt were the most unattractive and dangerous aspects of the stereotypical Irishman. In *Huck Finn*, Twain presents a complex study of Irish-American identity, showing it to be more versatile in dealing with cultural crisis, racial strife, economic hardship, and domestic tragedy, but also conversely incompatible with established social structures. The novel represents Twain's attempt to find a way to preserve the best qualities of Irish identity while also transforming the ethnic other into an American.

On the seventy-fifth anniversary of *Huck Finn*'s publication, Norman Podhoretz proclaimed the book "a key to the very essence of the American imagination" (BR5). Here, we were to understand, was the text that laid out exactly the contours and intricacies of American identity and represented the pinnacle of American literary achievement. The book has maintained its celebrated cardinal status among literary texts and been showered with affection by readers and critics right through to the present day. Lawrence Howe caps off a century of literary discussion by observing that, "Huckleberry Finn is not only the most representative boy in our literature, he is also the character with whom American readers—white American readers—have most deeply identified" (20).[1] This sentiment—that *Huck Finn* is the quintessentially American book, and the protagonist the quintessentially American hero—pervades the culture. Yet, this sentiment also glosses over the importance of Huck's ethnicity.

Given the scholarly obsession with racial dynamics in *Huck Finn*, it is surprising that few studies ever acknowledge Huck's Irishness. Scholars almost universally build their ethnic analyses on a black–white binary, with many presuming Huck and Pap Finn to be unambiguously white and lumping them together with the Anglo characters in opposition to the novel's slaves and freed blacks.[2] Others seem to sense that Huck and Pap are not quite the same kind of white, but lack the terminology to describe the phenomenon.[3] And some, faced with this racial ambiguity, even suggest that Huck is black.[4] Few critics consider the possibility of a third term outside of a black–white polarity that might explain Huck's racial position in society.

Ralph Ellison soundly argues that *Huck Finn* depends on an African voice and influence, adding that "without the presence of blacks, the book could not have been written. No Huck and Jim, no American novel as we know it" ("What America"). I would add that the same is true of an Irish presence. Without the metaphoric figuration of the Irish-American character and its associated features, Huck would not exist and the course of American literary history would look very different indeed.

An Irish identification, which in the context of the nineteenth century implied a uniquely ambiguous racial status, accurately signals a character who does not seem to be fully white, but at the same time cannot be considered black. As David Roediger observes in *The Wages of Whiteness* (1991), the Irishman was popularly considered "a 'nigger,' inside out" who came from dark, possibly African, origins (133). Though the Irish were not thought of as black skinned (or subject to the legal discrimination blacks experienced), they had, according to Frederick Douglass, assumed the degradation of blacks (qtd. in Roediger 150). Even the U.S. Census Bureau recognized the bizarre status of the nineteenth-century Irish and classified them as a racially distinct group (Roediger 133). The Irish in Twain's novel function in this liminal capacity, slipping across racial categories and complicating the ethnic make-up of a community that knows how to deal with blacks, but is still unsure what to do with these uniquely problematic "white negroes."

This critical silence regarding Huck's Irishness implies that readers and scholars downplay or ignore such issues either because of a general obliviousness of the American racial context of nineteenth-century Irishness brought about by the near total assimilation of the Irish into a more generic white culture in the twentieth century, or because they are uncomfortable with how such issues might complicate Huck's status as an all-American, and unambiguously white, boy. In the past century, Huck's identity has been whitewashed and de-ethnicized, resulting in a re-characterization that is both inaccurate and unsettling. Critics have over-emphasized Huck's class to the exclusion of his ethnicity, and as a result, readers have largely come to assume that Huck is a member (albeit an unruly one) of the white hegemony, when he is in fact very much an ethnic outsider. Being Irish was a stigma in both Huck's day and Twain's, and given that the Irish were considered neither truly white nor fully American in the nineteenth century, Howe's claim of Huck's status as the epitome of white American identity is anachronistic; Huck was the dangerous, uncivilized other with whom the community did not know how to deal. In truth, the contemporary readers who should best be able to claim kinship with Huck Finn are not those "white American readers," but rather those Americans whose social and community status are similarly questioned: immigrants and racial minorities.

Traditionally, Huck's resistance to being civilized has been read as his resentment of conformity, but it can also be read as an Irish boy's refusal to be assimilated into mainstream society. Huck's dilemma is the same as that of many immigrants: he wants to be American, but he does not want to give up his cultural heritage to do so. In many ways, *Huck Finn* can be read as a manual for resisting assimilation. Reexamining *Huck Finn* in such a manner complicates much of the scholarly conversation regarding the novel and moves away from stale literary dogma. We can abandon the traditional interpretations of *Huck Finn* as a story about a white boy and a runaway slave traveling the Mississippi and replace it with a story about two marginalized ethnic outsiders escaping from an oppressive community.

What makes Huck so recognizably Irish? The first and most obvious signal of his Irish heritage is his surname, which is "joyously and unmistakably Celtic" (Colwell 72). Hugh J. Dawson, who contributes the most thorough exploration of Huck's Irish identity to date, further adds that the name *Finn* has strong origins in Irish mythology and literature and even linguistic ties to the word *Fenian* ("Ethnicity" 1). More importantly, Dawson notes that among the sixty plus surnames to be found in Twain's novel, "[Huck] and his father are all but unique in being without what would have been a recognizably Anglo-Saxon surname" ("Ethnicity" 2). Among the book's *Sawyers, Thatchers, Grangerfords, Shepherdsons,* and the like, *Finn* does stand out as the odd ethnic marker in St. Petersburg, Missouri. For Twain, the *Finn* surname signified that Huck and Pap were outsiders and not part of the dominant social class. In an interview from 1895, Twain makes clear this absorption of nativist sentiment and the association in his own mind between Huck's Irish surname and low social status. After acknowledging that Huck is based on a boy he knew—who also was named Finn and was the son of the town drunk[5]—Twain goes on to say, "You see, there was something about the name 'Finn' that suited, and 'Huck Finn' was all that was needed to somehow describe another kind of boy than 'Tom Sawyer,' a boy of lower extraction or degree" (Colwell 72). In this context, readers are to understand that Huck bears the brand of bad genealogy. Unlike Tom Sawyer, whose ancestry seems to predestine him to become a prince of America, Huck must struggle against his nature and his name to achieve even the most basic degree of respect.

Importantly, the *Finn* surname is not the only, or the most significant, marker of Huck's Irishness. Twain presents numerous physical descriptions and behavioral quirks that, drawing on nineteenth-century racial taxonomies, explicitly signify the boy's ethnicity. Dawson thoroughly catalogues these physical manifestations of Huck's Irishness, among which he lists the boy's gregariousness, his pugnaciousness, his "experience of his parents, his physiognomy, anti-social ideas, behavior, style of dress and moral instincts," as well as his "unruliness, his small deceits, his pipe-smoking and preference for lazing about" ("Ethnicity" 1, 9). Pap is an even more explicit manifestation of the stereotype: "lazy, dirty, brutal, swinish, superstitious, bigoted, lying, illiterate, antireligious, foul-mouthed, financially irresponsible and destructive of himself and others in his craving for alcohol" (Dawson, "Ethnicity" 9). Twain—who also twice describes the Finns as living in a "shanty," a term with overt and unmistakable Irish connotations—did not try to obfuscate his characters' Irish heritage (*Huck Finn* 44, 54). Audiences who were thoroughly familiar with the Irish savage in their literature and primed to recognize this kind of ethnic coding would not have missed the outward signs of the characters' heritage.

For example, consider the specific ways in which Twain draws on popular stereotype to portray Huck as having hereditary predilections for poverty and squalor, in a manner similar to Jacob A. Riis' suggestion that the Irish were "hereditary beggars." Huck's happiness and satisfaction in his subhuman living conditions reflect a widespread belief that the Irish were content with living as squatters, paupers, and animals. When Huck is taken in to a proper home and given adequate food and shelter, he laments that "grub comes too easy" and that his newfound wealth is "just worry and worry, and sweat and sweat, and a-wishing you was dead all the time" (*Tom Sawyer* 167). Apparently, as an Irish boy, he should prefer starvation and poverty! Huck sleeps outside and dresses in rags, not because he (like other boys) is trying to frustrate his parents, but because he truly prefers filth over cleanliness. "Living in a house, and sleeping in a bed, pulled on me pretty tight," he says, "but before the cold weather I used to slide out and sleep in the woods, sometimes, and so that was a rest to me" (*Huck Finn* 27). Soon after, he expresses satisfaction in his reversion to his regular, seemingly natural and stereotypically Irish, ways. He moves back into the shanty with his abusive father, reacquires his habits of smoking and cussing, celebrates his laziness and ignorance, and proclaims it all "pretty good times" (37).

Though the text of *Huck Finn* makes explicit Huck's Irish identity, the illustrations by E. W. Kemble downplay ethnic signifiers.[6] It is likely that Twain and his publisher, concerned about audience reaction to such images, wanted to mute the outward signs of Huck's ethnicity. Beverly R. David proposes that Kemble's goal with the illustrations was to provide "socially acceptable images" that would make audiences "feel comfortable" with some of the more unappealing or dirty elements of Twain's characters (338, 341). Huck, who is one of the dirtier characters to be found in the illustrations for *The Adventures of Tom Sawyer* (1876), gets cleaned up a bit for his own novel's illustrations (see Figures 2.1 and 2.2). Henry B. Wonham argues that Twain was "thoroughly knowledgeable about an elaborate repertoire of conventions governing the comic representation of racial and ethnic difference," and his manipulation of Irish caricature in *Huck Finn* seems to reveal the knowledge Wonham describes (74). In reviewing the initial drawings of Huck, Twain commented, "All right & good, & will answer; although the boy's mouth is a trifle more Irishy than necessary" (David 338)—the implication here being that some Irishness in the character was desirable, but too much would turn audiences off. Of course Kemble does not clean up or de-Irish images of Pap since readers were intended to loathe such a figure and the familiar image of the stock Irish savage quickly engendered antipathy. David further argues that Twain's choice to mute Huck's visual Irish appearance was mostly a financial judgment:

> Realizing that contemporary local-colorists had limited their audience and therefore their monetary gain by geographically and ethnically restricting their subject matter, Mark Twain directed his editing toward a larger audience, a wider terrain and heavier sales. There would be little sense, in his mind, to limiting the appeal of Huck Finn to the increasing but unpopular urban Irish when the novel and its hero had a potentially limitless audience. The "Irishness" needed control, less prominence, especially in so promotionally visible a place as the cover design. (338)

Twain's goal, then, was to have Huck Finn pass as a generic, white, Anglo boy, at least as far as the book's illustrations were concerned; however, he filled the actual text of the novel with the adventures of an unruly, ethnic minority who refuses to assimilate.

Figures 2.1 and 2.2   The original True Williams illustration for Huckleberry Finn (on left) from *The Adventures of Tom Sawyer* shows a Huck who is much dirtier and more stereotypically Irish than E. W. Kemble's version (on right) for *The Adventures of Huckleberry Finn*. Notice the prognathic mouth/jaw, pug nose, bare feet, and ragged clothes in Williams' illustration. Kemble was instructed to make Huck less "Irishy."

I do not wish to ascribe to Twain a pro-Irish agenda; at best, his thoughts on the particulars of the Irish-American experience are ambivalent. Twain was well known for his anti-Irish/anti-Catholic beliefs and had absorbed certain aspects of nativist bigotry during his boyhood years in Missouri (Dawson, "Ethnicity" 7). In fact, he was fired from his position at the *San Francisco Morning Call* largely due to the anti-Irish bias in his writing, which upset the newspaper's large Irish readership (Camfield 522). Twain also supported the Know-Nothing Party during his early years and later criticized Catholics in *The Innocents Abroad* (1869), *A Tramp Abroad* (1880), and *A Connecticut Yankee in King Arthur's Court* (1889). As *The Oxford Companion to Mark Twain* notes, though he overcame his racism toward blacks and Chinese in his later years, he still "held to some bigoted opinions about the Irish" (Camfield 475).

Despite all this, Twain never demonized the Irish in his writings the way so many other writers did, and as a result, his works—which do traffic in common Irish stereotypes—often complicate and sometimes subvert the popular discourse on Irishness in the U.S. Twain offers a critique of the culture and morals of mainstream American society by highlighting its mistreatment of an Irish boy, and though I do not think it accurate to ascribe to Twain an honest sympathy for Irish-American social or political causes, it does seem that he came to believe, like the late-century social reformers, that the less desirable features of Irishness were a function of their environment and not their biology. Twain's critique, like that of Riis, focuses on the social majority who are to blame for the deplorable conditions that elicit immorality from the Irish; he shows that in the fictional world of St. Petersburg, it is the town folk who are corrupt, not Huck. In this sense, Twain presents a revolutionary take on Irishness by describing it as a cultural ideal to which Americans could aspire. At times Twain sentimentalizes the rustic, agrarian purity of the Irish, and in the end he does show Irishness to be fundamentally incompatible with American democracy as it currently existed, but through his Irish, boy hero he created a way for the Irish to participate in the imagined American community.

Twain's sympathy for the Irish is certainly qualified. He clearly admires certain supposed aspects of the Irish character, especially simplicity, rebelliousness, and free-spiritedness, and seeks to embody these traits in Huck. Yet, his writings also clearly show that Twain is wary of other stereotypical traits associated with the Irish, including dirtiness, drunkenness, violence, and Catholicism, which he embodies in Pap. By splitting the Irish character into two distinct persons in his novel, Twain is able to celebrate and condemn Irishness with little apparent contradiction. The worst part of the Irishman can be drowned in the river, while the best can go adventuring on the Mississippi. In addition, by splitting the Irish character between father and son, Twain maintains hope that the next generation will prove more adaptable to its environment. No one wants to see Huck turn out like Pap, and Twain suggests he does not have to by repeatedly emphasizing that Huck's fate is not tied to his biology. Twain rejects the popular belief in biological criminality (which formed the basis of so much anti-Irish prejudice in the U.S.) and suggests that Irishness is a kind of reformable ethnicity. The people of St. Petersburg may believe that Huck and Pap are inherently bad, but Twain does not share their opinion and seems determined to prove them wrong.[7]

To analyze the significance of Huck's Irishness and how it affects his community, we first must consider his father; after all, the fear of turning out like Pap motivates Huck throughout the book. Unlike most boys, Huck does not want to follow in his father's footsteps and would rather forego his biological inheritance. For years, Pap has been the town's stereotypical wild Irishman: filthy, greasy, long-haired, drunken, lazy, violent, more comfortable in the company of hogs than people, and prone to tirades against the government. Though he views himself, as Edward J. Piacentino observes, "as an honest, hardworking man" who has had his life intruded on by others, the community views him much as readers have viewed him to the present day: as a worthless father and monster who will never fit in (20).[8] He engenders such disgust and loathing that he is not permitted to live in town, but must find shelter out in the woods, a situation that physically reinforces the psychological and social distance that the locals maintain between this Irishman and themselves.

Despite the odds, the people of St. Petersburg try to reform Pap as a strategy for defusing the danger inherent in his Irish character. They attempt to civilize him in the manner of Charles Loring Brace, by rehabilitating his moral character and filling him with a proper sense of manhood. Their goal is not to make Pap a full-fledged member of their community (they would not think such an achievement possible or desirable); instead, they wish to break him in and domesticate him as they would an animal. Their manner of reforming him does not remove the stigma of otherness, but instead neuters it so that Pap can safely walk among them. Homi Bhabha describes this activity of encouraging mimicry in a subject as "*ironic* compromise" because it tries to get the subject to behave like the dominant culture while simultaneously (and paradoxically) remaining identifiably different. It represents "the desire for a reformed, recognizable other, *as a subject of a difference that is almost the same, but not quite*" (122). When Pap mimics the behavior and appearance of the typical Anglo townsperson, he becomes less Irish while also remaining identifiably different since his mimicry reveals him to be a pretender and not the real thing. This allows the townspeople to reduce the threat Pap poses to them while also reinforcing his position at the bottom of their social hierarchy.

The new judge announces that he is going "to make a man" out of Huck's father (*Huck* 33). This entails cleaning him up, dressing him in good clothes, teaching him proper manners, getting him to embrace temperance, and prompting him to repent his evil ways. The new judge, on completing his Anglo-style makeover, claims overwhelming success:

> Look at it gentleman, and ladies all; take ahold of it; shake it. There's a hand that was the hand of a hog; but it ain't so no more; it's the hand of a man that's started in on a new life, and'll die before he'll go back. You mark them words—don't forget I said them. It's a clean hand now; shake it—don't be afeard. (34)

Notably, the new judge here proclaims that Pap is no longer a sub-human animal or monster, nor is he a threat to the community. At this moment, the community welcomes Pap and invites him to live among them. Of course, that very night, he goes out, sells his new clothes for whiskey money, gets drunk, and falls off of a porch, breaking his arm in two places.

Carl F. Wieck suggests that the community exiles Pap once again because he "proves incapable of growth or renewal," to which I would add that Pap also proves incapable of adequately mimicking an Anglo identity, which is what they really expect of him (16). Pap's resistance to assimilation terrifies St. Petersburg because if they cannot deal with him, what hope do they have of dealing with other immigrants, much less freed blacks, who might come to their community?

Unlike the book's black characters who only ever can hope to be, as Huck labels Jim, "white on the inside," it seems at first possible to the people of St. Petersburg that Pap could wash the filth from his skin and achieve a semblance of actual whiteness and respectability. The fact that he fails, and that Huck fails too, likely proved satisfying to some nativist readers anxious about miscegenation and the unique threat of the Irish being able to pass so easily as Anglo American. As Ignatiev points out, though white skin made the Irish eligible for membership in the white race, it did not guarantee it (59). In fact, Pap's anxiety regarding freed blacks expresses his own uneasy sense of working-class whiteness and draws attention to his recognition that, as an Irishman, he maintains uneasy relationships with both blacks and whites.[9] Pap Finn exemplifies degenerate whiteness, and though his skin color keeps him socially above blacks, he never can rise to the level of civilized whites. Matt Wray importantly warns scholars not to make the mistake of oversimplifying the boundaries constructed between whites and urges us to "define *white* as a social category, not a racial category" (139). Many readers would have viewed Pap's failure to assimilate the way the people of St. Petersburg view it: as evidence of hereditary, even racial, weakness and proof that the Irish were observably different than mainstream Americans. In other words, it assured the general population that they would be able to spot the "hand of a hog" no matter what clothes the hog wore; however, all it really proves is a commitment to the maintenance of social categories of whiteness that Twain forces his readers to reevaluate when they see Huck put through the same gauntlet as his father and it is revealed that it is the reformers themselves who have made an error.

For the people of St. Petersburg, Huck might not appear to be as threatening a figure as his Pap, but they believe that the father predicts what the son will become. Dawson argues that Twain carefully arranges this dynamic, playing on his reader's belief in determinism:

> By splitting many of the most distinctive of the alleged Irish characteristics between the Finns, assigning the negative traits to Pap and investing his son with features readers would secretly find endearing even as they felt they were to be scorned, Twain succeeded in favoring Huck with a personality that the book's early readership would have straightaway recognized as suspect. The traits that mark Huck and his Pap off as different from and unacceptable to the settled American culture were conspicuously those of "the wild Irish." What is manifest in the mature condition of his father is latent in Huck, whose personality is heavy with the latent pathology of his people. (9)

It is this "latent pathology" of the Irish that lurks behind the text of *Huck Finn* as an implicit threat; the Irishman destabilizes communities, corrupts good people, and brings crime and filth into a clean society. As an adolescent, Huck has the potential to become a monster like his father and already shows the first signs of deviance. The people of St. Petersburg try to curb his nature while he is still young in order to protect their own children and the future of their community.

When Twain introduces Huck in *Tom Sawyer*, he describes the boy as "a juvenile pariah . . . idle, and lawless, and vulgar and bad" (40). This description evokes several stereotypical Irish traits to mark Huck as an outcast and threat. He is different and living among a group that prizes homogeneity, so it is no wonder that he is "cordially hated and dreaded" (40). The mothers of St. Petersburg worry that Huck will corrupt their sons, so they urge their children to avoid the Irish boy's "forbidden society" (40). Like so many Irish characters before and after him, Huck is described as socially contagious, liable to cause degeneration in even the most wholesome Anglo-Saxon child. All of the boys in the book yearn to be like Huck, and he becomes their instructor in many aspects of youthful delinquency, including cussing, smoking, fighting, skipping school, skipping church, and disobeying adults.

At first, the scorn heaped on Huck seems disproportionate to his crimes. Why is he so hated and feared? What makes him so different from other boys? After all, Tom Sawyer seems just as much of a scoundrel, perhaps even more so. Tom is the one who swindles other children, manipulates adults, and dreams of attacking his own community as either Indian, robber, or pirate. Huck mostly stays to himself and rarely gets into any mischief in St. Petersburg that Tom does not instigate. Yet, there is an implied essential difference between the boys that explains Huck's ostracism. Tom's challenges to social norms are nothing but playful testing of limits. Huck's challenges to social norms, on the other hand, are seen as serious attacks on community standards. Here was a boy who was not just playing at rebellion, but was actually rebellious.

Being Irish means that Huck Finn is not just another generic "bad boy" like Tom Sawyer.[10] Tom is a merry prankster whose misbehavior is treated with a kind of mock-scorn by adults. He is naughty, not dangerous, and therefore never receives real punishment for his actions. Judith Fetterley aptly calls Tom a "sanctioned rebel" who "entertains his world" and has a "remarkably positive" relationship with the community (282). Huck is something different and altogether more threatening to the community. Unlike Tom, Huck does not play at disobedience in order to shock adults or misbehave for the pure joy of it; rather, it is believed, he does these things because he has a hereditary predilection to do so. As the wayward son of the town's Irish drunk, Huck's misdeeds are seen by the populace as a fulfilling of biological and sociological destiny. None of Huck's people were civilized or literate, and Huck's pretensions to good manners and education are just attempts to "let on to be better'n what *he* is" (*Huck Finn* 32). And though Huck is only a young boy whose misdeeds might seem like youthful indiscretions, the townspeople people know too well that such playful misbehavior, if left unchecked, will become the foundations of a full-grown, anti-social Irishman.

Tom wants to transform his world through his imagination and adopt new identities for himself, but Huck only ever wants to be exactly who he is. This, more than anything else, causes the boys to grow apart. Tom's playful adventures mock the reality of Huck's life: Tom *plays* at being an outsider and criminal, but Huck *is* an outsider who actually commits crimes out of necessity; Tom treats abolition as a theatrical game, but Huck actually helps a runaway slave escape; Tom fakes his death for fun, Huck does the same out of self-preservation; Tom misbehaves because he enjoys upsetting adults, Huck misbehaves because he is ignorant of social rules. Ultimately, Tom enjoys a leisure Huck will never know; at the end of the day, Tom can stop pretending and go home to his family and his good life, but Huck only can retire alone to his damp hogshead barrel. And when Tom stops pretending, he also stops being friends with Huck, because it is only within the context of playful adventure that he can safely tolerate the Irish boy's company. In the real world, Huck threatens Tom's reputation. Twain writes that Tom "did not care to have Huck's company in public places," an indication that the boys' friendship could never transcend certain prejudices (*Tom Sawyer* 132). Though Tom enjoys Huck's company as a kind of forbidden fun, he also accepts the belief that he is entitled to, even destined for, a better life than his friend, and that the public association with someone so loathed by the community threatens his future success.

Twain makes explicit the schism between Tom and Huck during the boys' pirate island adventure in *Tom Sawyer*. This particular passage validates the community's worst fears about the wicked Irish boy's predilection for corrupting good children. Along with Joe Harper, the boys find a secluded spot in the middle of the river, far away from prying eyes and meddlesome adults. It is the first opportunity that Tom and Joe have to live like Huck. Away from the safety of their homes, Huck inducts them into the life of a vagabond Irishman teaching them to scrounge, keep warm, and even smoke tobacco. At first, Huck's lifestyle attracts them and they enjoy the freedom it offers. Tom says, "It's just the life for me . . . You don't have to get up, mornings, and you don't have to go to school, and wash, and all that blame foolishness" (75). Yet, after only a couple of nights away from their warm beds and loving parents, Tom and Joe lose their enthusiasm and yearn for home. Given the chance to live like Huck, Tom and Joe grow sick of it. They become painfully uncomfortable when they realize that what has been make-believe fun for them is actually the good life for Huck. Huck remarks that roughing it on the island with them "suited him" and that he didn't want "nothing better'n this" (75). But Tom and Joe do want something better and soon realize that living like an Irish outcast meant giving up all the privileges they were accustomed to.

During the boys' island adventure, Joe Harper remarks that swimming had lost its appeal because "there ain't anybody to say I shan't go in" (86).

In much the same way, Huck Finn loses appeal for Tom and Joe because there is not anyone to scold them for associating with such a pariah. A great deal of Huck's appeal is that he is forbidden. Boys want to be around him because they are told by their parents not to go near him. After a couple of nights on the island living with Huck, Tom and Joe realize that what was once a forbidden novelty was now boring, unappealing, and uncomfortable. Without anyone else around to see them associating with Huck, Tom and Joe realize that they are not really being rebels anymore; rather, they have simply become, like Huck, homeless social outcasts. On the island, they come to realize that (out here) they are Huck's equals, not his superiors. When a mother tells her son not to play with Huckleberry Finn, implicit in her command is that her child is better than Huckleberry Finn. When the child hears this, it reassures him that he is good, loved, and socially accepted, and not at all like that bad Irish boy. It is no wonder that Tom and Joe choose to go back home after only a couple of nights on the island. Without that implicit reassurance from their families that they are better than Huck, they likely start to feel their sense of superiority slipping away.

All three boys soon return to civilization, showing up at their own funeral; however, the return means something different for Tom and Joe than it does for Huck. Tom and Joe had been missed, and their absence had inspired testimonials from their friends and tears from their family. On their return they are greeted with overwhelming love at home and popularity at school, but the same is not true for Huck, who was not missed. On his return, he tries to shyly slip out of the celebration because he knows he does not belong there. Tom exclaims, "[I]t ain't fair. Somebody's got to be glad to see Huck" (94). Aunt Polly then gives Huck some momentary attention, but apparently quickly forgets the boy again. He goes right back to being homeless and hungry—the same conditions he and the boys experienced on the island—and no one seems to care. While his friends become local heroes, Huck slinks back to the margins, back to his life as the unwanted outsider. Twain clearly positions readers to sympathize with Huck here, in a manner that predicts the more focused criticism of the community found in *Huck Finn*. While not overtly celebrating Huck's ethnic otherness, Twain uses this scene to criticize the shallowness and cruelty of insular American communities.

Faced with such an alien threat in their midst—a threat validated by Tom and Joe's episode of "going native" because of the Irish boy—the people of St. Petersburg respond by trying to assimilate Huck. In fact, much of the plot of both *Tom Sawyer* and *Huck Finn* develops out of the community's attempts at, and Huck's resistance to, that assimilation. The nature of the assimilation is Anglo-conformity, and the hope is that Huck is young and malleable enough to change, unlike his father who was too old and set in his ways. If Huck can be cleaned up and curbed of his errant behavior, he will cease to be a threat. As a subplot, the salvation of Huck Finn enticed many readers when they discovered the character in *Tom Sawyer*. William Dean Howells, in his review of the book for *Atlantic Monthly*, finds Huck "entirely delightful" as a subordinate character, because "in his promised reform his identity is respected" (266). Howells possibly misses Twain's subtle irony and critique; there is no "promised reform" of Huck. Twain would never let such a thing happen and, in fact, indicates that the boy embodies a morality that far surpasses the community's. Yet, what initially attracted Howells and others to the character, at some level, was the notion that the aberrant ethnic minority could be made safe. Readers in the 1880s living in an era of mass immigration were just as anxious about ethnic friction as the people of St. Petersburg are in Twain's novel and just as interested in the notion of a "promised reform" of the alien element in their midst. Twain plays with this expectation while dismantling the precepts it is built on, setting readers up for the realization that it is not the boy who needs reform, but the community.

There is a certain violence inherent in assimilation in that it presents the dominant social group as embodying superior cultural standards that require the minority to relinquish the "deficient" aspects of their cultural heritage. This kind of cultural mentality dominated American thinking on immigrants in the nineteenth century; after all, it was John Quincy Adams who in 1818 instructed immigrants to "cast off their European skin, never to resume it" or "return to the land of their nativity and their fathers" (qtd. in M. Gordon 94). Without question, the people of Missouri in Twain's novels believe that Huck is void of any cultural worth, and they evaluate his success and his personal value by the degree to which he assimilates. When Huck resists assimilation, he resists everything the community believes is good and decent, and therefore he becomes, by default, the opposite: bad and indecent.

Another factor that likely fuels the community's sudden interest in reforming the "local pariah" is Huck's new wealth. Throughout most of the novel, the people of St. Petersburg are content to let Huck sleep in a hogshead and forage for his food in their trash. By today's standards, this kind of neglectful treatment of a child is unconscionable, but even in the novel's context, the good people of Missouri at times come off as more abusive than Pap Finn; at least Pap fed Huck and put a roof over his head. Twain highlights the community's hypocrisy by showing how no adult takes any real interest in Huck until he has money. It is no coincidence that the Widow takes him under her protection immediately on his receipt of six thousand dollars. Huck acquiring money elevates him to a new status in the community; he can no longer be ignored. Yet, having money also means that neither can he be allowed to continue as he was. Huck's sudden change in economic status requires a change in his ethnic status too because the people of St. Petersburg conflate ethnicity and economic class. Because of his new wealth, Huck Finn now can be introduced into society, not as the son of an Irish drunk, but as the respectable ward of the Widow.

The assimilation of Huckleberry Finn is evidenced by the community's repeated attempts to "sivilize" him. They try to un-Irish the boy by removing all external signs of his bad heritage, and hopefully some of the internal signs too:

> The widow's servants kept him clean and neat, combed and brushed, and they bedded him nightly in unsympathetic sheets that had not one little spot or stain which he could press to his heart and know for a friend. He had to eat with knife and fork; he had to use a napkin, cup and plate; he had to learn his book, he had to go to church; he had to talk so properly that speech was become insipid in his mouth; whithersoever he turned, the bars and shackles of civilization shut him in and bound him hand and foot. (*Tom Sawyer* 166)

They hope to produce a good, Protestant, Anglo-Saxon boy. They focus on cleaning him up so he does not *look* Irish, teaching him etiquette so he does not *act* Irish, and forcing him into their church so he does not *think* Irish. By removing all difference, they remove that which threatens them. Huck will become as harmless as Tom Sawyer.

In one of the earliest reviews of *Huckleberry Finn*, Brander Matthews observes that Huck thinks of Tom as the "ideal of what a boy should be" (331). Frequently, Tom does serve as the model of acceptable boyhood for Huck, but more often he serves as an agent of assimilation. Frequently, it is Tom—not the Widow Douglas or Miss Watson—who curbs Huck's behavior and encourages him toward conformity. When Huck runs away from the Widow for the first time, it is Tom who tracks him down and drags him back. Tom encourages Huck to come back and just act like everybody else, to which Huck replies, "I ain't everybody, and I can't *stand* it" (167). Tom goes on, promising Huck that he will grow to like being civilized, and then he finally threatens him with complete ostracism from not only the town, but also the company of the local boys. Tom says, "[W]e can't let you into the gang if you ain't respectable" (168). Tom comes across like a practiced social reformer at this moment, promising certain dividends in exchange for the immigrant's adherence to a certain code of conduct. Of course Huck agrees. He might be willing to forego the company of a broader society, but he does not want to be alone. Though Huck prefers a life apart from the town, he also frequently complains about being lonesome. This apparent contradiction at the heart of the character explains much of his internal turmoil. Elaine Mensh and Harry Mensh observe that Huck's "yearning to be outside is not entirely free of a wish to be inside" (20). Membership in Tom Sawyer's Gang promises a sense of belonging that Huck has never known while also allowing him to exist outside of mainstream society. The life of a robber, like the life of a pirate, would be the good life for Huck. It is with this in mind that he accepts Tom's bribe and returns to the Widow Douglas' house to be civilized.

The continual stress assimilation places on Huck leaves him depressed and makes him remark, "I felt so lonesome I most wished I was dead" (16). The changes forced on him do not bring a sense of belonging or inclusion in society, but the opposite. The Widow Douglas and Miss Watson, rather than creating a vital, well-adjusted new member for the community, create a miserable boy obsessed with thoughts of death. Their attempts at reforming his Irish character do not achieve the desired results.

Ultimately, of course, the community fails to civilize Huck, just as they fail with his father, and in this, Twain's critique of such methods of social reform is revealed. Ethnic otherness cannot be washed away with soap and water nor can it be made safe by dressing it in new clothes and taking it to church. Such methods only alienate the subject even further and ignore the beneficial qualities that he could bring to the community. The assimilation of Huckleberry Finn fails because such a project of social reform starts with flawed objectives. Huck is not the one that needs reform; it is the world he lives in that needs to change. Clearly, Twain shows Huck to embody the greater sense of social morality, and describes the townspeople's attempts to stamp out his character as nothing short of criminal negligence. Our sympathies logically gravitate toward the boy, who, despite his age and upbringing, displays greater reserves of empathy and common sense than anyone else in the book. We do not want Huck reformed; we want him freed of the confines of corruptive civilization.

Huck goes west into the Territories, not because he is not good enough for society, but because society is not good enough for him. Twain's proposition is that the only way for the Irish to be made American is for them to go to the very edges of America where corruptive, bigoted civilizations do not yet have a hold. On the frontier, Twain imagines, the very qualities the community hates in Huck will become the means to his success. Through such a radical change in context, the Irish can be made American.

Most critics opt to view the ending of *Huck Finn* as a triumph: having matured on the raft, Huck manages to escape from a corrupt society and goes west to further discover himself. His moral awakening at this point includes the realization that a slave-owning society is inherently immoral, that Miss Watson's theology is flawed, and that Tom Sawyer is not the friend he appears to be. Huck's great success, we are to understand, is that he finally rejects the society that has always rejected him.

Yet, there is a bittersweet quality to Huck's choice to leave.

At the end of the novel, Huck realizes that the only way to preserve his identity is to go into voluntary exile; it is his final tactic for resisting assimilation. The community makes one last-ditch effort to pull him back and civilize him; however, this time he is beyond their reach. He's "been there before" and knows he will not ever succeed in being the boy they want him to be (296). Not even Tom Sawyer can entice him back, because his rejection of civilization is also a rejection of Tom, who in the later portions of *Huck Finn* proves himself shallow and cruel and very much an agent of the flawed morality and biases Huck comes to hate.[11] In this context, Huck's "lighting out for the Territory" on the final page of the book is also a moment of profound resignation. He loses hope of ever fitting in and accepts that he is fundamentally different from everyone else. His experience here builds from an earlier scene in the novel, the climactic moment when he chooses to help Jim and "go to hell," rather than turn the runaway slave in to Miss Watson. During this frequently analyzed crisis of conscience, Huck also experiences a crisis of identity, and disturbingly, his moral triumph at this moment is simultaneous with, even necessitated by, his acceptance of his own social inferiority. In doing what he feels is right by protecting Jim, he is forced to acknowledge that he is inherently bad and deserves to be punished. After hearing adults accuse him of bad heritage his whole life, it is no wonder that he himself comes to the same conclusion, that "wickedness . . . was in my line" (223). The fact that Huck makes the right choice, a choice that leads to great joy at the end of the book, does not change the fact that he loses something here too. No one ever tells Huck he made the right choice or that he is not going to hell, and so, by the end of the novel, he comes to believe in the essential difference between himself and others and blames his bad behavior on his genealogy and upbringing too. Huck comes to see himself as nearly everyone else sees him—a no-good, dangerous Irish boy destined to break society's cherished rules and incapable of reform—and accepts that he has no place in a civilized community.

So, Huck ends the book by taking up the role of an outcast, leaving behind not just Missouri, but also civilization in its entirety. As much as he wanted not to grow up to be like his father, Huck adopts the same position and attitude as his old man. As Huck goes west to the Territories, Scott Donaldson notes, "he also goes to fulfill his destiny, as the son of his father" (32). After all, it is Pap who teaches Huck how to survive in a hostile social environment. Locked away in a shanty with his father, Huck listens to Pap rant against the government, freed blacks, and voting officials. More than just drunken rambling, this speech from Pap provides specific instruction for Huck on how to deal with a society intent on keeping the Irish down. "A man can't get his rights in government like this," Pap says. "Sometimes I've a mighty notion to just leave the country for good and all" (39). And this is exactly what Huck chooses to do.

Huck's voluntary exile can be read, in the same instance, as a triumph of ethnic fortitude, as well as a tragedy of social inflexibility. In order to succeed at being free, he must also to some degree fail at being civilized. No reader wants to see Huck morally reformed, but no one wants to see him remain a perpetual unwanted, even monstrous, other in the community either. So, exile seems like the best, but not perfect, alternative. In the west, we trust, he will find the freedom he needs to grow into a prosperous independent man. Frederick Jackson Turner characterized the frontier as an agrarian paradise where someone like Huck would thrive, because it was only on the edge between civilization and savagery where democracy really existed. Yet, as Henry Nash Smith points out, the frontier may have had mythological associations with primitive freedom, but it also carried a stigma for being socially, ethically, and culturally inferior to the east (251, 260). To which version of the American frontier does Huck light out for?

The one that will make him, as Turner promises, truly American? Or the one that will forever deny him a civilized existence?

And what of St. Petersburg? Are they better off for Huck's absence? I suspect that most of us think not, but his exile does promise to restore the social stability that he and his father had thrown into turmoil. There will be no more savages living in the woods just outside of town or in the back alleys; there will be no more danger to the wholesome upbringing of the town's children; there will be no more beggars or drunks in the street; there will be no more junior abolitionists or anarchists. With Huck gone and Pap dead (not to mention Injun Joe dead and Jim freed), St. Petersburg can settle back into its comfortable existence as a white, Protestant, Anglo-Saxon community.

F. Scott Fitzgerald lauds Huck's journey west because he believes it allows the boy to become "the first to look *back* at the republic" with objectivity (*In His Own Time* 176). Certainly this reading holds merit, but there is a downside to it as well: in order to be the first to look back, he must be alone in looking back. Twain displays optimism for Huck's future, but also suggests that that future cannot occur in Missouri (and by extension, civilized America east of the Mississippi). Huck's Irish nature, while joyously and perfectly equipping him for American ideals, makes him ill-suited for American social structures. Twain obviously lays the blame for this at the feet of the American community which has not lived up to its highest aspirations and moral obligations. Yet, his plan for making the Irish American by sending them to the borderlands feels inadequate, because eventually civilization will follow, and then what will America do with its ethnic others?

In his introduction to Twain's novel, T. S. Eliot writes, "Huck Finn is alone: there is no more solitary character in fiction" (349). Huck's loneliness resonates with ethnic significance. His pain reflects the pain of generations of immigrants, and the children of immigrants, who struggled to find a place in the American community, but were denied the opportunity or subjected to contradictory and confusing methods of social reform. Huck heads west, like so many Irish did, with the hope that somewhere on the frontier there might be a place for him. In literature, he is one of the first Irish characters to make this journey, but many others soon follow.

MAKING AMERICA IRISH: HAROLD FREDERIC'S *THE DAMNATION OF THERON WARE*

Harold Frederic's *The Damnation of Theron Ware* (published in England under the title *Illumination*) extends the line of thinking begun by Mark Twain regarding those Irish qualities that seem like the realization of American ideals, but paradoxically prove inaccessible to the Anglo majority of the country.[12] One of the most provocative aspects of Twain's work is his suggestion that it is the community that needs reform, not the supposedly aberrant ethnic minority, but Twain sends Huckleberry Finn west at the end of the novel and thereby excuses the people of St. Petersburg from having to change. Yet, the very idea of such radical social reform proves tantalizing. What would it entail or look like? Could a predominately Anglo population be "Irishized" so as to reap the benefits of those desirable Huck-like qualities (self-confidence, rebelliousness, independence, humanistic thought, simplicity, wittiness, democratic spirit, congruity with nature) without being subjected to Huck-like degradation? Was such transformation even possible? In *Theron Ware*, Frederic attempts to answer these questions and shows such inter-ethnic dynamics to be fundamental to the formation of a truly democratic American identity.

Theron Ware stands out among nineteenth-century American novels for its remarkably sympathetic portrait of the Irish. On the surface, it describes the experiences of a Methodist minister who "goes native" living among the Catholic Irish of upstate New York, and it plays on nativist fears of counter-conversion, degeneration, and moral corruption like a "belated Protestant panic attack" (Ferraro 1). Yet, it subversively works against Irish stereotypes and anti-Catholic propaganda, and undercuts the pervasive anxiety about the suitability of the Irish for inclusion in a civilized national community. Frederic demonstrates an understanding of the complexity of the Irish-American experience unique for his time and presents a view of it that is unlike anything else written by his contemporaries. Herbert J. Smith aptly describes *Theron Ware* as "a thoroughly unconventional portrait of the Irish unique in American fiction" (97). The anomalous existence of such a sympathetic portrait of Irishness from a non-Irish writer during this period demonstrates the author's foresight regarding American nationalism. Though Frederic himself has often been characterized as a lesser Hawthorne and his book pigeonholed as a bit of local color, he manages to present one of the most rich and intricate explorations of the relationship between ethnicity and national identity, accurately predicting the issues that would obsess American writers throughout the next century.

In *Theron Ware*, Frederic tells the story of a young Methodist minister assigned to a new congregation in Octavius, New York, a remote town in the upper Mohawk Valley. No sooner have he and his wife arrived and settled into their new home then they are informed about the problems the Methodist community has with the ethnically undesirable element living among them. One church elder tells Theron that the town "is jest over-run with Irish" and that during his sermons he should "pitch into Catholics" whenever he can (35). Yet, when Theron actually meets some of the local Irish men and women, he finds that he needs to "revise in part the arrangement of his notions" about them (52). In particular, Theron develops relationships with the Catholic priest, Father Forbes, a beautiful young pianist, Celia Madden, and a local philosopher, Dr. Ledsmar. As the novel progresses, Theron comes to ascribe more and more to the intellectual, religious, and social opinions of his Irish friends and progressively loses faith in the Methodist Church, his marriage, and his profession. The novel culminates in his choice to pursue a romantic relationship with Celia, but he fails to fully understand the implications of his recent transformation and is rejected. After experiencing such a substantial shock to his character, Theron chooses to leave behind all that he knows in the east and go west in order to reinvent himself.

Like Twain, Frederic shows the Protestant community to be deeply concerned with assimilating others into its body while being in need of significant social reform itself. The action of the book takes place during Methodism's Third Great Awakening and details this community's explicit attempts to gain converts through evangelical sermonizing and revivalism; however, Frederic shows this group to be so firmly entrenched in the past that they cannot succeed in the present. Yet, the Irish of Octavius do succeed because they embody a more modern American spirit. Again like Huck, the Octavius Irish highlight a deficiency in the general population that indicates a need for significant social reform. Of course, Frederic's trio (Forbes, Madden, Ledmar) is aware of their social superiority in a way that Huck never is, and so they lack the humility that made Twain's Irish boy so universally appealing. Nonetheless, Frederic's readers can learn from Octavius' Irish community, as Theron does, how to transform identity through modern, liberal ideology.

The effects that Frederic achieves in *Theron Ware* depend on his reader's familiarity with anti-Irish prejudice. In fact, the structure of the novel is built around an old racist anxiety: upright, moral persons would transform into savages through prolonged contact with the Irish. Since the time of the Anglo-Norman invasion of Ireland, many Englishmen believed that those "who stayed too long in Ireland were bound to go to seed or be corrupted and dragged down to the primitive, if not barbaric, culture of the 'mere Irishry'" (Curtis, *Anglo-Saxons* 18). In America, this fear found expression in popular literature and social commentary. In Hugh Henry Brackenridge's eighteenth-century novel *Modern Chivalry*, Teague O'Reagan exhibits this kind of degenerative effect on innocent country girls, who, in proximity to Teague, experience a sensation "affecting the nerves, and deranging the brain," and as a result come to prefer "bogtrotters" to "the most accomplished men" (252–3). In Herman Melville's *The Encantadas* (1854), Oberlus, the Celtic Caliban, rules an island in the Galapagos and transforms wayward sailors into savages and murderers, "wholly corrupt[ing]" them in his "mold of baseness" (58). In 1916, Madison Grant, the notorious eugenicist, made similar statements about the Irish while discussing their corruptive influence on the modern world and claimed that they had always had a "primitive and ancient" ability "to absorb newcomers" and cause them to sink to a lower cultural level (202).

Frederic's readers were adequately primed to read his novel as another such story of corruption. As Theron and his wife travel to their new home in rural Octavius, they travel into the heart of Irish darkness and take it for granted that "most of the poverty and all the drunkenness, crime, and political corruption were due to the perverse qualities of this foreign people" (52). Readers would have been prepared for the worst and feared for the safety of the couple's bodies and souls; after all, the book was labeled a "damnation." Yet, Frederic's novel radically defies expectations, refutes stereotypes, and departs from all literary precedent. He makes clear that it is indeed the Irish who are responsible for Theron's radical transformation, though, in the end, he undercuts expectations by showing that transformation to be beneficial, an "illumination" rather than the more expected corruption. Readers might have expected an indictment of Irish culture and Catholicism in support of long-held popular prejudices, but were presented with something very different. Thomas J. Ferraro asks, "How was it, then, that Frederic, a left-leaning journalist but no crusader, came to see such things *that* differently?" (4). Frederic was clearly aware of audience prejudices and was willing to play with them for ironic effect, but he created an imagined concept of Irishness unlike anything else in American literature, which seems all the more remarkable given popular sentiment toward the Irish of his day. Ferraro explains why such a portrayal of Irishness should surprise modern scholars:

> he saw beyond the immigration-and-liberty panics of late nineteenth-century xenophobia, saw beyond the shanty/lace typologies identified by mid-twentieth-century historiography, and saw beyond the invidious self-distancing from black folk that we now insist was central to European immigrant assimilation. (4)

It seems equally surprising that Frederic also saw beyond the positive stereotypes of the Irish embraced by other culture-defending writers of the time. There was precedent for benevolent representations of Irishness, but *Theron Ware* owes very little to them since it refutes the stereotypes, but does so without sentimentalizing the Irish character. Frederic wrote his novel during the beginning years of the Irish Literary Revival, but seems to reject the romanticized notion of the Celt (as conceived by writers like Matthew Arnold and W. B. Yeats) almost as vigorously as he rejects the negative clichés. Instead of inverting the stereotype and valorizing previously derided characteristics as primitive virtues, he re-imagines the Irish character in a completely new form, one that accorded with his own personal experiences.

Frederic grew up in Utica, New York, which served as the model for the Octavius of *Theron Ware*. The city had a robust population of Irish, many of whom descended from the immigrants that dug the Erie Canal. Notably, the Catholics and Protestants of Utica had better relations than was normal for that time in America, which may have encouraged Frederic to form cross-cultural bonds (Pula 83). He greatly admired Utica's Irish community and counted local Catholic Priest Edward Terry (the prototype of *Theron Ware*'s Father Forbes) among his closest friends. In later years, Frederic was acclaimed a hero by the Utica Irish community, among whom his claims to a quasi-Hibernian identity and status as a self-proclaimed "Irishman" were accepted (Garner 61, 63).

Frederic's close association with the Irish of Utica in his childhood led to a lifelong interest in Irish issues. In addition to *Theron Ware*, the Irish feature prominently in his novel *The Return of the O'Mahony* (1892) and several stories that chronicle life in Ireland during medieval times.[13] Smith notes that Frederic's work constitutes "the only fictional record of [Irish history and legend] by a major American novelist during the nineteenth century" (99). In addition to his literary work, Frederic also reported on Irish politics while working in London for the *New York Times* and vocally supported Home Rule. He made clear his belief that British oppression was the cause of Ireland's misery and described Ireland to Americans as the most "tearful, sorrowful land on the globe" ("Ireland As It Is"). Perhaps not surprisingly, among his close friends he counted numerous Irish nationalists, including Timothy Healy, T. P. O'Connor, and Charles Stewart Parnell. In the last decade of his life, he traveled regularly to southwestern Ireland to visit the family of his mistress, Kate Lyon, and he became so enamored of the island that he considered moving to Dunmanus Bay shortly before his unexpected death in 1898 (Garner 64).

Being such an admirer of the Irish, Frederic defends their reputation and culture in his work. His characters bear little resemblance to derogatory stereotypes: they neither speak with brogues nor carry shillelaghs; they do not engage in blarney or revolutionary activities; they are not the kind to incite violence, succumb to superstition, or let their emotions rule them; they are not drunks, soldiers, servants, or clowns. They also bear little resemblance to the "hereditary beggars" of the social reform movement. Frederic shows readers a view of the Irish beyond the "nurseries of crime" which Jacob A. Riis describes or the "fever-nests" which Charles Loring Brace studies (66, 26). In *Theron Ware*, there is no inherent deficiency in the Irish character, no lack of moral strength, no natural acceptance of poverty, no distrust of social structures, no degradation because of the "spiritual lifelessness of Romanism," and no degenerate appetites that can be blamed on heredity (Brace 155). In short, Frederic's Irish do not need reform.

Frederic's portrayal of Irishness differs most significantly from precedent in its focus on group identity. Whereas Twain's admiration for the Irish is restricted to specific qualities of an individual, Frederic lavishes praise on the Irish as a community and thus demonstrates a greater willingness to speak directly to their social context. He of course lauds specific Irish men and women in *Theron Ware* for possessing certain individually positive Irish traits (rebelliousness and poetic spirit in particular), but it is his repeated admiration for their strength as a community that marks his views as unusual and noteworthy. Many American texts (including the other two novels considered in this chapter) focus on the lone Irishman struggling to make his way through society, despite the historic reality that most Irish Americans lived within extensive social networks. In contrast, *Theron Ware* depicts the Irish as a functional and supportive community distinguished by their cultural richness, loving spirit, cohesiveness, and social superiority to the plain, boring, anti-intellectual, in-fighting Methodist population. In this way, Frederic identifies the source of Irish-American cultural power in the communalism that many nativists feared and shows it to be beneficial (not antithetical) to American society.

Theron's first contact with the Irish during the scene of MacEvoy's death speaks to this admiration of the Irish as a collective unit. When Theron sees the injured man being carried home, he "instinctively" joins himself to the procession and follows it into the house to witness the last rites being administered (45). Theron finds himself unexpectedly moved by the keening of the women, the murmuring of prayers, the chanting of Latin, and the presence of a crowd at this poor man's deathbed. He is impressed, even overwhelmed, by the sense of communal grief in response to the death of an individual and thinks to himself that though he "had stood face to face with death at many other bedsides; no other final scene had stirred him like this" (48). Theron's response to MacEvoy's death reveals for the first time his fascination with the Irish people and his awe of their social cohesion. The beauty and majesty that emerges from their confrontation with adversity pulls him in, against logic and Methodist sensibilities, and makes him part of something bigger and more inclusive than anything else he has ever experienced. In the end, he reflects that the experience made "a very powerful impression" on him, and we can trace all of Theron's subsequent actions in the novel back to this moment, as if the rest of the book is simply his series of attempts to re-attain the pure bliss of this one moment of communal belonging (50).

Theron's desires reflect a complex and conflicted inclination toward assimilation, since he wants the social benefits of Irishness without the blemishes of "Pagan Catholicism." In the same moment, the Irish represent a source of authentic cultural power, as well as spiritual debasement, and like Huck Finn, they seem to embody the very ideals of American modernism while also threatening the Protestant foundations of American identity. Ferraro sees this conflict in *Theron Ware* as predictive of the Irish Catholic relationship with Protestant America in the next century, describing it as

> that complex give-and-take between the increasing outreach and Protestant-entailed modernization of an initially ostracized but also self-isolated and thus sectarian Catholicism on the one hand (Vatican II representing the great breakthrough) and the increasing embrace of lay Catholic structures and feelings (Notre Dame football games, Mighty Macs basketball games, and Springsteen concerts as holy rites; the martyred alienation of city bars and mean streets, Capra's redemptive sentimentality

and Cagney's hard-boiled sacrifice and Crosby's celibate eroticism) by a once-Puritan and still-Victorian Protestant middle America. (13)

What attracted twentieth-century American Protestants to Irish culture, in Ferraro's formulation, was the same thing that attracts Theron to Celia, Forbes, and Ledsmar: a "sumptuousness" of thought that allows for secular (even profane) social structures to co-exist with religious devotions (14). Theron does not want to be Catholic, nor does he ever attempt a religious conversion. Instead, he attempts a secular conversion that will give him the social benefits of Irishness and associated intellectual freedoms without the potentially un-American allegiance to a foreign church enmeshed in pagan ritual. At one point, he fears that Celia is making a "deliberate suggestion that he should become a convert," but then he comes to understand her version of Catholicism as a vessel of liberal philosophy, rather than traditional theology, which makes it more of an intellectual standpoint than a spiritual one, and therefore less threatening to him (237). Celia's version of Catholicism does not require him to worship, only to think and to appreciate, and so it proves a palatably secular alternative.

Frederic celebrates the secular appeal of the Irish community during Theron's visit to the Catholic picnic. He had spent the past several days in another part of the woods attending a Methodist Revival meeting, which afforded him little intellectual stimulation or joy. During the meeting, he and other church elders were expected to attract new converts, but Frederic ironically shows the Irish to be more capable of facilitating conversion. Theron comes on the Irish celebration, which seems so inviting and good, and every bit the antithesis of the revival meeting he had just left. Frederic describes the scene as an American idyll with paradisiacal overtones:

> The bottom of the glade below him lay out in the full sunshine, as flat and as velvety in its fresh greenness as a garden lawn. Its open expanse was big enough to accommodate several distinct crowds, and here the crowds were,—one massed about an enclosure in which young men were playing football, another gathered further off in a horse-shoe curve at the end of a baseball diamond . . . Closer at hand, where a shallow stream rippled along over its blackslate bed, some little boys, with legs bared to the thighs, were paddling about, under the charge of two men clad in long black gowns. There were others of these frocked monitors scattered here and there upon the scene,—pallid, close-shaven, monkish figures, who none the less wore modern hats, and superintended with knowledge the games of the period . . . He gazed in mingled amazement and exhilaration upon the spectacle . . . The noises which arose from the multitude—the shouts of the lads in the water, the playful squeals of the girls in the swings, the fused uproar of the more distant crowds, and above all the diligent, ordered strains of the dance-music—charmed his ears with their suggestion of universal merriment. (216–7)

Unlike the congregation at the Revival who are being economically manipulated and spiritually chastised, the Irish seem joyful, and their gathering seems an occasion for social celebration. In this passage, Theron seems particularly envious of the Christian Brothers, who are religious leaders like himself, but who referee games and look after the children instead of spending their time sermonizing or pleading for money. Theron only spends a few moments watching from afar before he is invited to join in the festivities. He soon finds himself among friends, has a beer put in his hand, and remarks to Forbes and Celia, "I am in love with your sinners . . . I've had five days of the saints, over in another part of the woods, and they've bored the head off me" (218). Though he couches his admiration in religious terms, what really appeals to Theron here is the secular social dynamic of the gathering. He cannot help thinking that this is how communities should gather and behave. In this moment, Theron gives voice to Frederic's deep admiration for the Irish by rejecting their disparaging reputation and affirming them as "good, decent, ordinary people, just frankly enjoying themselves like human beings" (220).

Frederic's passion for the Irish must be considered alongside his evolving sense of what it meant to be American. Several critics note that he had a deep concern regarding America's rapidly changing demographics, immigration policies, and the possibility of over-civilization.[14] Carrie Tirado Bramen suggests that *Theron Ware* is "an intervention into these anxieties" (65). Theron's transformation in the novel is remarkable not because he transforms into an Irishman, but because he transforms into an American. The unmaking and remaking of Theron Ware allows Frederic to suggest a new definition of Americanness. Bramen states,

> [*The Damnation of Theron Ware*] destabilizes regional, cultural, and national identities through a series of chance encounters with the alien other. Frederic, who has been ironically perceived by his contemporaries as well as his critics as incontrovertibly American, produced a novel at the height of the "nationalist nineties" that actually explores the plasticity of national identity. (67)

It is this plasticity that I wish to explore here, more specifically the way in which Frederic conceived Irishness as essential to, and enabling of, that plasticity. Like Twain, Frederic explores Americanness through a lens of Irishness and, more so than his famous predecessor, suggests that the two are essentially connected. Theron passes through an Irish gauntlet that strips away his outmoded, anti-modern, European habits and leaves him ready to develop a progressive American identity. It is only by trying to "go Irish" that Theron can eventually "go American."

In large part, Frederic satirizes popular Anglo-colonial discourses of the late century by inverting conventional narrative patterns. He published *Theron Ware* during a period in which David Livingstone's missionary adventures in Africa still loomed large in the English imagination and shortly after both Rudyard Kipling and Joseph Conrad had started their careers with tales of foreign encounters. The humor of *Theron Ware* emerges from its playful irreverence for the conventions of this genre. It challenges readers to view colonization from the perspective of the colonized subject, rather than that of the colonizer. Through Theron, readers experience what it is like to undergo cultural scrutiny and radical social transformation. Theron's status as a white, Protestant, Anglo American allowed many early readers to identify and sympathize with him, only then to find themselves aligned with an identity subversively shown to be in need of reform. Frederic deconstructs the superiority and stability of the Anglo-Protestant identity by subjecting it to the same colonial power which it normally wielded.

Frederic's novel is a story of counter-conversion, a kind of reverse colonial narrative in which the Irish assume the role of colonizer and Theron becomes their colonized subject. Within this framework, Theron develops into what postcolonial scholars call a "mimic man." He spends the majority of the novel mimicking the behavior of his new Irish friends, imitating their cultural and intellectual interests, following their lead in scholarly arguments, accepting their literary and musical opinions as his own, even replicating their radical approaches to theological practice. Though Forbes, Madden, and Ledsmar are often described as Theron's corruptors, they more accurately should be considered his models. Theron believes that the trio "had lifted him bodily out of the slough of ignorance, of contact with low minds and sordid, narrow things, and put him on solid ground" (126). They do so by encouraging Theron to read the books they read, think what they think, and believe what they believe. They give Theron contact with high minds and progressive ideas, all of which he quickly adopts as his own. Theron pursues his libratory enlightenment by trying to know everything the trio knows and mimicking their approach to life, a project that "made Theron tremble" with excitement (126). Theron as much admits this to Forbes: "I date such a tremendous revolution in my thoughts, my beliefs, my whole mind and character, from my first meeting with you, my first coming here. I don't know how to describe to you the enormous change that has come over me; and I owe it all to you" (255). Theron is bright enough to recognize that the Irish are responsible for his transformation, but does not at first realize that he is merely mimicking their behavior. As he takes to drinking beer, listening to Chopin, and reading George Sand, he never questions whether these actions are innate desires or mere cultural performances to impress his new friends.

Theron's mimicry of the Irish leaves him less willing to fulfill his original marital and religious duties, which now seem beneath him, since he believes himself to no longer be that man he was, but rather "quite another being" (230). His wife, Alice, appears backward and foolish to him, and though he appeared to be happy with her at the start of the novel, Theron later describes his mind as "cramped," his "nerves harassed," his "ambitions spoiled and rotted," and his "whole existence darkened and belittled" by his marriage to her (231). He even hints at a fascination with celibacy and a desire to live more like a Catholic priest. Theron comes to think derisively of his job as a minister, and he further considers his religion a fraud and his congregation delusional fools. He proudly states to his Irish friends what he thinks they want to hear: "I am not a Methodist minister . . . at least not today,—and here—with you!" (230). Like the mimic men found in the novels of later post-colonial writers, Theron's mimicry separates him from his own community while drawing him toward a new community to which he can never truly belong.

In *The Location of Culture*, Homi Bhabha describes mimicry as "one of the most elusive and effective strategies of colonial power and knowledge" (122). Encouraged by the authority of the colonial state, the other imitates the culture and identity of the colonizer; however, the other's performance of the colonizer's identity is never perfect duplication, and mimicry creates a kind of "hybrid" or "bastard" that is similar to, but not quite the same, as the colonial culture. In relation to *Theron Ware*, Bhabha's articulation of mimicry is useful for two reasons. First, Bhabha's conception of mimicry and its role in the creation of performative hybrid cultures offers a concise way to examine the nature of Irish culture without resorting to discussions of inherent or essential Irishness. Second, Bhabha's explanation of the disciplinary function of mimicry allows us to better understand the motives of Theron's Irish "corruptors" and further helps us to make sense of the often misunderstood ending of the book.

Theron believes that he can gain total access to Octavius' Irish community and be fully embraced as one of their number, and he thinks that his transformation, if completed, will allow him to walk among them as an equal. At the scene of MacEvoy's death, Theron is astonished that no one "seemed to regard his presence there as unusual," which allows him to experience something profound as a member of a group, and he later seeks similar communal experiences at Irish picnics, Irish homes, and even the Catholic Church itself (46). Early in the novel, Theron is "dazzled" by the "sensation of having been invited to become a citizen of this world," but of course this sensation is erroneous as no one has actually invited him to join the Irish community (127). Theron conceives of Forbes and Celia as gateways and evaluates his success in Octavius by the degree to which he believes he is accepted into their world. Yet, he does not realize his folly. The Irish have not accepted him as one of their own, and several of them—including those he thinks of as close friends—believe his transformation to be "degeneration" (296).

Theron mistakenly believes he can achieve authentic Irishness, which in his mind means becoming mystical, romantic, "poetic . . . given to songs and music," polished, intellectual, progressive, good-humored, genial, prone to "pleasingly human" fisticuffs, hardworking, thirsty for alcohol, capable of good-natured sin, and obedient to strong authority (54, 218). In addition, Theron (like Frederic) seems to distinguish between the Irish and other Europeans and views the former as more modern and less entrenched in history. Theron describes his love of the Irish as "instinct" and "impulse," couching the change in his character in naturalistic terms (45, 49). In the end, he thinks his whole identity can be translated from the world of repressed Methodism to liberal Irish Catholicism and sees no obstacle to his fully becoming a part of their shared ethnic identity. Yet, mimicry of Irish culture can only lead to an ironic failure to achieve an authentic Irish identity; as Bhabha states, "The desire to emerge as 'authentic' through mimicry . . . is the final irony of partial representation" (126). Though Theron believes he has transformed into an authentic Irishman, in truth, his mimicry of the Irish has turned him into something else, a monstrous other reviled by the very people he wishes to be like.

Celia shows Theron the reality of his situation when he confronts her in her hotel room after following her to New York. Her chastising lecture of Theron had been a long time coming, but turns cruel when she describes him as just like "the fable about the donkey trying to play lap-dog," by which she means that he is not a transformed being, but just a deluded creature pretending to be something that he is not (296). And like Aesop's donkey, Theron unwittingly causes harm while pretending to be something he is not. In the original fable, the donkey decides that it is time "to enjoy the finer things in life and to command the respect of everyone," so it imitates the much adored house dog by leaping on the master and licking him all over, which of course results in gross injury to the master (Aesop). Celia accuses Theron of similar chaos and harm, saying that in his actions—which he thought of as authentically Irish—he had actually embarrassed herself, Forbes, and Ledsmar. She accuses him of being vain, egotistic, cruel, deceitful, and vulgar. Her verbal rebuke leaves Theron crippled, like the donkey who was beaten for harming its master, and Theron too is forced to learn Aesop's moral: "Unworthy people should not try to usurp the position of their superiors" (Aesop).

Of course, Frederic does not intend for his readers to lay all of the blame at Theron's feet. Lionel Lacker points out that the end of the novel is not "a scornful condemnation of Theron," but also acknowledges that there is no clear redemption of the protagonist (87). This ambiguity between damnation and salvation at the end of the novel has long confused readers and critics.[15] Are we supposed to agree with Celia's rebuke and celebrate Theron's subsequent mental and physical collapse? It seems unlikely. Frederic himself had a great deal of sympathy for Theron and stated in a private letter, "I think I like best of all the judgment of those who, like you, feel that our friend Theron was badly treated. I couldn't save him from it, but it was a grief to me none the less" (Bennett 174). It is Forbes, Madden, and Ledsmar that have "badly treated" Theron and reexamining their actions with a post-colonial framework clarifies their culpability in Theron's collapse and makes clear why Theron can neither be condemned or redeemed at the end of the book.

Celia expresses her and Forbes' interest in Theron in very condescending, colonial terms. In a passage that sounds like it could be an excerpt from an imperialist's diary, she says,

> We were disposed to like you very much when we first knew you . . . You impressed us as an innocent, simple, genuine young character, full of mother's milk. It was like the smell of early spring in the country to come in contact with you. Your honesty of nature, your sincerity in that absurd religion of yours, your general *naïveté* of mental and spiritual get-up, all pleased us a great deal. *We thought you were going to be a real acquisition* . . . We liked you, as I have said, because you were unsophisticated and delightfully fresh and natural. Somehow we took it for granted you would stay so. (295, my emphasis)

The appeal of Theron's natural purity and innocence as stated here casts him as a noble savage and reeks of the kind of essentialism and prejudiced outside observation that Edward Said famously criticizes in *Orientalism*. This is not surprising, perhaps, from a woman who divides people into two categories with implicit imperial connotations: Greeks (conquerors) and Jews (slaves). When asked to explain what she means by these categories, she only offers vague generalizations, but clearly privileges being a Greek over being a Jew (187). She, of course, considers herself a Greek and tells Theron that he is (at least partially) a Jew (180). Of course, ever the mimic man, Theron expresses his desire to be exactly like her: "I want to be a Greek myself, if you're one. I want to get as close to you—to your ideal, that is, as I can" (188). When Celia tells Theron that she is "Hellenizing" him, he does not recognize the cultural condescension implicit in her project, nor does he acknowledge the concept of Hellenization as imperial by design (183).

Celia studies Theron as if he is a specimen of an inferior culture and perceives his differences as fascinating signs of cultural weakness. She, Forbes, and Ledsmar think of Theron as an "acquisition," not as a friend, a colleague, or even a person. Theron's value to them is as something to be acquired and conquered, and, like many conquerors, they grow disappointed when the other's purity seems to fade during the colonial process. They assumed that their own actions would not fundamentally change the object of their fascination. Bhabha says that this kind of assumption contributes to the colonizer's "ambivalence," their belief that the colonized's social reality "is at once an 'other' and yet entirely knowable and visible" (101). The trio can only remain amused as long as their dutiful subject keeps his ambitions in check, because what they liked about Theron was his simplicity and his deference to them as superior beings. As soon as he starts making claims to his new identity and social status, he poses a threat to the cultural monopoly they maintain in Octavius, and as a result, they must remind him of his place. They squash his insurrection like practiced imperialists, leaving him humiliated and broken in the process.

Theron was set up to fail from the beginning. Forbes, Madden, and Ledsmar enact changes on him that precipitate their need to reject him. The colonizers undermine their own project, since, as Bhabha states, colonial appropriation and mimicry ensure "strategic failure" from the start (123). By trying to articulate a new identity for Theron, the trio deprives him of the ability to make any claim to an authentic identity. It amuses and flatters them to play with Theron by Irishing his character. *Acquiring* him requires that they do so, since in order to possess him they need to instill in him the kind of obedience that colonial mimicry ensures. But the very act of Irishing Theron guarantees that he will never actually be Irish. Bhabha observes that "to be Anglicized is *emphatically* not to be English" (125). In the context of *Theron Ware*, to be Irishized is emphatically not to be Irish. The Irish are those who do not need illumination. As Theron takes on Irish characteristics (which he believes are progressive, liberal, and good), he simultaneously creates a boundary between himself and the Octavius Irish that can never be transcended.

Theron's situation is made worse by his alienation from the Methodist community. As he becomes Irishized, he finds himself increasingly estranged from the people to whom he is supposed to be a leader. He passes beyond pretending that "there was anything spiritually in common between him and the Methodist Church of Octavius," and as the divide grows, he becomes "saddened and humiliated" by his own people and experiences "a dawning sense of shame" (127, 147). Theron tries to maintain his position in the community, despite his growing feeling that he is a "fraud" (168). He goes as far as describing his life among the Octavius Methodists as "my slavery,—my double bondage" (240). When Theron meets with Celia's brother Michael, the dying man repeatedly tells him to "keep among your own people . . . Go back to the way you were brought up in, and leave alone the people whose ways are different from yours" (273–4). As earnest as Michael's deathbed plea is, the suggestion is ludicrous. Theron has changed too much to ever go back, and as much as he can never be part of the Irish community, he can no longer be part of the Methodist community either.

Not really Irish and no longer truly Methodist, Theron becomes one of Bhabha's hybrids or bastards, his new identity created in the slippage between Irish and Methodist culture. Importantly, Bhabha does not consider hybridity a bad thing; rather, he suggests that hybridity enables the ability to discursively challenge authority and results in the performative creation of cultural identity. At the end of *Theron Ware*, Frederic's protagonist is not a cultural tabula rasa simply because he does not fit in with any existing community in upstate New York; instead, Theron performs a new cultural identity that has both legitimacy and agency. I believe it is this kind of new cultural identity that gave Frederic hope regarding America.

Frederic, anxious about the developing character of American culture, displays contradictory feelings regarding the role of immigrants in American society. Bramen suggests that he was "both repulsed by and attracted to the possibilities of cultural intermingling," and she further argues that, though Frederic did not want to relinquish the idea of a "homogeneous American spirit," he also believed that the kind of cross-cultural friction found in *Theron Ware* was necessary for the country (66). She calls Frederic a "reluctant modernist" and describes his contradictory position on America's heterogeneity in clear terms:

> [H]e is at once a nativist and a pragmatist, concerned about the demographic changes of the nation yet also aware that these changes are unavoidable. His response is not to advocate an outmoded, agrarian-based notion of Americanism . . . but to redefine a national identity that recognized, however reluctantly, the inevitability of cross-cultural encounters and intermingling. (67)

For Frederic, cultural hybridity was a necessary step in achieving a new kind of American identity. Of course, his fondness for the Irish and dislike of other immigrant groups likely prompted him to want to imagine American cross-cultural encounters with a primarily Celtic bent. In Frederic's novel, the Irish exemplify certain "impulsive, imaginative, even fantastic qualities" that America needs (221). The Octavius Irish's progressive attitude leaves them more suited than others for "modern go-ahead American civilization," especially when compared with the Methodists who "walk here . . . in a meek an' humble spirit" (213, 33). Meekness and humility were not the traits the country needed to succeed; instead, what was needed was a bold, richness of mind and spirit, and the desire to progress into the future without being shackled by the chains of history.

In *Theron Ware*, the Irish embody these traits. Forbes goes so far as to predict that the Irish will transform the country:

> The lager-drinking Irishman in a few generations will be a new type of humanity,—the Kelt at his best. He will dominate America. He will be *the* American. And his church—with the Italian element thrown clean out of it, and its Pope living, say, in Baltimore or Georgetown—will be the Church of America. (222)

The provocative nature of the priest's speech would have frightened anyone with nativist leanings, including Frederic himself. Forbes predicts the nightmare scenario for nativists: a country run by drunken Irishmen with the Pope ensconced uncomfortably close to the White House. This is not the kind of America Frederic hopes for in *Theron Ware*. He does not want an *Irish* country, but he does want an *Irish-like* country. He envisions the new American as having the best qualities (and none of the weaknesses) of both Anglo Americans and Irish Americans, only possible through cultural intermingling.¹⁶ Theron fails to become an Irishman, but succeeds in becoming the "new type of humanity" that America needed going forward.

When Theron goes west to his new life, he goes with a new identity and insights that will allow him to thrive. Though he is not truly Irish, his hybrid Irish identity leaves him uniquely suited to succeed on the frontier. Frederick Jackson Turner calls the frontier "the outer edge of the wave" where old outmoded European identities are broken down and replaced with new American ones (200). By sending his protagonist west at the end of the novel, Frederic wants readers to realize the place of the cultural hybrid in America's future. It is also a reminder, as Bramen notes, that "the native needs to be Americanized as much as the foreigner" (69). Though Frederic is at times critical of the Irish and even reinforces some nativist anxieties regarding their unsuitability for American communities, he also clearly shows that Anglo Americans are equally (if not more) unsuited for the country's modern period. If Theron had gone west at the start of the novel, while still a naïve and culturally isolated individual, he would have failed spectacularly. At the end of the novel, having experienced what he does, readers are inclined to believe in the possibility of his success and might even think it possible that he will fulfill his promise to go into politics and become a senator before he is forty (315).

Though some critics see the ending of *Theron Ware* as an unmitigated tragedy, I believe Frederic implies something more complex. Bridget Bennett describes Theron's going west as "the bleakest ending Frederic could conceive of, worse, even, than suicide" (181). Yet, this view tends to overstate the case and ignores certain indications of hope in the closing pages of the novel and Frederic's own professed sympathy for Theron, who he felt was "badly treated" during his time in Octavius. Would critics ever consider Huck Finn's similar flight to the frontier bleaker than suicide? Obviously not, even though the narrative trajectory of the two characters is remarkably similar: they both break rules and defy their superiors; they both are seen as needing reform; they both consort with ethnic others that they are not supposed to; they both are thought of as deviating from white, Protestant norms; they both undergo radical attempts at social rehabilitation; they both experience public ostracism; they both pursue intellectual enlightenment and independence; they both lose faith in their community and their friends; they both come to question their identity; and they both come to the realization that there is no place for them in the civilized regions of the country and so choose exile as their only alternative. Theron's journey west, like Huck's, seems a mix of tragedy and triumph, resignation and opportunity. Without any doubt, Theron has failed in all of his goals and proven himself weak and callow in the process, and so it is hard to feel too bad for him since, as William Dean Howells describes, "the author never for a moment represented him anywhere to you as a good man, or as anything but a very selfish man" ("My Favorite Novelist" 278); however, Theron's failures have broken apart his stifling, anti-progressive Methodist identity and left him ripe for transformation in the frontier. Frederic clearly saw in the Irish certain social characteristics he believed America needed to adopt; yet, he was not ignorant of the difficulty and dangers in such cultural change, which is why his novel can be both "illumination" and "damnation." The process of intellectual, secular, and social illumination would almost ensure damnation of the spirit by the standards of nineteenth-century conservative Methodism. The two titles of Frederic's book reflect this pull between the secular and the sacred and indicate how the Irishing of America could be viewed, depending on context, as either positive or negative.

Though Theron fails in the east, there is hope for him in the west. In the final pages of the book, he recovers from the shock and illness brought about by his confrontation with Celia, and though significantly and permanently changed, he seems poised for success. We learn that he had "an air of restored and secure good health about him," and his friends express their confidence in his embarkation on a new career and the likelihood that "he'll thrive in Seattle like a green bay-tree" (313–4). When Theron thinks about his future, he smiles and experiences a "little delighted tremor" (314). The novel ends on a note of possibility, not just for the continued transformation of Theron's identity, but for the social and political rejuvenation of America out west.

THE BRUTE IN THE CITY: FRANK NORRIS' *MCTEAGUE*

Mark Twain's and Harold Frederic's protagonists head west to escape from oppressive societies and to search for new communities in which being Irish is not taboo, but Frank Norris' novel *McTeague* begins with the title protagonist already having made this journey. As the novel opens, readers learn that McTeague left behind a life in the mines to pursue a career as a dentist in San Francisco. He has reinvented himself as a respectable, hard-working professional, and despite his faulty heritage and, as Clare Eby observes, the simple fact that his "passing" as a professional is "worse than plagiaristic—it is a total sham," McTeague has thrived and grown comfortable in his new home (136). Norris presents a vision of what Huck Finn and Theron Ware eventually might have found on their journeys—a land of opportunity where, perhaps, the Irish could succeed. Yet, as the novel plays out, Norris presents the bleakest vision of Anglo–Irish relations in literature of this period and suggests that the Irish would find no refuge in the new cities of the west.

The plot of *McTeague*, built on an unwavering faith in the science of degeneration, requires the Irishman to fall off the evolutionary ladder and hit every rung on the way down. McTeague's initial success must be revealed to be a temporary illusion, and the character must devolve into a stereotypical Irish monster, prone to slothfulness, drunkenness, deviant sexuality, and murderous rage. Norris takes away everything McTeague achieves (job, home, money, friends, health, marriage, happiness) and blames it all on his ethnicity. Before the dentist's atavistic nightmare begins, readers are warned that his racial identity forecasts doom: "Below the fine fabric of all that was good in him ran the foul stream of hereditary evil, like a sewer. The vices and sins of his father and of his father's father, to the third and fourth and five hundredth generation, tainted him. The evil of an entire race flowed in his veins" (22). Irish heritage predestines McTeague for failure, and his foul blood guarantees that, no matter how hard he works to climb the social ladder, he will wind up at the bottom. When McTeague is revealed to be an essential brute, it validates nativist fears and justifies anti-Irish policies in urban America. McTeague's inability to maintain an assimilated identity marks him—and all Irishmen, since his name suggests his representative function—as unfit for civilized life.

Despite Norris's pointing toward McTeague's racial shortcomings throughout the text, few critics explore the degeneracy plot of the novel in terms of the main character's specific ethnic heritage. McTeague's Irishness soaks almost every page of Norris' novel, yet it often is overlooked. In approaching *McTeague*, scholars too often ignore, downplay, or misinterpret the title character's ethnicity, while at the same time emphasizing the influence of nativism, evolution, and criminal anthropology on Norris.[17] This omission is strange, considering that ethnicity is central to all of these concerns.

Hugh J. Dawson provides the most comprehensive examination of McTeague's Irish heritage and considers the ways in which McTeague's simian appearance, prognathic jaw, sentimentality, idleness, drunkenness, and proclivity for violence play directly into nineteenth-century readers' expectations of Irish characters. Dawson also notes the importance of McTeague's name, which incorporates the word *Teague*, the title frequently given to stage Irishmen and a common derogatory slang term for Irish Catholics (41). Dawson argues for reconsidering the importance of McTeague's ethnicity, but still leaves mostly unexplored the impact of that ethnicity on the novel itself. Once we recognize the protagonist's Irishness, how does it change the way we read the book?

An understanding of the themes of *McTeague* must include a discussion of the pervasive Irish stereotypes that Norris appropriates. In particular, it is essential to consider the intersection of McTeague's ethnicity and Norris' project of composing the narrative of the modern city. In writing "A Story of San Francisco," Norris presents what he believes the American city should be; he presents his ideal imagined community. I wish to examine very specifically how Norris constructs this ideal by denying membership in that community to the Irish and by using them as a foil against which to build his new vision of America. The contrapuntal movement at work in the novel (McTeague's decline and San Francisco's ascendancy) is not coincidental. In fact, the success of Norris' San Francisco depends on the marginalization of McTeague. By denying McTeague a place in San Francisco, Norris denies the Irish a place in the modern city, and by extension, the increasingly urban American community. *McTeague* contradicts other literature of the period, including *Huck Finn* and *Theron Ware*, by suggesting that the attempt to assimilate the Irish was not just misguided, but also dangerous to the integrity of the nation.

Like Twain and Frederic, Norris uses his novel to meditate on the cultural anxieties surrounding Irish assimilation. The questions he asks are familiar: can the Irish be made safe? Can they be made American? Is civilization antithetical to the Irish character? What is the best way to reform the aberrant ethnic minority? How can Protestant Anglo-American values be preserved? Joseph R. McElrath and Jesse S. Crisler write in their biography of Norris,

> As had Harold Frederic in *The Damnation of Theron Ware* (1896), he [Norris] focused on the manners and mores of representative Americans, observing the stresses felt by those in the midst of an increasingly pluralistic society undergoing rapid transformations that called into question the values, truths, and ultimate certainties with which they had been reared. (6)

Of course, Frederic and Norris come to starkly divergent understandings of how America should respond to pluralism and express equally differing opinions on the role of the Irish in a national community. In Frederic's work (and in Twain's), the Western Frontier held promise for immigrants seeking Americanization, but the Frontier was also, according to Henry Nash Smith, a "constantly receding area of free land" (251). By the time McTeague leaves the Big Dipper Mine and journeys west, the Frontier has already started to transform into an urban landscape. There were still opportunities in such a place, but in Norris' imagination, the savage Irishman had little claim to them.

According to McElrath and Crisler, "Norris repeatedly enunciated his belief in the racial superiority of the Anglo-Saxon, which over time had become the Anglo-Norman, the British, and the Anglo-American type" (30). Norris went as far as to credit the conquest of North America and western expansion to an effort begun by fifth-century Frieslanders in Europe as they undertook a "Great March" toward Britain (McElrath 30–1). Norris believed that the Anglo-Saxons in the ensuing centuries proved their vigor by continuing west around the globe. In this context, *McTeague* can be read as a celebration of Anglo-Saxon triumphalism, but it can also be read, as McElrath and Crisler suggest, as an effort "to rehearse the shortcomings of the lowly Irish American" (31).

Like Twain, Norris absorbed nativist prejudices while still quite young. He was born in Chicago in 1870, when the city was the fourth largest Irish urban center in America and the seat of widespread anti-Irish prejudice. The Chicago Irish did not do as well as those in the "urban frontier" (i.e., San Francisco) because of pronounced nativism in the city, which was the result of the perceived stress the Irish were placing on the city's schools, hospitals, prisons, and charitable institutions (McCaffrey 8). In only two decades, the Irish population of Chicago had grown nearly eightfold its original size, from 6,000 Irish natives in 1850 to 40,000 in 1870 (the year Norris was born) (Funchion 9). This sudden boom in the Irish population, and the perceived threat of new Catholic Churches and political organizations like Clan na Gael, created friction with Chicago's Anglo population. As an adolescent, Norris might not have been aware of the political nuances of Chicago's Irish problems, but he certainly would have been aware of the popular view of the Irish as a social threat.

In 1884, Norris' family moved to San Francisco, a city where the Irish thrived socially and politically. The Irish community of San Francisco, which accounted for one-third of the city's total population, found greater satisfaction and opportunity on the west coast than they had on the east coast. Irish journalist and politician John Francis Maguire visited America in the 1860s and observed that the Irish were "better off in all respects" in San Francisco than anywhere else in the Union (274). Maguire noted that the city had been laid out by an Irishman and that the police force, hotels, banks, philanthropic organizations, street railways, gasworks, foundries, and government all were run largely by Irishmen (273). There were not as many obstacles to Irish social mobility in San Francisco, and the Irish who came there were not as committed to a "defensive-ghetto mentality" as their eastern counterparts (Sarbaugh 173).[18] By the time Norris' family moved there, San Francisco had become home to an Irish community unlike any other in the U.S.

Yet, despite San Francisco's general hospitality to the Irish, there persisted a strong current of anti-Irish sentiment among the city's broader population, apparent in the nativist rhetoric of the city's newspapers. In 1893, Norris—like many other San Francisco residents—became entranced with the story of Patrick Collins, a local Irishman who murdered his wife in the cloakroom of a kindergarten.[19] The local newspapers provided physical descriptions of Collins that strongly resemble Norris' later descriptions of McTeague.[27] *The Morning Call* described Collins as "surly and defiant . . . a perfect brute" ("Perfect"). *The Examiner* reported that he "is as surly a brute as ever was locked behind bars" ("Surly"). *The Evening Bulletin* reported,

Collins is unquestionably one of the most brutal-looking men ever brought into the City Prison. His face is of the bull-dog character: flat nose, thick lips, heavy jaws and small, fierce-looking eyes. He is a strong, muscular-looking man. He gave his age as thirty-two years and Ireland as his place of nativity. ("Collins Arrested")

The various accounts of the Collins murder emphasized the racial/ethnic aspects of the criminal, both in the text and in the illustrations, and evoked the popular ethnic caricature of the Irish (see Figures 2.3–2.6). Norris had an interest in ethnic caricature, and according to Henry B. Wonham, his Irish brutes "betray literary realism's uncertain relation to the magazine culture that made ethnic caricature a staple element in late nineteenth-century American intellectual life" (35). Some of these news articles trafficked in this "staple element" so explicitly that, predicting Norris' approach in *McTeague*, they blamed Collins' criminal impulses on his genetic destiny and condemned, not one man, but an entire ethnic group in the process. For instance, a follow-up article from *The Examiner* proclaimed that Collins was "born for the rope" and went on to suggest that "[i]f a good many of Patrick Collins' ancestors did not die on the scaffold then either they escaped their desert [*sic*] or there is nothing in heredity" ("He Was Born"). The same article further suggested that Collins belonged to another species of man entirely, twice compared him to a black man (evoking the "white Negro" concept), and then invited readers to simply picture Collins as a cousin to the thuggish John L. Sullivan (the most famous Irish athlete of the time). Norris would do more than just use the events of the Collins murder to plot his story; he would also appropriate the nativist rhetoric of San Francisco newsmen to help him construct McTeague as a racial other.

Though *McTeague* owes much to Norris' formative readings of nativist journalism, it is also the product of his study of criminal anthropology, particularly the school of thinking developed by Cesare Lombroso regarding atavism, hereditary criminality, degeneration, and criminal physiognomy. According to Donald Pizer, by the time Norris wrote *McTeague*, he had developed a "preoccupation" with the themes of atavism and reversion, and "particularly with the role of heredity in causing either an obvious physical or mental devolution or a return to an earlier family condition" (*Novels* 59). Suddenly, Norris had a way to explain the behavior of his murderous protagonist—he was born a criminal, having inherited the degenerate traits and predilections of his Irish ancestors. Combined with the newspaper reports of the Collins murder, criminal anthropology gave Norris all the tools he needed to write, what Pizer calls, "that mythical creature of literature, a naturalistic tragedy" (*Novels* 63).

Norris began writing *McTeague* while living in Boston and attending Harvard University. Though he was only there for a year (1894–1895),

Figures 2.3–2.6 These courtroom illustrations of Patrick Collins were paired with the nativist rhetoric of the articles: *The Morning Call*, 12 October 1893: 10 (top left); *The Morning Call*, 13 October 1893: 8 (top right); *The Examiner*, 11 October 1893: 4 (bottom left); *The Chronicle*, 11 October 1893: 4 (bottom right).

Boston, like Chicago and San Francisco, influenced his sense of how the Irish fit into American society and further encouraged his nativist leanings. When Norris arrived in the city, Bostonians generally considered the Irish an unwanted, peasant minority, and took action against them through hostile political and social organizations: the American Protective Association (APA), a nativist anti-Catholic group, opposed parochial schooling; the Immigration Restriction League, formed by three recent Harvard graduates, sought to curb Irish immigration to the city;

and the Anti-Saloon League forwarded prohibition as a way of stifling Irish success in business (O'Connor 153–7). In addition, Norris likely would have been aware of the local remnants of Know-Nothing politics and the popular anti-Irish/anti-Catholic sentiment at Harvard itself.[20]

Having been born in a city that saw the Irish as a major social threat, having grown up in a city in which the Irish were considered hereditary criminals, and having sat in a classroom in a city where the Irish were frequently and publicly vilified, it seems unsurprising that Norris' murderous dentist would turn out to be an Irishman who embodied all the worst elements of the stereotype.

When *McTeague* was published, some notable writers, including William Dean Howells and Willa Cather, thought highly of it, but many other reviewers labeled it "vulgar," "gruesome," "gross," "sordid," "revolting," and "stomach-turning," primarily due to its "novelistic violations of Anglo-American taboos" (McElrath 4). In the text, readers are exposed to murder, rape, drunkenness, uncouth bodily functions, deviant sexuality (including sadomasochism), greed, violence, and fundamental challenges to the standards of professional and domestic life in America. The novel gives grotesque focus to all seven of the deadly sins and forces readers to witness, if not participate by proxy, in some of the most heinous behavior that had ever seen print in America. Like the plays of Ned Harrigan, Norris' novel takes readers on a tour of the sordid streets of the city where ethnic minorities live, but unlike Harrigan's plays, *McTeague* makes no attempt to lessen the impact of ethnic difference or emphasize the positive aspects of slum dwellers. Norris certainly intended to shock his readers with his "realistic" depiction of the depraved underbelly of America, and in doing so, he invited them to join with him in rejecting those ethnic aberrations that he felt were threatening the purity of the nation.

Norris' novelistic vision of a lone Irishman floundering about the civilized world begins with the establishing of a barrier between McTeague and the world. In the first chapter of the book, Norris presents his protagonist as isolated and out of place, someone who can observe the world but not participate in it: "Day after day, McTeague saw the same panorama unroll itself. The bay window of his 'Dental Parlors' was for him a point of vantage from which he watched the world go past" (9). Like an animal in a zoo, McTeague can only watch people walk by and initially lacks the ability to enter the civilized world. Much of the novel describes his repeated attempts to join the world he sees from the window of his Dental Parlors; yet, McTeague's various strategies fail due to hereditary shortcomings. Though McTeague has the ambition to assimilate (an ambition that the Irish characters in Twain and Frederic lack), he will never fit in with the people of San Francisco. Norris makes this painfully obvious from the start. McTeague's attempts to become just like everyone else give rise to much of the novel's humor, but more significantly, they highlight insurmountable obstacles to the social reform and cultural assimilation of the Irish. His differences are dangerous to those around him, and the more he tries to force his essentially Irish identity into this world, the more damage he does to the American community.

In Norris' imagination, the Irishman is a threat to America because he pretends to be something he is not. Instead of truly assimilating, he merely passes as a civilized member of society, but his true monstrous nature lurks just below the surface and inevitably reemerges to wreak havoc on his community. *McTeague* is a nativist nightmare given form; the novel fulfills the worst fears of those who viewed Irish immigration as an attack on the principles of American life. In particular, Norris shows the Irishman to be a threat in four different contexts—physical, professional, social, and domestic—which play directly to four popular nativist beliefs: the Irish are biologically flawed; they are job thieves; they are disruptors of the peace; and they are destroyers of traditional family values. All of these fears depend on a belief in the biological and social inferiority of the Irish and a fear of the dilution of Anglo dominance in America, and in each of these contexts, Norris highlights how the Irishman proves not only woefully deficient but also insidiously destructive of American standards and values. McTeague embodies those undesirable traits, Dawson observes, which "nativist ideology had long taught were the 'race impulses' of the Irish" (36). Though he at times appears to be just like everyone else, Norris' Irishman is revealed to be a physical, professional, social, and domestic monster. It is in this way that *McTeague* can be read as fundamentally concerned with Irishness in America, as it uses the perceived major shortcomings of the Irish people as the tentpoles of its plot structure. McTeague attempts to reform his character in all four contexts, but his essential Irishness causes him to fail over and over again, and in this way, the plot of the novel becomes a rehearsal of Irish incompatibility with fundamental American cultural norms.

The physical context of McTeague's monstrosity is the most obvious. Norris begins his project by demonstrating just how awkward the Irishman is in a civilized context. McTeague's body does not fit (metaphorically or literally) inside the city. By repeatedly drawing attention to its monstrous dimensions and animal-like qualities, Norris shows McTeague's physical body—the body of the stereotypical Irishman—to be inappropriate for life in San Francisco. McTeague himself knows that a body like his does not belong in a civilized space. When he is invited to spend the night in Trina's room, he stands awkwardly in such delicate surroundings:

> McTeague was in his lady's bower; it seemed to him a little nest, intimate, discreet. He felt hideously out of place. He was an intruder; he, with his enormous feet, his colossal bones, his crude, brutal gestures. The mere weight of his limbs, he was sure, would crush the little bedstead like an eggshell. (46)

McTeague's presence in this room threatens the peace and stability of the Sieppe family's home.[21] What clean things will he dirty? What items will he break? In what way will he violate the privacy and decency of Trina's most intimate space? Eby links McTeague's awkwardness in this scene to his sexual arousal and suggests that being in Trina's room quickens his hormones "without the discomfort that attends being with her in the flesh" (130). In this sense, the grotesque presence of a bestial Irishman in the delicate bedroom of a young woman stands in for the threatened physical violation of that same woman (which is realized soon enough). Norris encourages readers who find McTeague's blundering through the bedroom to be comically inappropriate to see the implications of his physical threat to Trina; if he goes about brutishly fondling her things and crushing her clothes in his arms, what will he do to the actual woman? This short, but memorable, scene functions almost as a miniature model for the rest of the novel: McTeague is "an intruder" on a "clean," "white," "ordinary" space who is "seized with an unreasonable impulse" that incites actions which bring him pleasure and "contentment," but which everyone else regards as violent and perverse (46–8). Importantly, Norris builds this plot around the visual incongruity of the stereotypical Irish ape-man within a delicate, civilized, feminine space, and thus equates McTeague's insertion into Trina's life with the Irishman's equally inappropriate insertion into the American city. In both cases, the Irish penchant for emotionality, violence, and irrationality threaten the status quo, but, more importantly, the Irishman's body poses an overt physical threat to his fragile surroundings.

Dawson suggests that Norris' repeated descriptions of McTeague's monstrous body are attempts to "reproduce exactly the caricaturist's cliche-figures" of the Irishman (36). There is obviously a certain efficiency in making use of easily recognized stereotypes, but such a strategy validates the most demeaning ethnic images by transferring them from the comical context of publications like *Harper's Weekly* and *Puck* to a realist literary tradition. McTeague's physique is cartoonishly disproportioned to his environment, which only heightens his awkward presence in civilized spaces and emphasizes his ethnically odd features, which are repeatedly described in terms that blend recognizably Irish signifiers with gross physical distortions to such a degree that monstrosity and Irishness become one and the same thing. Norris also repeatedly emphasizes McTeague's physical difference through comparisons to animals: a draught horse, an anaconda, a bear, a Saint Bernard, an elephant, an ass, a bull, an ox, and (of course) an ape. Dawson finds McTeague's "animal features" to be evidence of Norris' attempt to remove the character's individuality and make him distinctively of an Irish-American type (34). While some of Norris' Darwinian rhetoric was relatively new, the animalizing of the Irishman was an old cliché of Anglo literature which sought to construct Irish identity as something naturally wild and filthy. Who would invite an animal into their living room or entrust to him their daughter? Norris uses the cliché of the animal-like

Irishman to set McTeague physically apart from his civilized neighbors, patients, friends, and ultimately the whole human species.

The professional context of McTeague's monstrosity is less visually striking than the physical context, but equally, if not more, threatening to the city. Since leaving the Big Dipper Mine, McTeague has set up shop in San Francisco as a dentist in the hope of achieving financial success and the respect of his community, but his ambition of adapting to a civilized environment does little to mitigate his crude path into the profession. The people of Polk Street believe Doctor McTeague to be a skilled and trustworthy professional, and by all appearances he is the embodiment of the self-made man; however, he never earned a dental degree, nor did he study dentistry in a formal manner. The most he can claim is that he sharpened excavators and hung advertisements for a traveling charlatan who operated out of the back of a wagon (145). He later also read many books on dentistry, but "he was too hopelessly stupid to get much benefit from them" (6). When Trina tells McTeague he has no legal right to practice dentistry, he simply cannot comprehend what that means: "What's the law? . . . Ain't I dentist? Ain't I a doctor? Look at my sign, and the gold tooth you gave me. Why, I've been practicing nearly twelve years" (146). McTeague believes that the appearance of being a dentist is enough. He has the tools and the outfit, he subscribes to the trade journal, people call him "Doc"—so what is the problem?

McTeague understands neither the danger in his shortcut to the top of the professional ladder, nor, as Eby argues, the importance of a diploma as a "sign of his professional authenticity" (136). It is not enough to look the part, as McTeague simply believes; there also must be legitimacy behind the identity. In the world of men like McTeague, substance apparently does not matter. Eby traces McTeague's desire for a fraudulent professional identity to early twentieth-century anxieties regarding authenticity and explains why his "passing" as a dentist was so particularly threatening to the public:

> Norris' plot—tracing the transformation of a bogus professional with nascent middle-class aspirations, to a real criminal on the lam—is extreme, yet strangely plausible, for in trying to appropriate a public identity that wasn't rightfully his, Mac had already twice broken the law. Besides illegally practicing dentistry, Mac comes very close to breaking the law by appropriating an identity that wasn't his . . . he steals an identity from the profession as a whole. (139–40)

The problem, once again then, is that McTeague tries passing as something that he fundamentally is not. Norris formulates McTeague's entire career as a kind of identity theft in which a crude, fraudulent Irishman usurps the persona of a legitimate, educated American. This makes McTeague's entire effort to professionally assimilate nothing more than pretend.

As Eby observes, McTeague's attempt at passing would have struck a nerve with American readers anxious about authenticity. The formalizing of dental education and licensing in the middle of the nineteenth century resulted from a desire to protect the public from "the evils of quackery" (Dalton 150). When the first College of Dental Surgery opened in the U.S. in 1840, its founders specifically described their mission as safeguarding communities from "totally incompetent individuals" like McTeague who "unjustly disparaged" the profession and worked "to the detriment of the community" (Horner 26). The era of barbers performing wisdom tooth extractions or traveling merchants moonlighting as cavity-fillers was over. As McElrath and Crisler note, McTeague was "born too late in a century" that stood "as a Rubicon in many respects" for quasi-professionalism (8). Norris positions McTeague's fraudulence as anti-progressive and anti-American. His circumvention of the law upsets the social equilibrium and threatens to hold his community back from new progressive standards. His brand of folk dentistry would have been acceptable in the old world, or during an earlier period in American history, but at the turn of the century in a growing city like San Francisco it simply has no place. The formalizing of the dental profession excludes him, and those like him, from the new urban professional orthodoxy.

American progress thus reveals the Irishman's fraudulence. According to McTeague's logic, anyone could claim any identity they want through a simple proclamation. Of course, such an idea proves threatening because it is only a small step from an Irishman claiming a professional identity to which he was not entitled to an Irishman claiming an American identity (to which many nativists also felt the Irish were not entitled). As Eby rightly argues, the issue at stake in *McTeague* is authenticity, but this extends well beyond the professional sphere. If McTeague was a fake dentist, might he also not be a fake American, a fake husband, a fake friend, even a fake human being?

The social context of McTeague's monstrosity reveals more fraudulence and subhuman features of his character, as he forces his way into polite society in an effort to become "a man of the world" (58). He equates personal success with social advancement and clearly sees his friendship with Marcus, his association with the Sieppes, and his marriage to Trina as potential paths for upward mobility. Yet, just like his professional ambitions, his social ambitions prove too lofty for him and his gentlemanly persona proves to be yet another identity he cannot legitimately fulfill. McTeague's essential incompetence causes him to repeatedly blunder through delicate interchanges and disrupts the stability and peace of all social gatherings he joins.

The most explicit example of the inappropriate nature of McTeague's presence in formal society occurs when he attends a Sieppe family picnic. After lunch, Marcus invites McTeague to engage in friendly wrestling. Yet, as soon as McTeague is injured, he reveals his true nature to Trina and the others:

> The brute that in McTeague lay so close to the surface leaped instantly to life, monstrous, not to be resisted. He sprang to his feet with a shrill

and meaningless clamor, totally unlike the ordinary bass of his speaking tones. It was the hideous yelling of a hurt beast, the squealing of a wounded elephant. He framed no words; in the rush of high-pitched sound that issued from his wide-open mouth there was nothing articulate. It was something no longer human; it was rather an echo from the jungle. (132)

McTeague's body gets in the way of his words in this scene, and having lost the ability to communicate on a human level, he must instead express himself through animal-like howling and posturing. McTeague's rage, his "evil mania," completely disrupts the social fabric of the park and stuns his fellow picnickers, and when he brutally injures Marcus it becomes clear that they have allowed a monster into their society. Given the right provocation, any of them could become the victim of his wrath.

Fundamentally, McTeague cannot even make himself understood even under the best circumstances. The majority of his social incompetence stems from an inability to speak coherently, as if, like an animal, he lacked that fundamental marker of human society: language. Pressured to make himself understood, he almost always reverts to base instinct, animal posturing, and angry blustering: when he is unable to place an order with a ticket broker, he threatens to "thump" the man on the head (57); when he tries to describe his feelings for Trina to his friend Marcus, he cannot find the poetry to express his passion and instead makes a series of "fierce, uncertain gestures" while wordlessly opening and closing his "enormous jaws" (34); when he asks Trina to marry him, all he manages to do is repeat the phrase "Ah, come on" over and over while she shakes her head no, which forces him to scoop her up in his arms, thereby "crushing down her struggle with his immense strength" (50); and when asked to give a speech to mark the occasion of Trina winning the lottery on their wedding day, McTeague only manages to stutter his way through a series of platitudes. He rises to his feet and attempts what should be a simple verbal exchange:

> I don' know what to say—I—I—I ain't never made a speech before; I—I ain't never made a speech before. But I'm glad Trina's won the prize . . . I—I—I'm glad Trina's won, and I—I want to—I want to—I want to—want to say that—you're all—welcome, an' drink hearty, an' I'm much obliged to the agent. Trina and I are goin' to be married, an' I'm glad everybody's here to-night, an' you're—all—welcome, an' drink hearty, an' I hope you'll come again, an' you're always welcome—an'—I—an'—an'—That's—about—all—I—gotta say. (71)

After this speech, McTeague collapses into a chair and wipes the sweat from his face, clearly exhausted by the effort of making sentences. Norris describes McTeague's inability to communicate in overtly physical terms, as if his body simply cannot produce the words needed. From the beginning, his social ambitions appear ludicrous and his beastly nature undercuts his pretensions to refined romance, friendship, and other social interactions.

McTeague's incoherent ramblings remind readers of the stereotypical Irishman prone to logorrhea, attributable either to drunkenness or stupidity. Like Pap Finn (who makes impassioned, but illogical speeches of his own), McTeague mutilates the English language on a regular basis. For centuries, the Irish people's perceived mutilation of language served to separate them from Anglo societies, and since language often served as an instrument of political unity, linguistic corruption positioned the Irish as a threatening presence outside such a union.[22] After brute physical appearance, the Irishman's verbal handicap is the most significant sign of his difference. June Howard argues that McTeague's mental shortcomings, revealed in his linguistic gaffs, deprive him of a "distinctively human capacity" to reason, effectively relegating his mind, like his body, to the status of an animal (91). Norris reinforces this idea through repeated descriptions of McTeague as weak minded; even his own wife describes him as "the stupidest man" she ever knew (140). Ultimately, McTeague's intellect and inability to communicate erect yet another barrier between him and society at large while simultaneously marking him as a dangerous other.

The domestic context of McTeague's monstrosity is the most tragic and the one requiring the most scrutiny, since it is by marrying Trina that he hopes to achieve happiness and prove himself a man capable of all the responsibilities of a husband, but by which he alternately proves himself definitively inhuman. Norris once again shows that McTeague's aspirations do not change his fundamental hereditary predilections. The Irish, we are to understand, cannot form and maintain proper family structures, an idea reflective of Jacob A. Riis' claim that the Irish were uniquely unsuited for domestic life. What stood in the way for the Irish, apparently, was a penchant for drinking and lazing about, animal-like sexual behavior, an innate inability to manage their own affairs, and an inclination toward avoiding responsibility. McTeague's courtship, marriage, and eventual murder of Trina give substance to fundamental nativist fears about what was happening behind closed doors in the ghetto.

McTeague does not marry Trina because of passion, romance, or even a desire to have children; rather, he does so to satisfy cravings for creature comforts and physical pleasures.[23] Such an attitude undercuts the possibility of love or intimacy in his marriage and reduces it to a relationship of convenient satisfaction, hedonism, and animal rutting. McTeague believes that Trina is simply "part of the order of the things" in his environment and that her main function as his wife is to appease his desires for food, comfort, and sex (158). Such a relationship does not require him to love her, merely dominate her. This sentiment finds extreme and disturbing proportions in the rape fantasies underlying much of the novel. In *The Gold Standard and the Logic of Naturalism* (1987), Walter Benn Michaels describes *McTeague* as "probably the first representation of masochism in American

literature," an accurate assessment given both McTeague and Trina's pleasure in their brutal sexual encounters (119). McTeague loves to dominate
Trina, and according to Michaels, though Trina "doesn't love the tyrant . . .
she loves the tyranny" (120). From the beginning, the attraction between
McTeague and Trina is described in violent terms: "The male virile desire
in him tardily awakened, aroused itself, strong and brutal. It was resistless,
untrained, a thing not to be held in leash an instant" (19). Norris evokes
here, and elsewhere, the image of McTeague's sexuality as that of an enormous, unstoppable beast. This bestial sexual power is counterbalanced by
Trina's status as a helpless and virginal victim, first as seen in her position
of absolute defenselessness as a patient in McTeague's dental chair and then
later as a bride in their wedding bed where she lay "in the hollow of his
arm, helpless and very pretty" (103).

Obviously, the rape fantasy extends beyond just descriptions of domina-
tion and helplessness and actually includes sexualized scenes of violence
between the two characters. Importantly, their relationship begins with
McTeague inflicting pain on Trina by filling a deep cavity which causes
her to "wince and moan," and it is during this visit to have her teeth fixed
that McTeague first becomes aroused (20). With Trina etherized and helpless in the dental chair, McTeague "leaned over and kissed her, grossly, full
on the mouth" (22). From this first encounter forward, McTeague equates
hurting Trina with his own sexual gratification. From the crushing hugs he
smothers her with to his persistent gnawing on her fingers, he finds pleasure
in her pain. Of course, after McTeague conquers Trina, he has no interest in her anymore. As early as their first kiss (of which both parties are
aware), McTeague starts to lose interest: "McTeague released her, but in
that moment a slight, a barely perceptible, revulsion of feeling had taken
place in him. The instant that Trina gave up, the instant she allowed him to
kiss her, he thought less of her" (50). When violence is no longer required
to obtain the object of his desire, McTeague becomes sexually unsatisfied.
He gains no pleasure from the simple romance that an idealized, gentle life
with Trina could offer, and he instead longs for the violent sexuality that he
likely imagines is a normal and healthy expression of romantic love.

Given the disturbing proportions of this marital mess, perhaps it is not
surprising that McTeague's most elaborate fantasy of domestic bliss involves
the physical abuse of his wife. As much as he is one of the earliest sadists in
American literature, he is also one of the most explicit wife beaters:

> His hatred of Trina increased from day to day. He'd make her dance yet
> . . . She couldn't make small of him. Ah, no. She'd dance all right—all
> right. McTeague was not an imaginative man by nature, but he would
> lie awake nights, his clumsy wits galloping and frisking under the lash
> of the alcohol, and fancy himself thrashing his wife, till a sudden frenzy
> of rage would overcome him, and he would shake all over, rolling upon
> the bed and biting the mattress. (201)

Of all the passages in *McTeague*, this is perhaps the most disturbing in its blending of sex and violence. It stands out because it is one of the only moments in the entire novel in which McTeague is shown to have an imaginative life, and it is also one of the few times that readers are allowed inside his head. His twisted fantasy of brutalizing his wife disturbingly culminates in a pseudo-orgasmic moment with him "[shaking] all over, rolling upon the bed and biting the mattress." By this moment in the novel, Norris forces readers to conclude that the relationship between McTeague and Trina is hopelessly and sickeningly askew.

A brutish sexual nature and an Irish indisposition to domesticity create a monstrous parody of the ideal family structure as imagined by the Anglo-American majority of the country. Many Americans looked at the Irish population of the cities and saw communities resistant to family formation, men more interested in drinking with the boys than marriage, and a huge number of orphaned or "half orphaned" children not being looked after properly. Irish Americans often were thought to have a pathological resistance to domesticity or to be "familially broken," even though many of the causes of their domestic problems could be attributed to economic conditions (Doyle, "Remaking" 238).[24] Similarly, Irish Americans had a reputation for unrestrained sexual behaviors even though, as historians have shown, they were pronouncedly more puritanical than average Americans in regards to sex and were more likely to wait for marriage or practice life-long celibacy.[25] Nonetheless, popular imaginings and stereotypes persisted and help explain why in the creation of McTeague such attention was given to failed domesticity and sexual deviancy. Whether true or not, there was already cultural currency behind the idea that the Irish were failures at family formation, and this allowed Norris to draw even more connections between McTeague's ethnic otherness and his inappropriateness for life in America.

In all four of these contexts (physical, professional, social, domestic), McTeague is revealed to be a monstrous threat to civilization, but he proves dangerous to the city in one additional way—he is contagious. Norris borrows the rhetoric of medical pathology to show that the Irishman's true danger to San Francisco was viral in nature. It was not uncommon in popular discourse of the time to characterize ethnic and racial otherness as a plague infecting the body of America or to describe ethnic and racial differences as functions of a disease. In particular, the Irish were popularly believed to be "shiftless parasites spawning large families that they were unable to support," which when considered along with the low birth rates among Anglo Americans resulted in the biologizing of ethnic anxieties and the conceptualizing of the Irish as a rapidly spreading cultural infection (Conners 2). It took little imagination to make the rhetorical leap from discussions of Irishness as a kind of cultural deviancy or social nuisance to Irishness as a disease to which even native-born Americans were susceptible. Stephanie Bower studies Norris' fondness for using a rhetoric of disease in writing about ethnic minorities and concludes that his "tales of degeneration function on one level as portraits of social and psychological pathology, but at the same time they represent these racial others as the source of this pathology and thereby racialized the language of naturalism" (33). This is precisely the case with McTeague; he is the "patient zero" of an outbreak of Irish deviancy in his community, which if left unchecked, could weaken national ideals, corrupt social institutions, ruin neighborhoods, undermine authority, and pollute the purity of the country.

McTeague's first victim is Trina, a wholesome, proper girl whom he infects and transforms into a cruel and degenerate masochist. Readers first observe the onset of the "McTeague virus" in Trina directly after the first sexual contact between her and McTeague, the disturbing etherized kiss in the Dental Parlors. When Trina awakes after her surgery, she becomes physically ill and is "suddenly taken with a fit of vomiting" (23). Her illness here is only the first of many symptoms. As the novel progresses, she becomes aware that McTeague had started something growing in her like a cancer, a "second self" that "shouted and clamored for recognition" (52). At first she thinks this is just a sexual awakening, but her desires have been thoroughly polluted by her husband and she comes to crave violence and demeaning pleasures unimaginable to her prior to meeting McTeague. She starts to worry that, having become infected, "she would come to be like him" (106). Of course, by the end of the novel, her fear is realized and she sinks both physically and mentally to an utterly debased condition.

Trina's story, like McTeague's, is a narrative of degeneration, but unlike McTeague, her degeneration is not caused by her genetics. Barbara Hochman argues against critics who claim Trina's downward spiral is the result of her Swiss-German heritage:

> Trina's transformation, one of the most powerful sequences in Norris's fiction, is not adequately explained by reference to her 'penurious' ancestors or her roots in a "hearty mountain race." The occasional references to her 'instinct of hoarding' or the power of Chance do not go much further in clarifying her destruction either. (4)

Taking Hochman's critique into consideration, we need to look elsewhere for the cause of Trina's transformation, and nothing seems more suspicious than her hereditarily impure husband. From him, she contracts the virus of Irish degeneracy as if it were a venereal disease. The "foul stream of hereditary evil" that ran in McTeague's veins, now runs in hers, and she becomes, like him, physically, professionally, socially, and domestically monstrous.

Bower explores the connections Norris makes between ethnicity, race, and contamination further:

> Sexual contact with these "aliens" thus becomes fraught with danger for "pure-bred" Americans, since every liaison jeopardizes their health, corrupts their principles, and weakens the genes responsible for

their racial superiority, a process of un-Americanization signaled by a system of representation that uses race as the external symbol of internal contaminations. Here, then, constructions of the other as diseased and theories about mongrelization work together to create an image of race-as-disease, a trope that equates an invasion of immigrants to an invasion of germs, both figured as deadly viruses that threaten the disintegration of the healthy organism, the transformation of self into other. (40)

The racial disease of the Irish that McTeague infects Trina with performs exactly the kind of disintegration that Bower describes. Trina's body is slowly destroyed and her beauty is stripped away, leaving her a monstrous creature with mangled hands, the result of literal blood poisoning. The image of Trina that Norris presents late in the book is that of a plague victim: "She grew thin and meager; her flesh clove tight to her small skeleton" (194). Her transformation is not just physical, though: she gives up her profession as a toymaker, she abandons society in favor of isolation, and she even turns her back on her family in their time of need. She experiences that weakening of the genes and that "process of un-Americanization" that leaves her morally, socially, and culturally destitute. Having experienced, as Bower suggests, a "transformation of self into other," Trina no longer resembles the wealthy, Swiss-German girl of the first half of the novel and instead comes more and more to resemble an Irish peasant woman. She takes a job as a scrub-woman in a kindergarten and also makes extra money washing the front steps of upper-class flats. These are jobs traditionally reserved for unskilled peasants and, in San Francisco, would have been the domain of Irish women. Having lost her ability to make a living as a skilled artisan and toymaker, Trina is forced to adopt the role of the unskilled Irish servant girl, the stereotypical Irish Biddy.[26]

The viral danger that McTeague poses does not end with his wife. He is the epicenter of a potential plague that could destroy Polk Street and potentially all of San Francisco. All of the characters in the orbit of the Polk Street Dental Parlors, with the exception of the two elderly Anglo-Saxons who are asexual and likely safe from the Irish virus, begin to demonstrate degenerate behavior—they become petty, cruel, violent, and murderous. In order for the city to remain safe, the Irishman must be removed and sent back into the wild where he belongs.

San Francisco protects itself by ejecting the monster from its midst. After killing Trina in the cloakroom of a kindergarten, McTeague is forced to flee the authorities and travels through a series of increasingly smaller communities until he is eventually alone. He makes a straight line from the modern city (San Francisco), through the rural work-town/labor camp (Iowa Hill/Big Dipper Mine), through the company of just one other man (Gold Gulch), to a final solitary existence (Death Valley). In the last few chapters of the novel, McTeague descends rapidly down both the social and evolutionary ladders and fully embraces his solitary animal-nature by becoming a beast who lives his life by the instinct of the wild, rather than the reason of the city. Like an animal, he senses danger when the authorities approach and runs deeper into uncivilized territory. His flight from San Francisco symbolizes his rejection of progress, modernism, Americanism, and human culture, and so he becomes, by default, the embodiment of everything Norris thought a modern society should reject. McTeague becomes a cultural boogey-man, lurking just beyond the frontier and reminding us what could happen to us if we stray too far from the country's Anglo-Protestant origins.

Norris' Irish monster ends the novel shackled to a dead man in the middle of a desert, finally trapped in an environment where he no longer can hurt anyone. Around him are scattered the symbols of his former life: all of his worldly possessions, including his pet canary in a gilt cage and a sack of Trina's lottery winnings, as well as the body of his former best friend Marcus who had chased him all the way from San Francisco. Yet, none of these things mean anything anymore, having lost all value the moment he left civilization. In the solitary wilderness, gold is worthless, friendship is meaningless, and past accomplishments earn him no quarter. McTeague asks, "What's the good of moving on?" since there is nowhere for him to go, even if he could survive the desert conditions (242). McTeague, we are to assume, will die here, and finally the undesirable ethnic other will be completely purged from the American landscape. Implicit in the ending is that the city is better off without the Irishman; San Francisco will thrive even as McTeague dies. In fact, McTeague has to die, as all monsters must die at the end of their stories, so that the angry town folk can get on with their lives. Norris labels his novel "A Story of San Francisco," not "A Story of an Irishman," and with this focus the ending of the book can be read as a success—San Francisco triumphs in surviving an ethnic onslaught—but what are we to make of such a conclusion? For ethnic minorities who, like Huck Finn, traveled west to find opportunity, there could be no bleaker message than the isolation and eradication of McTeague. His death signals an intolerance for pluralism and a rejection of assimilation and social reform.

An understanding of Norris' appropriation of Irish stereotypes in *McTeague* is useful to us because it highlights a crisis point in the history of the imagined American city and informs us of the particularly disturbing relationship between literary notions of "American progress" and the marginalization of ethnic communities. In this novel, Norris imagines a city plagued by ethnic minorities and implies there is a better community to be had if only the city could remove the dangerous elements. *McTeague* spotlights the fears of many nativists living in nineteenth-century America. As immigrants landed on the eastern shore and spread across the western frontier, nativists saw a dilution of what they perceived to be the real America. The cultural melting pot was a myth that did not match up with their own deeply cherished sense of American identity. In examining Norris' work from the distance of over a century, we are simultaneously struck by his passion to see the successful growth of the American city and by his passion for illogical, racist doctrines. It would be easy to dismiss Norris' imagined city as a product of a bygone era, but it would be more useful to consider it as a challenge to America to be more careful in imagining our communities and to always consider who is left behind when those communities progress into the future.

3   The Invisible Ethnicity

Joe Kennedy, patriarch of the Kennedy family, once rebuked a Boston newspaper for labeling him an Irishman, saying, "I was born here. My children were born here. What the hell do I have to do to be called an American?" (Shannon vii). His frustration was the frustration of many Americans of Irish heritage who experienced a kind of identity crisis in the early decades of the twentieth century. They were, as historian William V. Shannon notes, the ethnic group "closest to being 'in' while still being 'out'" (132). Since the Famine immigration, Irishness had changed from an identity implying a shared history to an identity connoting only vague, sometimes superficial, cultural similarities. As a result, many modern Irish Americans felt disconnected from the culture of their ancestors, but they also felt disconnected from American culture. Confusion emerged from this sense of being both deficiently Irish and deficiently American, and the challenge for this generation became reconciling their American identity with their cultural heritage in such a way as to show the two to be compatible, not mutually exclusive.

American literature of the early twentieth century reflects this complicated status of ethnic identity, with Irish Americans serving as exemplars of modernist identity anxieties. As figurative metaphors with established histories of embodying American social fear, Irish-American literary characters offered writers ready-made models of alienation that could perfectly represent the fractured personas, historic discontinuities, cultural isolation, economic despair, and national insecurities that typified the period. The two authors considered in this chapter describe the modern world as a disjointed, incongruent mess and modern man as futilely trying to stitch together meaning. In such an environment, even personal identity becomes unclear, more of "an ambition" than a certainty (Michaels, *Our America* 3). Writers found in the Irish-American condition something particularly relevant and resonant for broader American society, something that spoke both to the modernist dilemma and the consequent struggle to redefine personal, cultural, and national identities; and so they thrust the Irish-American character into his new role as the modernist everyman.

One of the most significant of these characters is T. S. Eliot's Sweeney, the morally bankrupt, spiritually empty, and physically grotesque beast-man who lumbers through several of the author's works. In the poet's imagination, Sweeney functions as the vulgar inheritor of the modern world and embodies the most degenerate qualities of humanity. Eliot links these qualities to the character's ethnicity, and readers are encouraged to understand his Irishness, as they did McTeague's, as a clear and immediate social danger.

Though F. Scott Fitzgerald, like Eliot, is a quintessential modernist, he describes his Irishman's confrontation with the modern world from the position of an insider and reaches very different conclusions. Amory Blaine, the semi-autobiographical protagonist of Fitzgerald's first novel *This Side of Paradise* (published in 1920, the same year that Eliot's first Sweeney poems appeared in book form), travels through his own fragmented American wasteland, and though he is far from heroic, he is nothing like the predatory monster of Eliot's imagination. Amory is cultured, educated, romantic, and self-conscious. He more closely resembles Eliot's effete, scholarly dandy, J. Alfred Prufrock, than he does Sweeney. It seems obvious that Fitzgerald would have more sympathy for Irish America than Eliot, but he does not merely defend Irish-American culture the way earlier writers like Dion Boucicault or Ned Harrigan do; instead, he problematizes our understanding of Irishness in America and suggests an entirely new way of approaching ethnic identifications in a modern context.

America's most famous Irish-American writer and its most famous anglophile writer positioned Irish identity at the intersection of modernity and human culture and thereby played out the fears of their generation on the body of the Irishman. The language of American modernism needed the language of Irishness in order to describe the socio-cultural trauma of the post-war world. Irish characters proved useful in narratives about cultural fracture, social collapse, and national change, and showed that there was still resonance in the Irishman as a metaphorical character in the American imagination. Though Eliot and Fitzgerald disagreed as to why Irish-American identity was pivotal in a modern context, they each saw something ubiquitous about it that spoke to broader conditions, something liminal in what Irish identity had come to represent in twentieth-century America. For them, the quintessential modern man was the Irish American, and whether he was hero or villain, the future of human civilization seemed tied to his ethnic inheritance.

By the time these two writers began their careers, the Irish population of the U.S. had changed significantly. The lines that separated "us" and "them" had become fuzzy, and for large numbers of Americans of Irish descent, their ethnic heritage had become increasingly invisible, by which I mean that their Irishness was less noticeable and seemingly less relevant as they entered mainstream culture. The Irish were no longer the newest or most obviously different immigrant ethnic group in America, and when compared to recent arrivals from Eastern Europe and other "exotic" locales, the Irish appeared more acceptable to Anglo-American social palates. In fact, the Irish became the model minority, having apparently learned English and adapted to American culture and customs quicker than any other group. In just a few generations, the Irish had gone from being dangerous interlopers to paragons of assimilation.

In addition, Irish immigration had finally tapered off and the population of American-born Irish now greatly outnumbered the population of foreign-born Irish, leading to what historian Timothy Meagher describes as an Irish America "dominated by people literally Irish American," that is, people who understood themselves not as a transplanted population, but as a native population (*Columbia* 95). The concerns of these second, third, even fourth generation people were not the same as their immigrant ancestors, and logically their sense of identity shifted as a result. According to Shannon, many of them had "ceased to be Irish in any significant sense" (viii). They moved out of the old ghettos and dispersed throughout cities, often engaging in new professions and marrying outside their ethnic group; they embraced American popular culture and gained footholds in the entertainment industry; they proudly rallied to American patriotic causes and pursued careers in politics; and they generally enjoyed social mobility and success unlike anything the Irish community achieved in America prior to the turn of the century (Meagher, *Columbia* 95, 106). Simply put, being Irish American in 1920 did not mean the same thing as being Irish American in 1860.

Yet, despite these changes, popular perceptions had not fully reconciled Irish identity with American identity, and many obstacles still remained for Americans of Irish heritage. "Newly revised categories of collective identity" in the 1920s complicated any ethnicity's claim to "Americanism" or citizenship (Michaels, *Our America* 6). In regards to the Irish, Meagher argues against conclusions that suggest they "had been neatly assumed, merged, and assimilated into American society," noting that their adaptation was more complicated than it might at first appear (*Columbia* 106).

One of the chief obstacles to Irish-American success was economic, because despite the prosperity of men like Joe Kennedy, the Irish in America had not achieved anything even remotely resembling economic equality. Instead, they consistently ran up against barriers put in place by the old guard, who would allow the Irish some measure of success, but not enough to threaten traditional economic and social hierarchies. Meagher observes that the Protestant establishment of America hardened itself during the early twentieth century to prevent the advancement of too many Irish into the upper echelons of power (*Columbia* 106–7). Irish Americans had achieved what Kevin Kenny calls "occupational and educational parity," but still had the highest rates of pauperism (*American Irish* 199–200); and though there were several notable Irish-American success stories during this time, the vast majority of Irish Americans lived working class lives, many below the level of subsistence (Shannon 131). As was also the case with African Americans, the Irish, having overcome the question of citizenship, now found the dimensions of their membership in the citizenry very much economically prescribed.

In addition to economic obstacles, Irish Americans also confronted a renewed questioning of their national loyalties during this period. The Easter Rising of 1916 and the following civil war in Ireland invited renewed attention to Irish nationalist causes in the U.S. Meagher sees this renewed interest, what he calls "nationalist mania," as evidence that "Irish Americans still understood themselves as a distinct group with links to the homeland" (*Columbia* 120); however, many Americans saw Irish nationalism as evidence of divided loyalties, if not an outright betrayal of America. By 1917, the U.S. was Great Britain's ally in World War I, and many questioned how Irish Americans could support a revolution against America's ally. Some Irish nationalists in the U.S. openly opposed America's entry into the war, arguing that Irish Americans had more in common (politically and religiously) with Germany than England. Exacerbating the problem of perceived Irish-American disloyalty were comments by President Woodrow Wilson, a pronounced anglophile himself, who openly and publicly questioned Irish-American patriotism and in a speech stated that Irish Americans "need hyphens in their names [i.e., Irish-American] because only part of them has come over" from Ireland (Shannon 329).[1]

Unquestionably, the Irish Americans of this era were not the target of the blatant kind of ethnic slandering that had been common in the nineteenth century, nor were they confronted with the insurmountable social, educational, occupational, and legal obstacles that the Famine generation immigrants experienced; however, these modern Irish Americans also were not imagined to be entitled to equality with the Anglo-American establishment. As Shannon suggests, Irish Americans were "accommodated" but not "accepted" (132). The debate of the previous century regarding the ability of the Irish to be Americanized, a debate that had concerned writers like Mark Twain, Harold Frederic, and Frank Norris, was for all intents and purposes over; the Irish were American. Yet, they were imagined to be a different kind of American. At first, this may seem a parsing of detail, but it actually amounts to a significant shift in public perception. The Irish were no longer an external threat, instead they were an internal dilemma, and the issues and anxieties of this generation, reflected in their literature, emphasize this shift in status.

In examining the literature of this generation, Charles Fanning suggests that there was a "general decline of Irish-American cultural self-consciousness" that resulted in Irish-American writers adopting an ambivalent attitude toward ethnicity that would last until James T. Farrell published the first of his *Studs Lonigan* books in 1932 (238). Fanning's description of this Irish-American "generation lost" provides important context for reading literature from this period; however, two issues complicate the ambivalence he observes. First, while it is true that the self-image of the Irish became increasingly indefinite during this time, the same cannot be said for images of Irishness imposed from external sources in popular culture (i.e., political cartoons, music, pulp fiction) or from literature by non-Irish writers. Second, ethnic ambivalence itself is a topic worth studying in detail because a lack of Irishness often can reveal just as much about the function and limits of ethnic identity as the presence of Irish traits; it is often the ambivalently ethnic characters who can teach us the most about ethnic boundaries and performative identities since they are the ones testing the boundaries and challenging the identities.

The literary construction of Irish-American identity during the 1920s reveals both a significant convergence of artistic agendas and a divergence of social ideologies. No two characters could be more radically different than Sweeney and Amory Blaine, yet they emerge, as it were, from the same cultural source. The conditions of their creation are remarkably similar, but with Fitzgerald writing as an internal witness to Irish-American life and with Eliot writing as an external observer of it, Sweeney and Amory develop into very distinct variations of the renewed Irish-American literary metaphor.

THE SAVAGE EVERYMAN: T. S. ELIOT'S SWEENEY MOTIF

When T. S. Eliot introduces his depraved, comic-monster Sweeney to his readers, he presents the character as a type rather than as an individual. Eliot resurrects old ethnic stereotypes, similar to the ones that Frank Norris uses in *McTeague*, to construct a savage inheritor of the modern city who carries with him some very specific cultural coding. While Eliot certainly attempts to speak to a broad modern condition transcending ethnicity, the fact that he chooses to express the worst aspects of that condition through a specifically Irish character cannot be ignored. Sweeney may be an allegorical character, but his body and behavior unquestionably carry ethnic significance, and though his ethnicity often functions as poetic shorthand for vulgarity, that fact should be the beginning, not the end, of analysis.

The character of Sweeney obsessed Eliot for much of his early career and was considered by the poet to be the subject of some of his most successful and "intensely serious" work from this period (*Letters* 363). For more than a decade he used the character as a vehicle to express his most personal observations and complicated doubts about his world. The character appears in four of Eliot's poems—"Mr. Eliot's Sunday Morning Service" (1918), "Sweeney Among the Nightingales" (1918), "Sweeney Erect" (1919), and *The Waste Land* (1922)—as well as the dramatic fragment *Sweeney Agonistes* (1926–7).[2] Few other Eliot characters seem as well developed, and no other appears so frequently or in such diverse contexts. Sweeney helped to unify Eliot's work and helped him to create a modern mythology, and because of the character's frequent appearances, we can follow the development of Eliot's thinking and craft in a unique way and uncover significant insights into the poet's perception of the connection between ethnicity and the decline of modern society.

Eliot broadly positions the Irish as monsters and villains in his imaginative landscape and characterizes them as the crude and vulgar inverse of the spiritual Anglo ideal. They are to blame for the filth of the cities, the corruption of the church, the debasement of women, the weakening of bloodlines, the ineffectiveness of men like Prufrock, the loss of heroism, the decline of history, and the infertility of the Fisher King. As Donald J. Childs observes, Eliot's "racist characterization of the Irish as the archetype of the prolifically unfit is ubiquitous" (108). In this sense, specific ethnicity and the prejudices and stereotypes associated with it stood in for general cultural vulgarity. Jonathan Morse describes Sweeney as "one of the great id monsters of modern literature" whose identity cannot be separated from his ethnicity (145), and he further argues that

> his name identifies him as an Irishman, one of the monsters who shambled through the nightmares of literary America during the second and third quarters of the nineteenth century. Sweeney is physically and morally repulsive, but his repulsiveness is generic, not individual. In evoking this repulsiveness, the Sweeney poems are not so much elliptical as allusive. (137)

Eliot alludes to very prejudicial conceptions of the Irish that could evoke cultural and social horror in the same way that the figure of Sweeney evokes immediate physical horror from those he meets. He is not just physically monstrous, but also ethnically monstrous. As Norris said of McTeague, his "hereditary evil" prefigures his patterns of deviant behavior.

Though Eliot's prejudices have been widely studied and commented on over the past half-century, relatively little attention has been given to his conception of the Irish, and few scholars give much thought specifically to Sweeney's ethnicity.[3] I propose to show the significance of Sweeney's Irish Catholic identity in Eliot's thinking, specifically highlighting the ways in which the character represents a conflation of racial and religious vulgarity. By placing the poems into the continuity of popular constructions of Irish-American identity in literature, I examine how Eliot participated in the reformulation of that identity in the twentieth century. Sweeney can be best understood when juxtaposed with characters like Huck Finn, McTeague, Amory Blaine, and Studs Lonigan because he is not an isolated ethnic figure, but rather a permutation of a literary stereotype who draws meaning from earlier Irish-American characters and gives new meaning to those characters who come after.[4]

Eliot was born into a respected Unitarian family in St. Louis, Missouri in 1888 and was taught that the world contained three types of people:

"Eliots, non-Eliots and foreigners" (L. Gordon 5). Among the most important "foreigners" in his life was his Irish Catholic nursemaid, Annie Dunne, who on occasion took him with her to the local Catholic Church and discussed with him the ways to prove the existence of God (J. Miller 27). In later years, Eliot recalled being very impressed by the spectacle and "lived-in atmosphere" of the Catholic Church (in comparison to the stark, simple style of Unitarian churches), and he also recalled the "secure intimacy" of his days with his Irish nurse, who he said was the "earliest personal influence" (L. Gordon 7) on his life other than his parents, and to whom he was "greatly attached" (J. Miller 27). Yet, despite personal attachments, Eliot was raised to believe that his family came from a different, more privileged, stock with prudent English Protestant roots, and as a boy he could trace his lineage all the way back to sixteenth-century English nobility. Eliot's family also had been influential in New England society since the colonial period, and he counted among his ancestors several notable American religious and political leaders, as well as a number of distinguished persons of literary fame (Gordon 13–7).[5] With such background, heritage, history, and (importantly) the stamp of colonial authenticity, Eliot believed himself to be the latest product of an elite Anglo-Protestant bloodline.

Eliot lived in Boston and attended Harvard University from 1906 to 1910, and again from 1911 to 1914. This period overlaps with what historians now recognize as a significant shift in Irish power and influence in the city. Eliot would have witnessed firsthand the three events that reshaped the landscape for Irish Americans in Boston: the 1906 election of John F. Fitzgerald (grandfather of John F. Kennedy) as Boston's first American-born Irish Catholic mayor, the 1911 elevation of William Henry O'Connell to the rank of cardinal (the archdiocese's first), and the 1914 election of David Ignatius Walsh as Massachusetts' first Irish Catholic governor. Of course, there was still lingering opposition to Irish advancement from Boston's Protestant Brahmin elite, but an important corner had been turned and Irish-American culture started to become part of mainstream city life. Such cultural transformation did not suit Eliot's sensibilities or family loyalties. His time in Boston strengthened his ethnic biases, and the city itself seems to have, to some degree, offended him. As Kinley E. Roby observes, Eliot's "revulsion against sex, against the world of sense, broadened at Harvard to a horror of the 'commercial city' and against its inhabitants'" (9). A significant portion of those inhabitants that horrified him were Irish Americans whom, harkening back to his childhood lessons, he classified as "foreigners." Sweeney's origins, like McTeague's, can be traced to his creator's time in Boston and at Harvard. Eliot, like Norris, saw social danger and cultural decay in Boston, the result of the increasing influence of "foreigners" like the Irish, and he created Sweeney so that his readers could share his nightmares.

During his lifetime, Eliot was protected from charges of bigotry by a cadre of loyal guardians, but in recent years, the issue of his prejudices and the influence they had on his poetry has been openly explored (L. Gordon 2). Morse argues that Eliot "grew up in a milieu . . . in which it was socially acceptable to speak one's prejudices aloud," and speak them aloud he certainly did (136). Recent scholarly work has taken aim at Eliot's pervasive racism, anti-Semitism, and misogyny and reevaluated his poetry and legacy in light of these factors.[6] Eliot himself was not coy about his prejudices, and once proclaimed, "I shall be untolerated, intolerant and intolerable . . . I think that the virtue of tolerance is greatly overestimated, and I have no objection to being called a bigot myself" (Ricks 52–3). Eliot's prejudices need to be studied because they directly informed the writing of his poetry and, as Christopher Ricks suggests, they take you "into the nature and boundaries of his imagination" (78). Yet, Eliot's prejudices require that we grapple with often uncomfortable ideas in order to appreciate his literary achievement. Lyndall Gordon acknowledges this problem early in her biography of the poet: "Undoubtedly, an infection is there in Eliot—hate—and we can't explain it away" (2). Gordon argues that the solution is not to "blast Eliot with political correctness," but instead to look at his flaws "without seeing flaws alone" (109). This methodology offers a productive way to explore Eliot's social and racial positions in his poetry because it moves the focus away from the prejudices themselves to the way in which those prejudices functioned in his texts. Such an approach allows for, as Morse puts it, a study of how Eliot "mobilized the energy of his prejudices" (145). In looking at his intolerance in the Sweeney poems, it is important to consider why it satisfied him to target the Irish and why he chose to make an Irishman—out of all the ethnic types he disliked—the ultimate expression of the savage everyman of the modern world.

Eliot's anti-Irish prejudice differs from his other prejudices, such as his well-studied anti-Semitism, in one important way: it expresses at the same time both repulsion and attraction. While Eliot's work clearly expresses a belief in the general inferiority of the Irish, at times a slight admiration, perhaps even jealousy, of the rugged masculinity personified in the tough Irish stereotype emerges. Though Sweeney is a monster, Eliot seems attracted to the character in a way he is never attracted to any of his Jewish figures, for instance. Whereas the poet repeatedly describes Jews in his poetry as vermin with no redeeming features, the Irish are described in his work as alluring in their degradation. Sweeney is an animal, but he is also strong, sexually potent, carefree, and feared by those around him—qualities that bring him closer to the masculine ideal than someone like Prufrock. One passage in "Sweeney Erect" emphasizes this combination of attraction/repulsion:

(The lengthened shadow of a man
Is history, said Emerson
Who had not seen the silhouette
Of Sweeney straddled in the sun.) (lines 25–28)

Eliot invites readers to gaze with him in awe and disbelief on the powerful naked form of an Irishman straddling the sun—an image so imposing that it prompts him to compare the man to other giants in history. The speaker of these lines is at once disgusted that Sweeney could ever be compared to the Emersonian ideal and impressed that the Irishman could cast such an impressive shadow (literally and figuratively) in the first place. The comparison asks us to be disgusted by Sweeney's intrusion into history, but also jealous of his achievement. A similar effect is achieved in "Sweeney Among the Nightingales" when Eliot elevates the character beyond historical greatness to mythological legend and compares Sweeney to Agamemnon. As critical as the speaker of these poems is about Sweeney, he cannot help but describe Sweeney's body and sexuality in jealous terms. Sweeney leads an uncomplicated and satisfying life, and the speaker of these poems expresses a desire for the same. The voyeuristic elements of the Sweeney poems in which the poet studies the naked body of the Irishman and his pre- and post-coital behaviors, suggest a desire to be like Sweeney, to take his place in the cabaret and the brothel, if only for a moment before better moral judgment wins out.

Eliot's poetry repeatedly describes an obsession with the masculine—the physically strong, the sexually potent, the violent—and in his own life he seemed preoccupied with his potential physical and sexual shortcomings. Critics have thoroughly analyzed Eliot's considerations of masculinity in his poetry, but what has been missing from the picture is the realization that in his Irishman, Eliot found a unique figure with whom he could express both attraction and repulsion. The Irish stereotype came pre-loaded with such associations and offered the most dynamic ethnic characterization available to him.

Several theories have been put forth to explain Eliot's inspiration for Sweeney, including literary influences like the penny dreadful character Sweeney Todd and Mad King Sweeney, the murderous pagan king of the ancient Irish legend *Buile Suibhne*.[7] Others have pointed to models in popular culture like Joel Walker Sweeney, the famous minstrel banjo player of the nineteenth century, and Dr. F. L. Sweany, a doctor whose advertisements for treating "nervous debility" in men (Figure 3.1) fascinated a young Eliot who then copied the advertisement's slogans and illustrations into his "self-published," homemade childhood literary magazine (Crawford 28).[8] However, the most frequently cited inspiration for Sweeney is a man Eliot knew personally. The poet once said, "I think of [Sweeney] as a man who in younger days was perhaps a professional pugilist, mildly successful; who then grew older and retired to keep a pub" (Coghill 119). Several critics latch onto this statement and argue that Sweeney is based on the Boston boxing champ turned bartender, Steve O'Donnell, who gave Eliot boxing lessons during his time in the city.

WHEN OTHERS FAIL CONSULT

DOCTOR SWEANY

THE OLD RELIABLE SPECIALIST.

Figure 3.1   Advertisement for Dr. F. L. Sweany. *San Francisco Call*, 4 July 1895: 5. In looking at Sweany's promise to restore men's energy, strength, and vigor, Robert Crawford exclaims, "Here is the doctor Prufrock required" (28).

Whatever Sweeney's origins, his resemblance to the derogatory Irish stereotype of the previous century is unmistakable. He comes from the same stock as Mark Twain's Pap Finn (though Eliot's Irishman lacks the satirical elements of Twain's) and bears all the hallmarks of a wild Irish savage like McTeague. Thus, Eliot draws particular attention to Sweeney's brutish physicality and animal-like features. In "Sweeney Erect," he is compared to an "orang-outang" and is further described as hairy, naked, and "broadbottomed" (11, 22). In "Mr. Eliot's Sunday Morning Service," he is portrayed as having ham-like thighs and buttocks. In "Sweeney Among the Nightingales," Eliot again simianizes Sweeney, describing him as having an "apeneck," long, hanging arms, and a hairy face (1). He also struggles with basic communication skills. Eliot only allows him to speak in one text, *Sweeney Agonistes*, and even there, the bestial Irishman, with telltale inarticulateness reminiscent of Pap's ranting and McTeague's stammering, complains, "I gotta use words when I talk to you" (84). There are several other signs of Sweeney's Irishness that leave little doubt as to Eliot's following the stereotype, including a blind devotion to Catholicism, a ravenous sexual appetite (Sweeney appears in the company of prostitutes in four out of the five Sweeney texts), a dualistic temperament that vacillates between child-like innocence and murderous rage, a proclivity for excessive drinking and eating (including human flesh), a weak mind, a penchant for violence, a blatant disregard for social manners and mores, and a cruel disposition toward women. Eliot's wife, Vivienne, was terrified of her husband's creation and once described Sweeney as an "absolute horror" that nearly made her faint (L. Gordon 288). As disturbing as Pap Finn and McTeague are, Sweeney outdoes them both in terms of sheer monstrosity and repulsiveness, and he proves a more immediate threat since, unlike his predecessors who lived outside of society, he lives very comfortably within it.

Though Eliot's portrait of the Irish might at first seem a throwback to the prejudices of the mid-nineteenth century, careful reading reveals that, despite initial appearances, Eliot's clichéd Irishman functions quite differently from precedent and addresses substantially different social fears. Eliot revives the classic stereotype but animates it with new purpose in response to modernist cultural anxieties. Whereas earlier writers were concerned about the friction between ethnic groups, Eliot seems concerned with the breakdown of ethnic categories themselves.

The racial and ethnic boundaries that had seemed so well defined and unchanging in the previous century had become permeable, vague, and unclear; it was getting harder and harder to tell the difference between "non-Eliots" and "foreigners." Walter Benn Michaels observes that in the 1920s, there were profound "shifts in racial logic" that manifested in somewhat vague and contradictory notions of "difference" and "pluralism" (*Our America* 11). The skewed logic of the period moved the American population toward a concept of a more homogeneous white "State" and a system of "essentialized racism" that tried, in often vague and confusing ways, to make distinctions between Americanism and mere entitlement to American citizenship (43, 64). Race and ethnicity, which had been the clearest markers of individual identity in previous generations, could no longer be depended on to delineate clear boundaries between groups, and the very terms themselves began to blur together. It was not easy for one ethnic group to look at another and label it "alien," when the defining characteristic of everyone living in the modern world was alienation. Modernism had transformed individualism into isolation, personal liberty into social dislocation, and the commitment to progress into a disorienting break with history. In America, the old social hierarchies, racial divisions, and ethnic boundaries offered no sanctuary for the alienated individual seeking the comfort of a categorical identity. There was too much slippage across categories for old definitions to endure, and it was increasingly common for individuals to have hybrid identities and claims to multiple cultural heritages, or for traits once seen as uniquely ethnic to become subsumed into broader and more abstract categories of "difference."

Nonetheless, many clung to their prejudices believing they could give some order to an otherwise disorganized world and help solidify individual identity. As a man committed to clear moral principles and social standards, Eliot found himself frustrated by increasingly unclear ethnic boundaries. He needed his prejudices in order to make cultural judgments in his work, but he lived in an age during which having prejudices had become so much harder. Ricks points to the heart of Eliot's problem:

> Eliot's work . . . is designed to incite its audience at once to strict judgments upon the world which it presents and to strict thought about the exact grounds on which anyone may validly pass such judgments. For Eliot writes always with a founded sense that the very conditions of modern life which make it more and more urgently essential to be able to pass strong judgments are themselves the conditions which make it less and less possible confidently or unmisgivingly to do so. (78)

In Eliot's estimation, the modern world needed to cultivate its prejudices in order to shore up its social standards and prevent the further decay of civilization. This decay, caused by cultural homogenization, could be seen particularly clearly in the assimilation of the Irish. Though the Irish were, in the mindset of nativists, as foreign as Jews or Asians and as ethnically different as African Americans, they were assimilating faster and more thoroughly than any other group. The perceived danger of the Irish was that they could pass as white Americans; they were not different enough to satisfy those clinging to traditional notions of American identity as fundamentally white American Protestantism. So much of Eliot's poetry yearns for moral clarity and tries to define the superior and the fallen, the in-group and the out-group, the socially good and the socially depraved, and in doing so it tries to reestablish very culturally defined social standards. These standards aim to filter the Irish back out of mainstream American society and once again isolate them as ethnic others.

Eliot's attempts to address the social ills of the time are inextricably caught up in the reestablishment of clear ethnic and cultural boundaries. As Gordon suggests, Eliot's hatreds and sense of perfection are "interfused" (475). He needed his prejudices in order to orient himself in an increasingly confusing environment. This was far from uncommon; as Michaels shows, though no law "could keep the vulgar from imposing themselves upon the genteel," 1920s America built an array of complex social systems that identified gentility with white, Anglo heritage and vulgarity with racial and ethnic otherness, and in the process it established moral and cultural righteousness as one of the defining features of racial/ethnic difference (*Our America* 57). In such a system, the clarification of acceptable morality and standards for behavior would functionally demarcate the line between Anglo and non-Anglo ethnicities.

America had become too ambiguous a concept for Eliot and American identity so muddled and watered down that it had no real value anymore. The "foreign races" that Eliot believed were invading the country could now claim American identity as easily as he could (*After* 16–7). He did not wish to ascribe to an American identity that had become so generic as to mean almost nothing, nor did he wish to stay in an environment in which being an Eliot hardly mattered anymore and old Yankee blood did not convey special status. These issues likely contributed to his search for a new identity in the 1920s and his conversion to a new national identity with more rigorously defined social and cultural boundaries.

When Eliot employs ethnic stereotypes in his poetry, he re-imposes unambiguous ethnic boundaries on the world. In the modern age, such clearly delineated stereotypes were uncommon, and so he had to reach back to an earlier time and pluck the old characters from their original contexts, just as he plucked old heroes from mythology and put them to work in new ways. Eliot once said that the repurposing of mythology in texts like *Ulysses* and *The Waste Land* was "simply a way of controlling, of ordering, of giving shape and significance to the immense panorama of futility and anarchy which is contemporary history," and he seems to use prejudice and stereotype toward a similar organizational purpose ("Ulysses" 483).[9] The old stereotypes were unambiguous representations of what society found unacceptable, and by inserting them into the modern world, Eliot imposed some measure of order onto the perceived social chaos of civilization.

The Irish stereotype had particular appeal for Eliot for several reasons, the most obvious being that the vulgar Irishman seemed like the natural counterpoint to the spiritually enlightened Anglo gentleman. Early stereotypes developed in eighteenth- and nineteenth-century British texts explicitly conceived the Irish as having opposing qualities to the English, so that Irishness came to be defined as the inverse of Englishness. Declan Kiberd observes that in literature, the Irishman came to be seen as "the anti-self of the true-born Englishman" (24). Eliot's affection for English culture and his general belief in Anglo superiority naturally inclined him to posit civilization's elite as having English qualities, and logically, when he needed to describe the opposite of his ideal man, he reached for the ready-made anti-Anglo stereotype: the Irishman.[10] More importantly, in an American context, the Irish stereotype appealed to Eliot because the Irish, more than any other ethnic group, represented the trends toward cultural homogenization and vanishing ethnic prejudice. It was harder now to point to what made the Irish different, and fewer and fewer Irish Americans saw any benefit in claiming a unique ethnic heritage or believed that there was anything specifically Irish in their identity (as is the case with Fitzgerald's Amory

Blaine, discussed in the next section). It was because Irish Americans had become so undifferentiated from Anglo Americans and because of weakening prejudices that Eliot chose to revive the Paddy stereotype. Eliot clearly saw the Irish as different, but it was not their difference he was worried about; it was their invisibility. They, more so than any other immigrant group, had rid themselves of the mark of otherness and proved that such transformation was possible. Eliot's opposition to the cultural homogenization of America led to the intense ethnic panic and doubt evident in the Sweeney poems.

Eliot constructs the Irishman as a monstrous other but also addresses a broader fear of the monstrous other becoming common or ordinary. Eliot's characterization of the Irish is insulting, but such characterization was merely a tool, not the objective. He once wrote in a private letter, "We live in an *impossible* age . . . a world of thugs" (L. Gordon 474). It is hard not to notice that he imagines it as a world of predominately Irish thugs. Eliot's poems are not just simple attacks on the Irish, but rather meditations on the undesirable homogenization of American society; the Irish just happened to be the most explicit example of the transformation Eliot wished to critique.

Eliot feared that social homogenization and the resultant lowering of moral standards would lead to spiritual and physical decay. In his poetry, the Irish serve as harbingers of the realization of his worst fears. As the Irish became a common and ordinary presence in American culture, Eliot saw evidence of the decay that would transforms the modern world into a wasteland. John Ower suggests that Eliot was obsessed with "the sordid contemporary reality which undercuts the Romantic dream," and argues that, in the Sweeney poems, "[m]odern man's gross materialism and spiritual degeneracy are figured primarily in terms of a psychic lapse from full civilized humanity into the fallen physical nature of egocentric and destructive appetite" (73). Who better to represent such a fall from spiritual grace than the literary Irishman who came prefigured for debasement and already had been used in tales of degeneracy for over a century in America? What we find in the Sweeney texts is Eliot's realized fears expressed through the language of Irish ethnic identity. All of these texts obsess over failed spiritual fulfillment and gross physical debasement, the result of society's increasing shift toward generic banality, which itself can be blamed on the collapsing ethnic barriers that have allowed men like Sweeney to flourish and become common. With Sweeney as the modern everyman, civilization will content itself with crudely physical pleasures and never achieve divine union.

An explicit visual example of this is found in "Mr. Eliot's Sunday Morning Service" where the Irishman washes his meaty buttocks in the same baptismal waters that had cleansed Christ's feet. Sweeney, who in this poem and others stands in for modern religious worshippers, has no understanding of the spiritual use of holy water and so uses it to wash himself as he shifts "from ham to ham / Stirring the water in his bath" (29–30). He degrades a sacred ceremony and pollutes the sanctified waters, and in the process he ruins salvation for everyone else; how could anyone find purification in the water he has sullied? Eliot criticizes modern religion here by suggesting that Christians had degenerated to the level of the Irish and that Christian ceremony had become akin to ignorant splashing in filthy bathwater. The most vulgar insult Eliot can lob at modern culture is to compare it to the ethnically specific vulgarity of the Irish. In effect, Eliot suggests that modern man was becoming the very monster that nineteenth-century American nativists had fought so strongly against.

Eliot believed in the principles of ascetic mysticism that advocated self-discipline and the curbing of physical desire as a path to spiritual fulfillment. Not surprisingly, he quotes ascetic mystic St. John of the Cross in one of the two epigraphs to *Sweeney Agonistes*: "Hence the soul cannot be possessed of the divine union, until it has divested itself of the love of created beings" (74). What is interesting in the Sweeney texts is Eliot's insistence that the "love of created beings," the love of physical pleasure, and the failure to achieve "divine union" all result from clearly ethnic influences.

The religious argument that Eliot tries to make with the Sweeney motif is built on certain characteristics of the Irish stereotype, chiefly the Irishman's reputation for physical excess and gratification. According to the stereotype, the Irish routinely engaged in unwholesome entertainments, drunken revelry, and sexual impropriety. Since Eliot's conception of spiritual enlightenment is so dependent on the rejection of physical pleasures and temptations, it does not seem surprising that he would make use of the one ethnic stereotype so explicitly linked with material excess.

In Eliot's work, Sweeney's presence is that of a crudely sexual beast. He is described in each situation as either pursuing sex, engaged in sex, or recovering from sexual exertion. Eliot even worried that he had gone too far in sexualizing Sweeney and that his mother would be shocked to read such poems (*Letters* 363). Eliot viewed lust as the worst of all sins, so clearly his modern boogey-man had to be a sexual monster, but there is also something of ethnic significance in this characterization. Childs' *Modernism and Eugenics* (2001) explores Eliot's fear that "the Anglo-Saxon race was about to be overwhelmed by Jews and Irish-Catholics" (107). The eugenic problem centered on differential birth rates between the less-virile Anglo Americans and the (supposedly) overly prolific Irish Americans, a situation exacerbated by the perceived loss of viable Anglo blood in the war (Childs 88). Many in Eliot's generation perceived the Irish as sexual monsters who spread through civilization and threatened the extinction of their betters. The best way to deal with such a threat was through programs of social hygiene (like those described in Chapter 2) as well as through the segregation and sterilization of defectives (Childs 79).

Eliot's fear of the Irish contribution to the dysgenic flood is evident in his descriptions of Sweeney. In "Mr. Eliot's Sunday Morning Service," Eliot begins the poem by using an unusual term that describes the ability to produce many children—"polyphiloprogenitive"—which Childs traces to a eugenical origin (109). Eliot echoes this concept of super-virility several times throughout the poem: in his suggestion of "Superfetation of τὸ ἕν" (multiple impregnation of the One), his description of reproducing bees who "With hairy bellies pass between / The staminate and pistillate," and the image of the sexually potent Sweeney naked in his bath (6, 26–7). In a poem ostensibly criticizing Christian theology, Eliot noticeably directs much of his attack at the biological proliferation of undesirable people, such as Irish Catholics. Similarly, when Sweeney inseminates a woman in "Sweeney Erect," she immediately convulses in a spastic fit:

> Jackknifes upward at the knees
>   Then straightens out from heel to hip
> Pushing the framework of the bed
>   And clawing at the pillow slip. (17–20)

The unnamed girl continues to suffer throughout the poem, "clutching at her sides" in "hysteria," while Sweeney goes about his business unconcerned (32, 37). The girl's suffering and illness warn against violent Irish sexual natures and the possibility of miscegenation. Just as McTeague is aroused by Trina's vulnerability and his ability to inflict pain on her body, Sweeney seems emboldened by what he has done to the girl. The overly fertile, but racially inferior, Irishman spreads his infection first at Mrs. Turner's house, but then in the encompassing city. In *The Waste Land*, Sweeney is a vision of sexual potency that stands in stark contrast to the Fisher King's infertility. He rushes off through "[t]he sound of horns and motors" to a sexual rendezvous with "Mrs. Porter in the spring" (197–8). Despite surrounding descriptions of a cityscape devoid of life and "[u]nder the brown fog of a winter noon," it is springtime for Sweeney (208). His fertility is the frightening counterpoint to the city's infertility, and is possibly even partially to blame for it. The filth that chokes the life from everyone else is the atmosphere in which the Irishman thrives. Eliot wants his readers to be horrified by Sweeney, because his gross sexuality and bestial nature allow him to dominate the Unreal City, but preclude the possibility for spiritual transformation and salvation. There is sex in the wasteland, but it ruins rather than saves the world.

Eliot's religious background provides an important context for reading the Sweeney poems for two reasons. First, he interpreted modern Catholicism as a fallen institution and a counterpoint to his own idealized sense of ascetic Christianity. Second, he, like many others, viewed Catholicism as a fundamental aspect of Irish otherness. For yet another reason, the Irish proved to be the perfect model of the worst aspects of modern man. Eliot was born into a family that practiced Unitarianism, and there was some expectation that he himself would become a Unitarian minister after completing his education, but the church disappointed Eliot. He believed that modern theology had tried to make following the example of Christ too easy when it should have been hard, and as a result, theologians had "boiled away" what was important in early Christianity (Gordon 109–10). He favored an ascetic approach to religion, believing it was the only way to achieve spiritual passion, and craved a religion that would provide an "exacting moral code" (Gordon 226). Even after converting to Anglicanism, Eliot tried to be a reformer within the church, calling for stricter dogmatic theology since he did not want a religion "watered down and robbed of the severity of its demands" (Gordon 227). His poetry, according to Thomas F. Dillingham, "is the product of a fastidious mind that is attracted to the potential beauty of the Christian religion, but repelled, at the same time, by the actual vulgarity of the debased institutions by which it functions in the world" (48). Eliot often points to the Catholic Church as the epitome of debased spiritual institutions and characterizes Irish Catholics as ignorantly obedient worshippers incapable of truly appreciating their own religious heritage. The Irish represented the very opposite of the ascetic ideal and their brand of Catholicism seemed to Eliot a dumbed-down version of Christianity that did not require enough discipline, only obedience.

The Sweeney texts give voice to Eliot's disgust with what religion had been reduced to in the modern world and particularly emphasize the banality and bureaucracy that had resulted from Catholicism's attempts to appeal to men like Sweeney, who in these poems stands in for the common, unenlightened, modern Catholic. The priests, who should have been spiritual vanguards instilling Catholic values into secular life, were now nothing more than "sapient sutlers," as Eliot labels them in "Mr. Eliot's Sunday Morning Service," who pass themselves off as wise men, but who actually are just shilling the word of the Lord to the hopelessly ignorant masses who cannot grasp true spiritual enlightenment (2). Dillingham observes that the priests in this poem lack the "joyous devotion of the apostle" and fail to achieve "the ideal pastoral virtues which should be inspired by and inspire the simple devotion Paul recommends" (42–3). Eliot also appears disgusted with the young worshippers who wait for the priests along the "avenue of penitence" believing that forgiveness and guidance can come from such "sable presbyters" (17–8).

In addition, Eliot is troubled by the broad public acceptance of theologians who distort the word of God but still are taken as voices of authority. It is the "polymath" qualities of theologians (as well as the "polyphiloprogenitive" qualities of men like Sweeney) who are destroying the Catholic community, because "anything 'poly' is a threat to unity" (T. Dillingham 41). In the second stanza of the same poem, Eliot laments the influence of Origen (Christianity's first theologian) on the church and the way his writings diminished the purity of "the Word" (5–7). Such flawed spiritual guidance, as revealed in the last stanza, results in the idiotic and spiritually empty worship of Sweeney. He understands nothing that he is told, and though he is dutiful to the Catholic Church, he is not obedient to the actual spirit of Christianity. The very qualities that Harold Frederic admired in Catholics and that he describes in *The Damnation of Theron Ware*—qualities that include liberal philosophy, obedience, and suspicion of outdated European theology—are the same qualities that Eliot believes undermine true religious faith. Though Eliot's rebuke here targets a specifically Irish Catholic individual, he clearly intends to chastise all Christians (including Anglo Protestants) who are no better off than Sweeney; targeting Irish Catholicism simply sharpens the barb.

Instead of the church lifting Sweeney up, he pulls it down. Eliot dreamed of a society in which Christian ideals would become secular values—again, a similar goal (in form, if not substance) to Frederic's vision of an America strengthened by Irish Catholicism. Yet, Eliot describes a world in which the worst secular behavior of a crude ethnic minority has corrupted the church and ruined his dream. Sweeney does not pursue spiritual goals, only physical ones, and in his worship, he reduces the most sacred aspects of the church to the level of the purely material, even carnal. For instance, in "Mr. Eliot's Sunday Morning Service," Eliot evokes the image of the "Baptized God," Christ in the Jordan River, and then contrasts it with Sweeney "stirring the water in his bath," effectively replacing the most vivid example of spiritual purification with the image of a naked and dirty Irishman playing in his tub like a child (11, 30). Anselm Atkins describes this as a "humiliating . . . comedown" for Christ, made all the more humiliating, we can imagine, because of the vulgar physicality and perceived spiritual emptiness of Sweeney's ethnic identity (33). Eliot might have placed any derided minority in that bathtub in the last stanza, but the Irish stereotype carried with it specific associations and affiliations which better captured the vulgarization of Christianity that Eliot wished to emphasize.

Eliot takes more explicit aim at the Catholic Church in some of the other allusions in the Sweeney poems and again evokes very old and crude stereotypes to make his point. In "Sweeney Among the Nightingales," Eliot alludes to popular anti-Catholic propaganda and literature from the nineteenth century that equated Catholicism with murder, prostitution, and debauchery. In the poem, Sweeney hears nightingales "singing near / the Convent of the Sacred Heart" (35–6). Since "nightingales" carries with it a slang connotation of "prostitute," Eliot invites readers to question what is actually happening within the walls of the convent and reinforces the connection between the Catholic Church and the Whore of Babylon. In the context of "Sweeney Among the Nightingales," readers are to understand that in the event of Sweeney's death, his afterlife will be negotiated by this grossly fallen institution. He has entrusted his spiritual guidance to a corrupt church, which, at his funeral, will let "liquid siftings fall" and stain his "stiff dishonoured shroud" (39–40). Sweeney, unlike Agamemnon, apparently avoids being assassinated in this poem; yet, he is not unscathed. The epigraph to the poem is Agamemnon's last words from Aeschylus: "Alas, I have been struck deep a deadly wound." The conspirators "thought to be in league" against Sweeney in the poem fail in their mission, but the insinuation is that it does not matter (26). Sweeney's "deadly wound" is spiritual; whenever and however he dies, his material existence and lack of real religious guidance have made him unworthy of "divine union."

In discussing Sweeney's function in Eliot's conception of human spirituality, a few critics have identified the character as a classical pilgrim in a modern context, but this seems to me a misreading of Sweeney's journey through Eliot's work.[11] Like many of his stereotypical stage Irish forebears, Sweeney functions as a vulgar buffoon who only acts on physical cravings and who has no ambition for self-improvement. If anything, Sweeney is much more of an anti-pilgrim in a kind of immorality play in which he refutes virtue and plunges deeper into sin and debauchery while corrupting everything around him. Sweeney is Eliot's everyman, but the poet repeatedly shows him to be the inverse of the medieval everyman.

One of the telling features of the various Sweeney texts is the character's insistent pursuit of sin and physical satisfaction. Eliot gives the character an appetite for sacrilege and gross material pleasure, and though his blasphemies and indulgences seem fairly tame in the early poems, they quickly escalate to something far more threatening in the later works. In "Sweeney Erect," Sweeney seems on the threshold of something far worse than his usual gluttony and sexual villainy. After finishing with a prostitute, he "tests the razor on his leg" and seems to consider adding murder to his list of sins. In *The Waste Land*, Eliot describes Sweeney rushing once more to the whorehouse and reveling in the physical depravity of the city. After describing the ruination of his surroundings, the narrator of this section of the poem says, "But at my back in a cold blast I hear / The rattle of the bones, and chuckle spread from ear to ear" (185–6). Who is it that is chuckling in the wasteland? Who could possibly find amusement and enjoyment in death and destruction? Eliot seems to identify Sweeney as the chuckler just ten lines later: "But at my back from time to time I hear / The sound of horns and motors, which shall bring / Sweeney to Mrs. Porter in the spring" (196–8). Sweeney's ultimate fall from grace is described in *Sweeney Agonistes* when he shows no remorse for his sins, which include adultery, murder, and cannibalism. After admitting his depravities, Sweeney proclaims,

> But if you understand or if you don't
> That's nothing to me and nothing to you
> We all gotta do what we gotta do
> We're gonna sit here and drink this booze
> We're gonna sit here and have a tune
> We're gonna stay and we're gonna go (84)

There is no repentance or salvation for Sweeney; he simply has "gotta do" what he has "gotta do," and he feels no one can judge him. In the play he repeatedly states that the only things he believes in are the purely physical.

He tells Doris, "Birth, and copulation, and death / That's all, that's all, that's all, that's all . . . That's all the facts when you come to brass tacks" (80). There is nothing for him beyond this physical world. The progress of this pilgrim has only led him away from God.

Importantly, though, Eliot's Irish everyman does not just damn himself; like McTeague, he threatens to take the world down with him. In his backward pilgrimage into corruption, he defiles everyone he comes into contact with. Again, this is most explicitly evident in *Sweeney Agonistes* in the early part of the conversation between Doris and Sweeney. In their playful word games, Doris proposes to bring Christianity into the life of the savage Irishman, but Sweeney says that it will actually be the other way around; he will bring savagery into her world:

> SWEENEY. I'll carry you off
>   To a cannibal isle.
> DORIS. You'll be the cannibal!
> SWEENEY. You'll be the missionary!
>   You'll be my little seven stone missionary!
>   I'll gobble you up. I'll be the cannibal.
> DORIS. You'll carry me off? To a cannibal isle?
> SWEENEY. I'll be the cannibal.
> DORIS. I'll be the missionary.
>   I'll convert you!
> SWEENEY. I'll convert you!
>   Into a stew.
>   A nice little, white little, missionary stew. (79–80)

Such a counter-conversion is inconceivable and abominable, as well as a mockery of the sacrament of the Eucharist in which Christians consume the body of Christ in order to be saved. Even worse, Sweeney admits that this is not his first attempt to "convert" a woman. He describes how he once drowned a girl "with a gallon of lysol in a bath" and then left her corpse to decompose there for several months in the bathroom of his apartment as he went about his normal routine (83).[12] What Sweeney has done is a reverse baptism of the girl, which only brings about horror and death, and which mocks the Christian sacrament. Lysol is a cleaning agent, but in the hands of Sweeney it—and Christian ritual—become murderer's tools. Apparently Sweeney was not content, as he had been in "Mr. Eliot's Sunday Morning Service," to dirty the baptismal waters alone anymore.

Some critics believe Sweeney achieves some sort of enlightenment in the end or that he is redeemable in some way, but again, this seems very unlikely.[13] In fact, Eliot emphasizes the fact that Sweeney got away with murder and that, in truth, men like Sweeney "don't all get pinched in the end" (83). This is not to say that there is no hope in Eliot. The truth of Christianity is still there, though it has been obscured by modern filth. In "Mr. Eliot's

Sunday Morning Service," Eliot proclaims that "through the water pale and thin / Still shine the unoffending feet" of Christ (13–4). Eliot's later poetry explores ways to recover this more perfect Christian spirituality, but in these earlier texts, we learn that salvation cannot come from men like Sweeney.

In the original excised opening of *The Waste Land*, Eliot begins the poem with a scene of Irish revelry, drunkenness, and violence.[14] It is hard to imagine *The Waste Land* not beginning with that famous line—"April is the cruelest month"—but in this earlier version it begins, "First we had a couple of feelers down at Tom's place, / There was old Tom, boiled to the eyes, blind." The narrator of this opening section then describes an evening of drinking and carousing his way through Boston with his friends. They sing show tunes, including a bit from George M. Cohan's "Harrigan"[15]: "'I'm proud of all the Irish blood that's in me, / There's not a man can say a word agin me'." It is a scene that could have been lifted from Joyce, if not for the fact that there is no humor, just bitter condemnation. Eliot evokes a stereotypical Irish presence and links the desolation of the modern world to the pride of the "Irish blood" in the city. This celebration of Irishness, which explicitly evokes the overblown Irish-American sentimentality of Ned Harrigan's Mulligan Guards, leads the young men to the Opera Exchange, a pub that Eliot frequented in Boston that, according to Valerie Eliot, was run by the model for Sweeney. In the rest of the section, the young men cause mayhem ("I tried to put my foot in the drum, and didn't the girl squeal"), solicit a prostitute ("Get me a woman, I said; you're too drunk, she said"), get in trouble with the police ("We'd just gone up the alley, a fly cop came along, / Looking for trouble; committing a nuisance, he said"), and are rescued by a corrupt Irish politician named Donovan ("What's this officer. You're new on this beat, ain't you? / I thought so. You know who I am?"). This original opening to *The Waste Land* is poetically crude when compared to the published version, which is likely why Eliot excised it; however, it reveals the same ethnic anxieties and fears as the Sweeney texts. It displays, once again, Eliot's fundamental obsession with the metaphorical significance of the Irish-American character. It is not actually clear who the speaker in this section is or whether he is ethnically Irish, but this might just be the point.

What Eliot particularly despised was the way generic American culture had come to resemble Irish culture. These young men, whatever their heritage, proclaim Irish pride and behave like stereotypical Irishmen. That this was common was itself the problem. The potential horror, according to Eliot, is that in this scene of young college boys drinking in Sweeney's bar, being American seems an awful lot like being Irish; and unlike Twain who envisioned an Irish boy better than American society and Frederic who believed that the Irish were the key to American progress, Eliot sees only corruption and despair in his imagined Irish characters.

By the time that Eliot created Sweeney, the Irish had become a significantly less marginal community in America. While it would be an exaggeration to claim that they had been neatly assimilated or fully de-ethnicized, it is fair to note, as historian Timothy J. Meagher does, that they had "largely dissolved into a broader American mainstream" (102). Yet, this process did not mean, as some early assimilationists hoped, that all ethnic qualities would be subsumed by American ones. In dissolving into the American mainstream, the Irish had changed American culture. Many Irish cultural values and practices had become mainstream American values and practices. In the process of becoming more American, the Irish had made mainstream America a little more Irish. For Eliot, the dissolving of the Irish into American society was a pollution, and the ambiguous line between Irish culture and American culture was unsettling. The Irish were becoming increasingly invisible as ethnic others, in part because they seemed more American, but also because Americans seemed more Irish. Eliot's fears originate from a position outside the Irish community; however, the increasing invisibility of the Irish also created problems for a new generation growing up within that community who could not determine the distinct boundaries of the identity into which they had been born.

"CELTIC YOU'LL LIVE AND CELTIC YOU'LL DIE": F. SCOTT FITZGERALD'S *THIS SIDE OF PARADISE*

Like T. S. Eliot, F. Scott Fitzgerald was born in a large Midwest city along the Mississippi River, grew up in a privileged household, attended an Ivy League school, and achieved fame in the decade after World War I. He saw many of the same things Eliot did—the blurring of ethnic boundaries, the fragmentation of individual identity, the breakdown of social hierarchies, the trend toward cultural homogenization—and again like the slightly older poet, he worried that the Irish were becoming an increasingly indistinct ethnic group. Both Eliot and Fitzgerald lived in a world in which the gulf separating Irish America from Anglo America had become much smaller and, in some contexts, negligible. Yet, whereas Eliot feared unclear ethnic boundaries because of the potential for cultural corruption and the decay of social and moral standards, Fitzgerald feared the phenomenon because it made it even harder for ethnic Americans to know themselves. Fitzgerald himself was Irish American, but as is clear in *This Side of Paradise*, he was not sure what that even meant anymore.

Fitzgerald represented the kind of ambiguously Irish American that Eliot feared was encroaching on the domain of the Anglo-Protestant elite.[16] He had come from a "new money" family, risen through society, attended a good school, achieved a modicum of success, and married a beautiful and wealthy Protestant woman. He did not speak with an Irish brogue or look like a vulgar savage, but instead was well dressed, handsome, and polite.

Even his name—Francis Scott Key Fitzgerald—evokes Anglo-American ancestry simultaneously with Irish heritage.[17] His reputation during his lifetime was as an American writer (not an Irish-American writer), and as an icon of the Jazz Age and a member of the Lost Generation, he was usually viewed in the context of writers like Ernest Hemingway and Sherwood Anderson and not in the context of Irish-American writers of the time like Finley Peter Dunne or John O'Hara.

William V. Shannon argues that Fitzgerald rose to fame so swiftly that "he never became identified in the public mind as Irish at all" (233). This is surprising given that Irish-American characters appear in nearly all of his novels and many of his short stories, and also given that his fiction repeatedly treats issues of ethnicity and identity as central themes. *This Side of Paradise* explicitly details a semi-autobiographical struggle with Irish Catholic identity and obsesses over the compatibility of Celtic heritage and modern American social values, but the novel has traditionally been read as a more generic story of a typically sad young man of the 1920s engaging in romantic excess. Amory Blaine, like Huck Finn, has had his character de-ethnicized by readings that ignore his Irishness. As a result, *This Side of Paradise* has been significantly undervalued as a narrative of ethnic experience.

Despite the relatively little attention given during Fitzgerald's lifetime to his ethnic heritage or the Irish elements of his works, many of his friends and colleagues considered his Irishness to be a focal point in his identity and writing. In an article from 1922, famed literary critic Edmund Wilson, who was one of Fitzgerald's close friends at Princeton, asserts that readers should know that "Fitzgerald is partly Irish and that brings both to life and to fiction certain qualities that are not Anglo-Saxon" (qtd. in Shannon 234). Wilson argues that these qualities include conflicting strains of romance and cynicism, a degree of vanity and wit, and "an Irish gift for turning language into something iridescent and surprising" (qtd. in Shannon 234–5). Malcolm Cowley similarly remarks that Fitzgerald's "Irishness was a little disguised, but it remained an undertone in all his stories; it gave him a sense of standing apart that sharpened his observation of social differences" (qtd. in Shannon 234). In considering the comments of Fitzgerald's friends and contemporaries, Shannon concludes that Fitzgerald's "work is intimately bound up with his Irish background but in a more complex and less obvious way than that of the earlier Irish writers" (234). Though these critics observe that Irishness is important to Fitzgerald, none of them articulate how it functions in his work. If the Irish elements of Fitzgerald's fiction are, as Shannon suggests, "more complex and less obvious," then how are they recognizable and why did they develop so uncommonly? Is Fitzgerald's Irishness really as "disguised" as Cowley argues, or is the ethnic slipperiness of Fitzgerald's writing indicative of something else?

Fitzgerald remains somewhat of an anomaly in Irish-American literary history because his work seems so different from the unambiguously Irish stories of other more canonical Irish writers. Yet, Fitzgerald experienced Irish identity as ambiguity, and in this sense, his work seems an authentic representation of a very common experience among Irish Americans of his generation. Charles Fanning argues that Fitzgerald "found his way in part by largely ignoring the possibilities for fiction of the ethnic dimension" (248). Yet, his work demonstrates a career-long obsession with the "ethnic dimension." The key to understanding Fitzgerald's conception of Irishness is to realize that his texts are not affirming Irish identity, but rather questioning it. The fact that Irishness seems faded and illusive *is* the point. Writing a novel that confidently celebrated Irishness would have been impossible for him, but writing a novel that honestly expressed his confusion about Irishness was not. It is a little erroneous to suggest that he ignored, disguised, or sublimated his Irishness, when it is evident that he was testing the limits of his ethnic heritage, rehearsing its characteristics, exploring its associations, and trying to reconcile it with his American identity. Throughout his career he maintained an uneasy sense of his own Irish identity and exhibited radically different feelings about it, ranging from slight embarrassment to overblown pride. Fitzgerald should be credited with the honesty and sophistication required to publicly grapple with his own ethnic insecurities—insecurities that turned out to be widely shared by his generation. In writing *This Side of Paradise*, he expressed both his desire for ethnic authenticity and his frustration at achieving such an impossible goal, and in doing so, he offered an understanding of Irishness in America that took nothing for granted.

Fitzgerald was born in 1896 in St. Paul, Minnesota, a city that attracted many Catholic families eager to escape common prejudices lingering elsewhere in the country (Shannon 237). After his father's business failed, Fitzgerald and his family were taken in by his maternal grandfather Philip Francis McQuillan, an Irish immigrant who had made a fortune in the grocery business, and they lived comfortably thereafter among St. Paul's social elite (Shannon 236).[18] Fitzgerald's family has been characterized as lace-curtain Irish due to their wealth and social status, and Fitzgerald generally enjoyed a privileged childhood; however, he was troubled in those early years by what he later described as a "two-cylinder inferiority complex" and an "intense social self-consciousness" resulting from his Irish heritage (Rhodes 31). His family's wealth and religion entitled him to general acceptance in the community, and he routinely socialized with wealthier non-Irish children and was well liked, but his Irish heritage still carried a bit of a stigma that embarrassed him. He was very conscious, and a bit snobbish, that despite his family's success, they were (in his words) "straight 1850 potato-famine Irish" (Shannon 237).

Fitzgerald's attitudes toward his Irish heritage began to change when he started attending the Newman School, a Catholic preparatory academy near Princeton University. While at Newman, Fitzgerald developed a close relationship with the school's headmaster, Monsignor Sigourney Fay (the inspiration for *This Side of Paradise*'s Monsignor Thayer Darcy), who became a kind of surrogate father to him. Fay had converted to Catholicism in 1908 and earned a reputation as a brilliant theologian, a "jolly monk," and a dandy-like aesthete (Meyers 17). Several Fitzgerald biographers describe Fay as a bit of an Irish rogue in the church and claim that he regularly recited mass in Gaelic, though this is likely fallacious (Meyers 17–8). On Fay's death in 1919, Fitzgerald described him as "the best friend I had in the world," and in 1920, he dedicated *This Side of Paradise* to him (*Letters* 374). Much has been written about Fitzgerald's friendship with Fay, particularly about the older man's influence on the author's perception of Catholicism, but in addition, it is worth noting that Fay also kindled in Fitzgerald an interest in Irish topics.[19] Fay convinced the young Fitzgerald that the Irish were a lively and romantic people, that Irish political causes were worthwhile, that Irish history and legends were noble, and that being Irish American was extraordinary. In Fay, Fitzgerald saw Irish identity as enabling of intellectualism, spirituality, mysticism, wit, artistry, and visceral pleasure. Shortly after Fay's death, Fitzgerald wrote that he felt the monsignor's "mantle had descended upon me" and that he had "a desire, or more, to some day recreate the atmosphere of him" (*Letters* 375).[20] A large part of recreating that atmosphere would require Fitzgerald to fully embrace his Irish heritage and to celebrate it the way Fay had done in his own life.

The other major Irish influence on Fitzgerald during this period was Irish-born author Shane Leslie. Having been introduced through Fay, the two men took an interest in each other's careers, and the older (and well-connected) Leslie served as a kind of literary sponsor for Fitzgerald and was largely responsible for getting *This Side of Paradise* published at Scribner's. Fitzgerald admired Leslie's Irish Catholic persona, much as he had Fay's, and likely saw in the Irish writer a model for his own developing identity. In particular, Leslie prompted Fitzgerald to ground himself in his Celtic ancestry and to take an interest in Irish politics and history. Fitzgerald described Leslie's book *Celt and the World* (1917) as a "sort of bible of Irish patriotism," and in a review of that book he took the opportunity to affirm his own status as an "Irishman" and to speak out in favor of Home Rule (*In His Own Time* 116). Leslie returned the favor of this compliment a few years later when he reviewed *This Side of Paradise* for the *Dublin Review* and tied the novel in to a protracted discussion of an "Irish bias" among several prominent British and American intellectuals (288).

It was largely due to the influence of Fay and Leslie that Fitzgerald became comfortable with his ethnic identity, so much so that during these early years of his career he began identifying himself as a "Celt" and would sign letters with the valedictions "Celtically" or "Gaelically yours" (Rhodes 35). His interest in all things Irish peaked during the years 1917–1919 while he was writing the early drafts of *This Side of Paradise*, but waned in the period after Monsignor Fay's death. He never again exhibited the same level of fervor or enthusiasm for Irish topics (or Catholic ones, for that matter), and his later novels describe his resulting uneasy sense of being Irish and his attempts to mediate between alternating poles of embarrassment and pride.

Fitzgerald used Amory Blaine's Irishness, as Eliot used Sweeney's, to metaphorically signal a crisis in broader American society. The issues at hand were not limited to the Irish-American community, but an Irish-American character provided a versatile test case. Amory's ethnic context, like Sweeney's, allows for the contemplation of a range of issues obsessing Americans. By symbolically figuring the Irish body as the site where these issues came to bear, Fitzgerald partook of the same stereotypes and rhetoric as Eliot, and like the poet, he repurposed old tropes for a more modern agenda.

Yet, the outcomes of Eliot's and Fitzgerald's literary projects are significantly different because the two writers did not have the same perspective of the existing metaphor of Irishness. Eliot's understanding of the Irish-American character never goes beyond superficial characteristics. Fitzgerald, on the other hand, knew Irish America in private as well as public spaces. He knew the stereotypes and could evoke them as well as Eliot, but he also found literary significance in Irish America's less obvious features: its insecurities, its divisions, its problematic relationship with Catholicism, its conflicting social agendas, its class assumptions, and its wavering sense of communal cohesiveness. He saw something very American in the breakdown and transformation of his community and opened up the Irish-American character to new metaphoric possibilities.

This Side of Paradise is a novel obsessed with inconsistency of character. As Fitzgerald's first major work, it marks the beginning of what would be a career-long exploration of how Irish ethnicity played into that inconsistency. Amory Blaine's search for the essential truth of his identity, what he repeatedly calls "the fundamental Amory," takes him from the Midwest, to Princeton University, to the battlefields of Europe, and back to the U.S. He tries to affirm his identity by immersing himself in a variety of environments, some intellectual, some spiritual, and some profane, and like many of his generation, Amory attempts to establish some sense of continuity in his life by linking himself to his ethnic heritage. Amory's attempts to understand, embrace, and even perform an Irish identity reveal a revolutionary shift in Irish-American characterization and the beginnings of a complex re-imagining of ethnicity in America.

As a child, Amory believed that he was extraordinary and he "wondered how people could fail to notice that he was a boy marked for glory" (24). His greatest ambition in life was to distinguish himself from the common rabble of the world, whether at childhood birthday parties, at university clubs, or at war. He even dreams that, one day, he "might be a really great dictator or writer or religious or political leader" (198). Amory needs to be admired, if not famous, but finds his ambitions repeatedly frustrated by a society that increasingly makes it impossible for individuals to distinguish themselves from the mass of common men. To survive as a child living in Minneapolis, he tells his aristocratic mother, Beatrice, "I adapted myself to the bourgeoisie. I became conventional" (27). However, what he assumed was a temporary survival strategy of his youth turns into a de facto condition of the rest of his life.

The obsolete caste system and snobbish pretensions that Amory learned from Beatrice do not sustain him once he leaves home. He repeatedly tries to assert his difference from the rest of the world but fails to realize that the race and class distinctions he wants to make really do not matter in his new context. For example, he complains about riding in a train car with New Jersey's "alien population" and resents their ethnic otherness, even though the train is taking him to Princeton where he himself, as an Irish Catholic, is the alien ethnic other (113). The next time he rides the train, he again decries the "stinking aliens" sharing his car and thinks to himself that wartime patriotism would be easier if Americans all shared the same racial background; he imagines "how much easier it would have been to fight as the Colonies fought, or as the Confederacy fought" (139). Again, his fantasy here runs counter to his own situation; he wishes America, like Princeton, was the domain of primarily wealthy, white, Protestant men, when he himself as a non-wealthy Irish Catholic would be a marginal member of such a community. Similarly, he tries to use economics and social class to separate himself from others, but this too proves problematic. He unashamedly admits, "I detest poor people . . . I hate them for being poor" and considers this attitude "natural and sincere . . . unchangeable, unmoral," but at this point in the novel, he himself is poor and is reduced to begging for a ride back to Princeton (237). Amory fails to realize the hypocrisy of his situation and stubbornly refuses to acknowledge the discrepancy between his ideal social hierarchy and his own ethnic and economic realities.

Amory's basic conflict is that he has a deep desire to believe in an American caste system, but he regularly finds himself blocked from inclusion at the top of such a hierarchy. When he arrives at Princeton and finds himself, for the first time in his life, to be at the bottom of the social ladder, he despairs at his vanishing sense of entitlement and his growing realization that he is part of "the damned middle class" (49). "I like having a bunch of hot cats on top," he says, "but . . . I've got to be one of them" (50). Up to this point, Amory had viewed himself as inherently one of American society's elite young men. His entire identity was formed around the belief that, on his maturity, he would be a prince of America. Yet, at Princeton, he is told that he is merely "a sweaty bourgeois" who will have to work to distinguish himself from the thousands of other boys who are equally (if not more) remarkable than he (50). Amory, accustomed to thinking of his extraordinariness as an inherent quality, not an earned achievement, remarks, "But I hate to get anywhere by working for it. I'll show the marks, don't you know?" (50). Unfortunately for him, as his friend Kerry observes, such "honorable scars" are increasingly necessary both at Princeton and in modern America as well.

Amory's Irish-Catholic background does not make the matter any easier. His ethnicity, compounded with his status as a freshman, makes him an outcast among outcasts. Like it was for Fitzgerald, Irishness for Amory becomes a dirty secret. It serves as a constant reminder of his difference from the older boys, and even when he dresses up like an upper-classman and adopts a characteristic "Princetonian" attitude, he remains conscious of the performance. Beatrice's tutelage did not properly prepare him for the ethnic hierarchies he encounters in southern New Jersey.

After losing much of his young egotism at Princeton and at war, Amory comes to believe that the extraordinary individuality he had craved as a child was impossible. He had arrived at Princeton "abreast of the best of his generation," but his generation's best were hopelessly ordinary; none of them were destined for greatness (88).[21] The post-war world created a "great protest against the superman" that he believes unfairly limits his potential (144). As an adult, he laments that the war had "killed individualism" and made it impossible for men to "stand prominence" (198–9). Amory complains that even men as extraordinary as Leonardo da Vinci and Lorenzo de Medici would wallow in obscurity in the modern world; so what chance does he have (198)? By the end of the novel, he accepts that there are "no more wise men" and "no more heroes," and that he no longer has an obligation to try to be either (242).

Pearl James describes Amory as suffering from the strain of "American nervousness" and "neuroticism" that had a particular effect on men from prominent New England families during the early part of the century (4). According to James, this "pandemic, if ethereal, malaise" resulted from changes in class structures that constricted how young men could define themselves in America. The socio-cultural structures that would have leveraged Amory to greatness in previous decades had collapsed, leaving him confused and frustrated, unsure of how to understand his own identity now that the criteria for success—even the criteria for mere differentiation— was vanishing. Amory offers an understanding of this phenomenon that emphasizes his anxiety about being left behind:

> Modern life . . . changes no longer century by century but year by year, ten times faster than it ever has before—populations doubling, civilizations unified more closely with other civilizations, economic interdependence, racial questions, and—we're *dawdling* along. My idea is that we've got to go very much faster. (251–2)

In this passage, Amory's chief complaint is that social change has made it impossible for an individual to stand out. He laments the breakdown of barriers between civilizations, social classes, and races and despairs at the increasing population—all factors that make individualism more problematic. Just like Eliot, Amory wonders how the truly elite men of America are to distinguish themselves when the country has made it harder to tell populations apart. Amory craves the same categorical clarity that Eliot desired. Without clear divisions between ethnicities and classes, everyone in America starts to seem the same.

In an interview from 1927, Fitzgerald expresses concerns similar to Eliot's. He argues that the "American race" has become "a mass product without common sense or guts or dignity," and that it needs a "national testing" in order to clarify what it means when an individual stands up and claims, "I am an American" (Salpeter 275). Fitzgerald's rhetoric here surprisingly blends nationality and race and sounds more like something Eliot might say; however, the concerns he voices are nothing new. He is simply once again lamenting what he believed was an increasingly banal and homogenous American culture and the apparent meaningless of Americanism in the twentieth century. Fitzgerald, like his literary alter ego, craves to escape the uniform mass of confusion and mediocrity that had subsumed American individualism. He shares this desire with Eliot as well, who for different reasons saw danger in the same phenomenon.

Like many literary protagonists of this period, Amory develops a fragmentary identity as a result of the trauma of living in the modern world. What makes Amory unique, though, is his incredible self-awareness of this problem. He describes his life as "a succession of quick, unrelated scenes" that would "take all time, more than he could ever spare" to glue together into a unified whole (215). Even as a young boy, he understands his own inconsistency of character and describes himself in almost schizophrenic terms as "a certain, changing person whose label, in order that his past might always be identified with him, was Amory Blaine" (24). The obvious goal of his life then is to try to discover the unchanging, essential core of his identity, which will solidify his sense of being, resolve his inconsistencies, and mark him as a unique entity in the modern world. Amory's search for this core identity forms the plot of *This Side of Paradise*.

Irish ethnic heritage enters the novel as a potential way for Amory to solidify his fragmented identity, as a way to glue together his sense of being, and as a way to establish his individuality.[22] One avenue to escape modern homogeneity, that great enemy of individualism, would be to identify oneself with a unique ethnic heritage. Having failed to distinguish himself in any other way, Amory turns to his Irish roots in the hope that the "fundamental Amory" might be fundamentally Irish if nothing else.

Of course, Amory's understanding of Irish identity is problematic. He has only a limited knowledge of his ethnic heritage, and that knowledge is distorted by misunderstanding and prejudice (a problem experienced by Studs Lonigan and Scarlett O'Hara, too, as discussed in Chapter 4). When he first considers adopting an Irish persona, Amory hesitates because of the preconceptions he has about the Irish:

He was rather skeptical about being an Irish patriot—he suspected that being Irish was being somewhat common—but Monsignor assured him that Ireland was a romantic lost cause and Irish people quite charming, and that it should, by all means, be one of his principal biases. (31)

Amory's dilemma is the same one faced by Celtic Revivalists: he must find a way to appreciate Irish culture despite suspicions that it is non-genteel. Prior to meeting with Monsignor Darcy, Amory assumes that Irishness is vulgar and undesirable, and he associates the Irish people with drunkenness, poverty, bourgeois social values, and bad manners—much the way T. S. Eliot does; however, there are some interesting differences in Amory's preconceptions since they were learned not just in the aristocratic social milieu he moved through in his childhood, but also through his experience of his own family.

Amory's mother, Beatrice Blaine (formerly Beatrice O'Hara), was an Irish American from Wisconsin who had been educated at the Sacred Heart Convent in Rome and subsequently lived a life of leisure supported by her family's wealth. Amory "had no illusions" about his mother and attributes the worst aspects of her behavior to her Irish origins (12). Even at age thirteen he is "ever *on* to his Celtic mother" whose nervous breakdown "bore a suspicious resemblance to delirium tremens" (15). Like Huck Finn who also as a child must deal with a parent's alcoholism and delirium tremens, Amory is forced into the role of caretaker, but he has it harder because social respectability matters to the Blaines in a way it clearly does not to the Finns. Drunkenness was not a sign of the kind of social refinement that the Blaines' high society context would permit. In American literature, the trope of the drunken Irish parent serves two major functions. First, it provides a reminder of the falsity of the Irish claim to civility. In *Huck Finn*, one night of drinking undoes all the work by the judge to clean Pap up; similarly, in Margaret Mitchell's *Gone With the Wind*, despite Gerald O'Hara's wealth and status, his drinking suggests that he is only a pretender among the Southern aristocracy (a notion discussed in more detail in Chapter 4). In *This Side of Paradise*, Beatrice's alcoholic binges similarly signal that she is not quite as refined as she lets on to be. Second, the alcoholic parent serves as a visible warning to the child about his or her substandard biology. It reveals the degenerate nature that lurks within the child and can be brought to the surface if the child makes the wrong choices. Beatrice frustrates Amory by persisting in her bad behavior and even touting her alcoholism as a badge of pride. After being released from the sanitarium, Beatrice proudly tells Amory that, "if any man alive had done the consistent drinking that I have, he would have been physically *shattered*, my dear, and in his *grave*—long in his grave" (27). Amory winces at this remark, embarrassed by his mother's stereotypically Irish pride in her predilection for drinking.

Amory similarly expresses frustration and shame at his mother's Catholicism since she treats her religion as a game and her faith as a tool for garnering attention. Amory, who is not raised Catholic himself, observes his mother's relationship with the church as an outsider, and he is appalled by his mother's frivolous and hypocritical faith. For Beatrice, the church is an amusing social distraction and her relationships with priests is a "favorite sport" (14). She feigns wavering belief because she discovered that "priests were infinitely more attentive" to her if they thought they were going to lose her (14). What Beatrice wants from the church is superficial satisfaction, and Amory loses respect for the Catholic Church for giving it to her. He condemns the priests in a way similar to Eliot's condemnation of empty, commercialized Catholicism in "Mr. Eliot's Sunday Morning Service." Amory's anger culminates in the moment he learns that Beatrice, "in a sudden burst of religiosity," has given half of his inheritance to various churches so they could buy stained-glass windows (153). Instead of ensuring her son's future, Beatrice persists in affirming what Amory believes is false faith in a lingering habit from her Irish Catholic upbringing.

As Amory grows up, he forms preconceptions about the Irish along three distinct lines, the first being social class. One of his principal fears is that being Irish is "being somewhat common" (31). He equates the Irish with peasantry, with ghetto life, with low-class culture and ideals, with unrefined tastes and manners, and with working-class employment. He has intense misgivings about embracing an ethnic identity that appears to him to be socially and economically inferior. Robert E. Rhodes argues that Amory's feelings were also Fitzgerald's and suggests that "[t]he simple, inescapable identification of the Irish with the middle-class is more than Amory can bear, and Fitzgerald shared his pain" (Rhodes 38). Amory never manages to overcome his class prejudices, and as a result, he never is able to fit comfortably enough into an Irish identity.[23]

The second preconception Amory maintains is that Irishness and Catholicism go hand in hand. In his mind, you cannot be Irish without being Catholic. Amory is not completely adverse to Catholicism; in fact, like Eliot and Harold Frederic, he admires the beauty of its traditions, but he cannot bring himself to truly believe. Walter Raubicheck argues that what appeals to Amory are the "medieval, Chestertonian qualities" of the church, but such qualities are not incentive enough to "compel him to any active practice" (56). Catholic symbolism and mythology appeal to Amory because he views them as part of Irish culture, but the literal act of worship and the necessity of faith escape him. Amory retains too many bad impressions of Catholicism in practice and cannot shake his fundamental conception of Catholicism as the bogus brand of faith practiced by his mother.

Amory, again like Eliot, sees a discrepancy between the ideal of the Catholic religion and the manner in which it is usually practiced in America; the beauty and respectability of the ancient faith seems debased and corrupted in its modern form. Darcy tries to reeducate Amory about Catholicism and urges him to become "anchored to the Church," and he almost succeeds (103). When Amory sees Catholicism through Darcy's eyes, he sees the wonder and glory, much as Fitzgerald did when he saw it through Monsignor Fay's. Fitzgerald describes his own illumination in an article from 1922: "[Monsignor Fay] made of that Church a dazzling, golden thing, dispelling its oppressive mugginess and giving the succession of day upon gray days, passing under its plaintive ritual, the romantic glamour of an adolescent dream" (qtd. in Allen 37). Unfortunately, just as Fay died before Fitzgerald's conversion was complete, Darcy passes away and leaves Amory with significant lingering doubts about his religion.[24] After the war, Amory writes to a friend that he is now a "passionate agnostic" largely because the Catholic Church proved "timidly negligible" during the war and because "they haven't any good writers any more. I'm sick of Chesterton" (153). Bored by Catholicism's romance and no longer under the influence of Darcy, Amory cannot sustain enthusiasm for Catholic belief, which proves crippling to his sense of Irish identity.

The third major preconception Amory harbors about Irish identity is that it should be romantic, mystical, and rooted in ancient culture (a bias shared by *The Damnation of Theron Ware*'s protagonist). Amory largely accepts as truth the vision of the Irish as presented by the Celtic Revival: heroic peasants with ancient souls, joyous spirits, and an almost magical connection with the land. In college, Amory's favorite writers are W. B. Yeats and J. M. Synge, but like Fitzgerald himself, Amory did not like James Joyce's frank, unromantic descriptions of the Irish.[25] When he reads *A Portrait of the Artist as a Young Man*, Amory finds himself "puzzled and depressed" (195). If Amory is going to be Irish, he does not want to be a Joycean Irishman, he wants to be someone with more romance and wit, closer in spirit to the mythical Celt. What attracts Amory to an Irish identity is the potential to link himself to a grand history. Somewhat problematically, Fitzgerald uses the terms "Irish," "Gaelic," and "Celtic" interchangeably, both in his public and private writings, and so do Amory and Darcy in *This Side of Paradise*. When Darcy claims that he and Amory share "Celtic souls and Celtic subtleties," he affirms that their fundamental character emerges from a pre-modern, unblemished source (150). In a letter to Amory, Darcy says that this "mystical element" of Irishness "flows into us" and "enlarges our personalities" (204). Largely because of Darcy's insistence, Amory accepts this idea of himself as a "Celt" heroically struggling against the modern world.

The most significant piece of romanticized Irish culture in *This Side of Paradise* is the poem that Darcy writes for Amory while the young man is preparing to embark on his journey to war in Europe. This poem is the most explicit attempt in the novel to insert Amory into a continuity of Celtic heroism and represents the kind of sentimentalism that was reinforcing Amory's preconceptions of Irish identity. Darcy's poem for Amory is actually a transcription of a lament that Fay wrote for Fitzgerald in similar circumstances

(*Letters* 469). The poem makes use of phonetic approximations of common Irish language phrases popularized in the "Oirish" songs of Tin Pan Alley.[26] Darcy's poem reads as follows (English translation of Irish in brackets):

A Lament for a Foster Son, and He going to the War Against the
    King of Foreign.
Ochone [Alas]
He is gone from me the son of my mind
And he is in his golden youth like Angus Oge
Angus of the bright birds
And his mind strong and subtle like the mind of Cuchulin or
    Muirtheme.

Awirra strhue [O Holy Virgin Mary, what a shame]
His brow is as white as the milk of the cows of Maeve
And his cheeks like the cherries of the tree
And it bending down to Mary and she feeding the Son of God.

Aveelia Vrone [One-thousand Sorrows]
His hair is like the golden collar of the Kings at Tara
And his eyes like the four grey seas of Erin
And they swept with the mists of rain.

Mavrone go Gudyo [My sorrow forever]
He to be in the joyful and red battle
Amongst the chieftains and they doing great deeds of valor
His life to go from him
It is the chords of my own soul would be loosed.

A Vich Deelish [Dear son]
My heart is in the heart of my son
And my life is in his life surely
A man can be twice young
In the life of his sons only.

Jia du Vaha Alanav [God save your life my child]
May the Son of God be above him and beneath him, before him and
    behind him
May the King of the elements cast a mist over the eyes of the King of
    Foreign,
May the Queen of Graces lead him by the hand the way he can go
    through the
Midst of his enemies and they not seeing him
May Patrick of the Gael and Collumb of the Churches and the five
    thousand

Saints of Erin be better than a shield to him
And he go into the fight.
Och Ochone.[27] [Alas] (151)

It is highly questionable whether Amory understands any of the Irish phrases or many of the references to Irish mythology and history, but he certainly does not misunderstand the basic idea that Darcy is inserting him into a pantheon of Irish heroes and comparing his very body to the land of Ireland. The poem is possibly unintentionally funny; it traces a lineage from an ancient god (Angus Oge) through Ireland's most famous hero (Cúchulainn) through several famous Irish monarchs (Maeve, the Kings of Tara) through the biggest religious icons of Ireland's history (St. Patrick, St. Columba) to a modern-age egotist who stumbles through adolescence, fails his way through school, and makes a mess of every social group he joins (Amory). As much as Darcy wants to believe Amory belongs in this kind of exalted company, it is apparent to readers, and probably to Amory as well, that he does not. I do not question Darcy's affection for Amory or his earnest desire to pay tribute to his "foster son," but the kind of heroism he describes was no longer possible in the modern world. Amory's experience of war is nothing like the picture Darcy paints. When Amory returns from Europe, the one thing he is sure of is that war had weakened his individualism, not strengthened it. He says he learned two things in the army: first, "that physical courage depends to a great extent on the physical shape a man is in," and second, "that I was as brave as the next man" (196). The battlefields of World War I did not transform him into a new Cúchulainn; if anything, they just made him even more ordinary.[28]

In addition, Darcy's attempt to valorize Amory in this poem is undercut by the overly sentimental, almost ludicrously clichéd, language and form of the piece. Darcy's use of stock "Oirish" lyrics places his lament in the context of popular musical numbers and evokes a commercial rather than "authentic" sense of Irishness. This lament, more than anything else in *This Side of Paradise*, highlights the problems within Darcy's own sense of Irishness. Though the monsignor repeatedly asserts the concept of essential Irishness and the eternal nature of the Celtic spirit, he reveals here the very constructedness of his own Irish identity—an identity heavily influenced by American popular culture. Darcy's Irishness, much like Amory's, is a performance of what he thinks Irishness should be in America. His lament should be a warning to Amory since it shows that the most noble and steady Irish-American influence in Amory's life is himself clinging to a woefully out-of-date and largely superficial sense of his own ethnic identity.

Before embracing an understanding of Irish ethnicity as a performative identity, Amory believes that it is an inherited trait naturally within him. Early in the novel, while still a child, he clings to a folk understanding of ethnic heritage that defines his own Irishness as a function of his blood. Amory thinks that since Beatrice is Irish, he too is Irish by default and that certain aspects of his behavior and personality can be attributed to his Irish bloodline. The very first line of *This Side of Paradise* enforces this fundamental belief in biological ethnicity and establishes Amory, like McTeague, as an inheritor of essential Irish traits: "Amory Blaine inherited from his mother every trait, except the stray inexpressible few, that made him worth while" (11). Fitzgerald then offers a lengthy description of Beatrice that emphasizes her Irish Catholic identity, and readers are to infer that these essential qualities are among the ones that Amory inherits. Beatrice's story is largely that of a woman attempting to escape her heritage and biological predispositions. She favors classically English behavior and tastes, but throughout her life she experiences certain lapses attributable to her Celtic blood. She believes that her history "must be thrown off" if she is ever to escape her Irish weaknesses (13). Amory spends his childhood believing that such biological dangers lurk within him too and that he must be ever vigilant to avoid being dragged down by the bad blood in his own veins.

When Amory meets Darcy, the monsignor reinforces this idea of Irish inheritance, though he obviously sees it as beneficial. For Darcy, Irish biology enables the continuity of the Celtic spirit. He attributes nearly every personal characteristic (physical appearance, intellectual preferences, emotional dispositions, cultural tastes) to ethnic identity and believes he knows the truth of Amory's identity by simple fact of the boy being Irish.[29] Darcy believes that Amory's fate is tied to his Irish nature and proclaims to him that the one thing he is sure of is, "Celtic you'll live and Celtic you'll die" (149–50). Such a statement implies that Amory does not even have a choice in the matter and that his life and death are prescribed by ethnic forces. In Darcy's mind, both he and Amory are essentially Celtic, and their whole identities are fundamentally defined by this single fact. This intense faith in ethnic heritage initially appeals to Amory because it seems to promise a stabilizing of identity; he envies Darcy's unwavering sense of self and craves to be a reincarnation of the monsignor so that he too can stand steadfast against the onslaught of modernity, but Amory's adult experiences force him to question his childhood belief in biological inheritance and teach him that Irishness is not so much in his blood as in his actions.

Rhodes claims that, "Born Irish, as it were, Amory spends a good deal of the novel shedding his birthright" (37); however, this seems an erroneous way to think of what happens in the novel. Amory does not try to shed his birthright, but rather tries to understand and embrace it. He wants to be Irish, especially after meeting Monsignor Darcy, and makes a serious effort to realize that goal; however, he learns that Irishness does not come naturally to him. Amory, like Huck, tries to remake himself to better fit in to society, but whereas Huck tried to attain a veneer of Anglo respectability, Amory struggles to achieve a functional façade of Irishness. What might look like Amory's shedding of his birthright is actually a series of failed attempts at achieving a supposedly authentic ethnic identity and his growing frustration at ever doing so. When Amory cannot find the Irishness inside of himself, he is forced to look outside of himself for models that he can emulate in performance.

Amory is no stranger to performative identity. As a child he is very aware of the necessity for adopting certain poses and social masks. Beatrice encourages many of his poses, but even when he is out from under her influence he feels a certain pressure "to conform to what others expect of him" (34). He does not even believe he has friends in his youth, merely "mirrors" that reflect his "posing" back to him and give him a chance to perfect his performative identities (33). In his childhood, he tries out several different identities, sometimes within moments of each other. At Myra St. Claire's bobbing party he starts out as a pretentious aristocrat ("My *dear* Mrs. St. Claire, I'm *fright*fully sorry to be late, but my maid . . . "), turns into a bad boy with a colloquial drawl ("I'm diff'runt . . . 'Cause I don't care, I s'pose . . . I been smoking too much. I've got t'bacca heart"), and finally he turns into a junior Don Juan ("Pale moons like that one . . . make people *mystériuse*. You look like a young witch with her cap off and her hair sorta mussed . . . Oh, leave it, it looks *good*") (17, 19, 20). At Princeton, Amory continues his performances. On his first day as a freshman, he dresses up and goes around acting like an upper-classman. His friend Tom later describes him as a "rubber ball" that easily adapts itself to its local corner of the world (83).

When Amory commits to trying out his Irish identity, he again treats the experience as a performance. Despite what Darcy tells him, there is no internal Irishness bubbling up from his soul or percolating in his veins, so the only way he can be Irish is to reflect the Irish characters he knows. Unfortunately, all of his Irish models prove difficult to successfully copy.

There are three significantly different Irish identities that Amory tries to perform, each one inspired by a different kind of Irishman. The first of these three is based on Monsignor Darcy. Darcy represents for Amory the intellectual, jolly monk whose life is filled with simple pleasures and stimulations of the mind. He is cut from the same mold as *Theron Ware*'s Father Forbes, and like Forbes, his greatest enjoyment is vibrant conversation with other brilliant minds over a glass of wine. On Amory's first meeting with Darcy, he is described like this:

> Monsignor was forty-four then and bustling—a trifle to stout for symmetry, with hair the color of spun gold and a brilliant, enveloping personality. When he came into a room clad in his full purple regalia from thatch to toe, he resembled a Turner sunset, and attracted both admiration and attention . . . He was intensely ritualistic, startlingly dramatic, loved the idea of God enough to be a celibate, and rather liked his neighbor . . . he was solid and enthusiastic and conservative . . . harmlessly modern, energetic and antic and entertaining. (29–30)

Amory adores Darcy, much as Fitzgerald adored Fay. The monsignor harkens back to a respectable and smart Irish identity completely unlike the vulgar and impoverished Famine Irish from which Amory wants to distance himself. Darcy is respected and, more importantly, as Amory realizes, he was "necessary to people . . . indispensable" (246). In every manner imaginable, Darcy exemplifies for Amory the very best aspects of the modern Irish American.

Amory is clearly flattered by the attention given him by Darcy and excited by the idea that the two of them really are very much alike. Darcy continually emphasizes their similarities, describes Amory as his reincarnation, and seems able "to guess Amory's thoughts before they were clear in his own head, so closely related were their minds in form and groove" (101). Darcy has the kind of life Amory wants, but there is one insurmountable obstacle to Amory replicating his mentor's identity and success: religious faith. Amory wants the lifestyle of the modern intellectual monk, but not the religion. He admires Darcy's life of the mind, but that kind of faith does not even seem possible anymore. The monsignor believes that Amory's "faith will eventually clarify" and that he will fully become Darcy's reincarnation; however, Amory does not share his optimism. "I'm rather pagan at present," Amory says. "It's just that religion doesn't seem to have the slightest bearing on life at my age" (196–7). After Darcy's death, Amory realizes that he "had leaned on Monsignor's faith" and that he never had any faith of his own. As appealing an Irishman as Darcy is, Amory cannot fully perform such an identity.

The second of the three Irish identities that Amory tries to perform is that of the Irish literary dandy. The dandy would seem to have refined sensibilities and tastes similar to the intellectual monk, but without the need for religion. Again, here was an Irish role model completely unlike the stereotypical image of Irish peasantry. Amory discovers the Irish dandy while at Princeton. A friend asks him, "Ever read any Oscar Wilde?" and Amory responds, "No. Who wrote it?" (54). Amory's subsequent reading of *The Picture of Dorian Gray* profoundly affects him. His world becomes "pale and interesting" as he tries "hard to look at Princeton through the satiated eyes of Oscar Wilde" (55). Amory even takes to pretending he is Dorian Gray and that his friend Kerry is Lord Henry, whose job it is to follow him around and "encourage in him wicked fancies and attenuated tendencies to ennui" (55). In Wilde, Amory finds another Irish persona he can admire, likely because Wilde, though an Irishman, seems so classically English. Amory was very comfortable with an English identity from his days of faux-British pretension in his childhood, and now he had discovered an Irishman who seemed so very like that sophisticated and romantic persona. Yet, here again, Amory struggles to perform such an identity.

At first, Amory's Wilde persona helps to reconcile his identity issues by offering him an Irish identity that had little to do with the Celt or common Irish culture. Through Wilde, Amory could claim a version of Irishness more palatable to his Anglo sensibilities. Yet, being an Anglo-Irish dandy proves too much work for him in the end. The ennui and the romance, especially, take too much effort and require Amory to limit his behavior in ways he is unwilling to do. Wilde's persona was great for an earlier era, but in Princeton during the 1910s, it seems anachronistic and counterproductive. Flapper girls do not seem to respond well to Amory's dandy behavior or his pretensions to romance, so he abandons the act. While attempting to seduce a young woman at a petting party, he realizes that his new romantic persona is counterproductive to the girl's expectations and changes tactics. He propositions her in very un-Wilde like terms: "Let's be frank—we'll never see each other again. I wanted to come out here with you because I thought you were the best looking girl in sight. You really don't care whether you ever see me again, do you?" (62). While the persona of Oscar Wilde has some appeal, Amory's goals are different than the Irish writer's. Amory believes that he is "temperamentally unfitted for romance," and so must look elsewhere for his Irish identity (92).

The third and final Irish identity that Amory tries to perform is that of the degenerate stereotype, a persona not unlike that of Sweeney. The stereotype, while foul, still holds some degree of appeal for Amory because he thinks it will make him uncommon and give him some sense of purpose. "A 'good man going wrong' attracts people," he says. "They stand around and literally *warm themselves* at the calories of virtue he gives off" (238). Amory always desires to be at the center of a crowd, and seems to consider spectacular failure and infamy as a possible alternative to glory. Amory's descent begins in the section of *This Side of Paradise* titled "Experiments in Convalescence" when he embarks on a drinking binge in response to his failed relationship with Rosalind (the character based on Fitzgerald's future wife, Zelda). Amory gives in to a "rather grotesque condition" and utterly abandons all pretensions to manners and society (185). In a drunken fit in a bar, he proclaims through slurred speech that he is now a "physcal anmal" who "don'givadam" about romance, and he claims his new philosophy is, "Seek pleasure where find it for tomorrow die" (186). Amory's binge seems at least partially predicated on the periods of alcoholic excess undertaken by his "Celtic mother" when he was a child, but more tellingly, he seems to be posing once again, living out the image of what he earlier thought of as the "somewhat common" Irish. Prior to meeting Darcy he had believed the Irish were vulgar, mindless, social misfits who consoled themselves with perpetual drunkenness. This original impression of the Irish was something Amory could actually replicate, and so he performs the role of a degenerate Irish drunk to perfection. Becoming an ignoble stereotype proves easier than becoming a noble personage.

Amory even searches for models for his degenerate persona and is "surprised by his discovery" of two American novelists who specialize in such characters: Frank Norris and Harold Frederic (195). During his "convalescence," Amory reads Norris' *Vandover and the Brute* and Frederic's *The Damnation of Theron Ware* and seems to cast his own life into the familiar mold of these stories. Like Theron Ware, Amory tosses aside his most cherished beliefs, abandons his allegiance to his church, and pursues (in vain) a smart and independent wild-Irish girl.[30] Like Vandover, another of Norris' atavistic protagonists, Amory falls from aristocratic heights to sordid poverty, sexual debauchery, and drunkenness, and he comes to imagine himself akin to an animal or monster, "a thing that frightened children and crept into rooms in the dark" (241). His performance of degeneracy gives him "an overwhelming desire to let himself go to the devil—not to go violently as a gentleman should, but to sink safely and sensuously out of sight" (242). This adopted identity of a reviled Irish monster seems like a last refuge that will allow Amory to "deteriorate pleasantly," but it too proves ultimately insufficient and a pose he cannot maintain (242).

Just as Amory believes there are no more opportunities for heroism in the modern world, he also believes there are no opportunities for tragedy. Amory wants to be a fallen, tragic monster, but his suffering, alas, is just too ordinary, and his fall from grace is not much of a fall at all. His new persona lacks the grandeur and pathos of a classically tragic figure like Faust or Oedipus; his story of romantic failures, thwarted ambitions, and subsequent alcoholic self-indulgence even pales in contrast to the stories of more contemporary figures like Vandover and Theron Ware. Amory wants to "go to the devil," but his ruination likely is not remarkable enough to get the devil's attention. His performance of a debased Irish identity is, ironically enough, "somewhat common." Everyone in his generation feels some degree of ruination, and so again the problem is that Amory cannot distinguish himself from the masses. He can never become monstrous enough or pathetic enough to evoke much sympathy or earn much attention. Even his most explicit attempt at infamy—a completely manufactured story about him spending the night with a woman in an Atlantic City hotel—only garners a few lines in the back of a newspaper. Simply put, no one cares if Amory Blaine goes to hell, which proves just as disappointing to the young man as when no one cared about his success.

At the end of *This Side of Paradise*, Amory learns of Rosalind's engagement to another man and a day later receives word that Monsignor Darcy has died. This "collapse of several pillars" in his life shocks him into his first earnest attempt at self-reflection (233). He realizes that "all enquiries" should have started "with himself," not with outside prototypes, and further concludes, "He was his own best example—sitting in the rain, a human creature of sex and pride, foiled by chance and his own temperament of the balm of love and children, preserved to help in building up the living consciousness of the race" (245). This moment marks Amory's abandonment of the search for the "fundamental Amory," his realization that he will not find fulfillment in performing external identities, and his acceptance of a more fluid, contextual understanding of his own self. At the same time, it marks a shift in his understanding of his ethnicity. Irishness proved neither an inherent element in his character, nor an identity he could wear like a mask. Ultimately, he could not feign Irishness any more than he could feign religious faith or academic interest or wartime courage or romantic attachment. He knows that "there had been a time when his own Celtic traits were pillars of his personal philosophy," but these traits had been the monsignor's, not his own, and as a result he grew "completely tired of the Irish question" (197). If he was Irish at all anymore, it was not because of biology or behavior, but because of his participation in a "living consciousness" that categorized him as so. He belongs to an invisible ethnicity that to him has no substantive defining features. Amory is Irish American only in so much as he is labeled Irish American. He represents a new kind of Irish character in American fiction whose defining characteristic is the very ambivalence of his Irishness.

Fitzgerald's description of Amory's ethnic anxieties and the character's ultimate realization of the instability of ethnic categories proves significant because it marks the beginnings of a major shift in thinking about Irish characterizations and more generally about the function of ethnicity in America. Fitzgerald describes ethnicity in *This Side of Paradise* as elusive, frustrating, and culturally constructed. Amory's desire to ground himself in the continuity of his ethnic heritage and his exasperation at trying to do so are predictive of the ethnic distress experienced by many literary characters that emerged over the next several decades, including Studs Lonigan and Scarlett O'Hara, who like Amory go in search of their own version of the "fundamental Amory," but find the endeavor just as problematic.

4 Replacing the Immigrant Narrative

The 1930s were a time of transition for Irish America, with 1931 being, according to historian J. J. Lee, a date that looms large in Irish-American historiography because it "marks the end of the immigration flow that had lasted since before the Famine" (36). The reduction in Irish immigration to the U.S. was extreme; in the 1920s, approximately 211,000 Irish immigrated to America, but that number declines to just 11,000 in the 1930s (Almeida 549). Though there were several contributing factors to this sudden drop-off, including more stringent U.S. immigration policies introduced in 1921 and 1924, the main cause was the Great Depression. With little to no prospects for work in America, fewer Irish emigrants came across the Atlantic.

As a result, the stories of the Irish in America came to depend less and less on an immigrant narrative. Kerby A. Miller suggests that Irish-American culture moving into the 1930s decreasingly focused on Irish nationalism while increasingly emphasizing specifically American concerns. Miller concludes that "[t]he long, dark winter of Irish exile in America was over," and he suggests that something new was beginning (555). As a community, Irish Americans no longer fundamentally imagined themselves to be the castoffs of national struggles on the other side of the Atlantic, victims of British oppression, interlopers on the American scene, or political and social outsiders in the U.S. They did not think of themselves as unwillingly displaced people whose loyalties belonged to an ancestral land. The Irish-American present, future, and even, to a large degree, the past were now rooted in American culture and history.

Irish-American literature after the Great Depression cannot be studied in quite the same way as what came before, because Irish-American identity, no longer rooted in an immigrant context, became increasingly indefinite and variable. As Lee observes, the study of Irish America in the twentieth century is "increasingly a study of generations long removed from Ireland," and as such, it requires different approaches than those used to study Irish-born generations (37). Lee suggests that it would be erroneous to assume that fifth- or sixth-generation Irish Americans behave as if they were Irish born. Though some may be inspired by Irish ancestry or influenced "to behave in a certain 'ethnic' manner," they are not necessarily comparable to what came before. He even argues that studies that ignore the differences between generations "lead to primitive stereotypes substituting for the complexity of historical reality" (37). Lee then suggests a reorientation of Irish-American studies that, instead of pursuing cross-generational similarities, would ask "how many [Irish Americans] consider their recorded ancestry a significant part of their sense of who they are. And insofar as they do, what exactly is their sense of the Irish dimension of their identity?" (37). This line of questioning allows us to investigate ethnic identity and literary representations of that identity without resorting to essentialist criteria.

In looking at the literature of the 1930s and beyond, we must not make the mistake of assuming that ethnic identity is static across time or of believing that the Irishness of a post-Depression character will be the same as a pre-Depression character; nor can we assume, for that matter, that the Irishness of one post-Depression character will look anything like that of another post-Depression character. We must instead distinguish between a character's "ancestral association" and "active identification" and ask in each individual case whether an Irish-American character considers his or her ancestry an integral part of their identity, and if so, we must then strive to discover how that character understands Irishness functioning within the self (Lee 38). This chapter turns its focus to the literature of the 1930s, specifically those novels that were written and published during the historic moment when Irish-American identity was in the process of shifting from an immigrant context to something altogether different. It focuses on the loss of the immigrant narrative and the often desperate need of Irish-American characters to find a replacement.

In abandoning the story of exile, Irish Americans had to turn elsewhere for narrative unity. Competing discourses of Irish-American identity emerged in the late 1920s and 1930s, many of which sought to subsume Irishness into pre-existent categories of politics, race, and social class. For some, being Irish American largely meant being part of the Democratic political party and being beneficiaries of New Deal policies of social reform; for others, Irishness primarily became a marker of whiteness and racial entitlement; and still for others, it implied working class honesty and an American value system derived from the virtues of the common man. Importantly, the identifiably Irish-American icons of the era—Al Smith, Henry Ford, and Jimmy Cagney among others—were all seen as primarily and unquestionably American. Their Irishness did not obstruct their national identities or mark them as others, but instead enabled their appeals to an American authenticity.

In literature of this period, Irish-American characters continue to display some of the ethnic uncertainties of modernist characters like Amory Blaine while also exhibiting a willingness to rewrite the story of their ethnic heritage. In these Depression era stories, we can see the start of a trend that would last through the rest of the century. Irish-American characters, cut off from Old World history and their own immigrant origins, redefine the stories of their families and communities with whatever materials are available to them. Instead of being ethnic outsiders, they remake themselves as racial, political, and social insiders.

Perhaps no other writer of this time was more closely associated with an Irish-American identity than James T. Farrell, and no character considered more iconically Irish American than his literary creation Studs Lonigan. Farrell's trilogy of novels—*Young Lonigan* (1932), *The Young Manhood of Studs Lonigan* (1934), and *Judgment Day* (1935)—chronicle life in a middle-class Irish neighborhood in Chicago and detail the struggles of the generation of Irish Americans who came of age between World War I and the Great Depression. Farrell responds to the increasingly ambiguous status of the Irish in America by showing Studs' ethnic confusion and social frustration in response to the rapidly dissolving Irish presence in his South Side Chicago neighborhood. In under a decade, what had once been an insular Irish Catholic enclave becomes a predominantly African-American community, and Studs, unsure what it means to be Irish in a non-Irish environment, redefines his ethnic heritage as a function of racial difference. Farrell presents Studs' short life as a study in ethnic trauma; it is a tragic portrait of a young man whose entire identity is defined by his connection to an Irish-American community, but who does not know what it actually means to be Irish anymore.

At first glance, Scarlett O'Hara may not seem all that similar to an urban tough like Studs Lonigan, but her complicated relationship with her ethnic past and her attempts to understand her own Irish identity during a period of radical social change reveal a familiar pattern; the struggle of an Irish-American woman from western Georgia in the 1860s proves not too different than that of a boy from Chicago in the 1920s since both are truly products of the 1930s. Margaret Mitchell's *Gone With the Wind* (1936) reaches back to the Civil War and the Reconstruction era to tell a story about an Irish-American family on a Southern plantation. Scarlett, like Studs, is a second-generation Irish American who experiences her ethnic heritage both as a mark of social otherness and as an enabling source of power. Faced with the destruction wrought by the Civil War and the implosion of the Southern aristocracy, Scarlett knits together a new personal identity that tries to use Irishness as a bridge between the Old and New South. Like Studs, she redefines her ethnic heritage as a fundamentally American narrative. Yet, Mitchell's rewriting of Irish-American history racializes Irish identity in America and results in an ending as equally troubling, if not as explicitly tragic, as *Studs Lonigan*.

Farrell's and Mitchell's novels, set in disparate locations and times, obsess over the same issues of Irish-American identity. They both attempt to reconstruct a new ethnic narrative that, while couched in the terms of the past, could speak to the present. Such historically removed stories featuring Irish-American protagonists of the imagined past had great appeal because they promised a kind of ethnic clarity missing in the modern world. Studs and Scarlett both live in time periods in which Irishness seems to hold more capital, in which Irish heritage more clearly signals difference, in which Irish communities still have static borders, and in which Ireland continues to loom large in the lives of immigrants and their children. In setting their stories in the past, Farrell and Mitchell help construct a notion of prelapsarian Irishness; readers are to understand that true Irishness had been lost before the modern era and that the current generation's claim to Irish ethnic identity required attempts to recover some of the authenticity of the past. As the protagonists of these stories strive to connect to their Irish roots, they allow readers to vicariously do the same. Studs and Scarlett, though figures of the Irish-American past, reveal more about Irish America of the 1930s and how it reconstructed the meaning of its own cultural heritage.

A PORTRAIT OF THE WRETCH AS A YOUNG THUG: JAMES T. FARRELL'S *STUDS LONIGAN*

In *A Portrait of the Artist as a Young Man* (1916), James Joyce recounts the semi-autobiographical coming-of-age of a young man raised in a middle-class Irish family who rebels against his society, his family, and his religion. Sixteen years later, James T. Farrell published a semi-autobiographical novel with the same basic elements. Studs Lonigan, like Stephen, is a young man from a middle-class Irish family raised in an urban environment of rigid social and religious governance. His family, like Stephen's, experiences financial hardship and physical dislocation, and his rebellion, again like Stephen's, includes bouts of social excess, sexual misadventure, and drunkenness. Studs wanders the streets of Chicago, much as Stephen wanders through Dublin, asking the same kinds of questions: should he join the priesthood? Should he go to school? Should he embrace the fervent nationalism and political causes so many of his friends embrace? Should he immerse himself in the culture of his Irish ancestors and find comfort in his heritage? Joyce imagines his hero as being able "to fly by those nets" of "nationality, language, and religion" that obstruct personal development (*Portrait* 206); however, Farrell imagines a protagonist who becomes hopelessly entangled in those same socially imposed constraints.

Studs Lonigan's story seems a whimpering echo of Stephen Dedalus'. Farrell appreciated Joyce's decision to describe the common, and even the vulgar, aspects of Irish life, and in *Studs Lonigan*, he seems to try to do something similar for Irish-American life. Those qualities of the Joycean Irishman that F. Scott Fitzgerald had found so disturbing seemed to Farrell to be the very basis on which twentieth-century Irish-American identity could be built. Unlike Fitzgerald, Farrell was not worried about discovering an Irish identity that was "somewhat common" since he was not in search of an extraordinary ethnic identity, only a practical one. He admired Joyce's irreverence toward exaggerated ethnic sentimentalism and emulated his approach and narrative style in order to present an American counterpoint to the most famous Irish coming-of-age story. Ezra Pound, who read the galleys of *Young Lonigan*, suggested to Farrell that his prose was too similar to Joyce's in *Portrait* and that he needed to find a way to make the language of his Irish characters different from Joyce's (Landers 105). Farrell responded,

> I had read Joyce, and pretty well forgotten him in all details at least a year, and the Portrait a year and a half before even starting the book, and any similarity was all unconscious. I reread most of the Portrait a month or so ago, and while doing so, I did feel that, with differences of time, climate, and country, there were certain similarities. (Landers 105)

Despite acknowledging the similarities between his work and Joyce's, Farrell believed that the story of the Irish in America was different than the story of the Irish in Ireland. In *Studs Lonigan,* he recasts one of the most uncompromising individuals of Irish modernism as one of the most compromised young men of American realism; he replaces a story of adversity and achievement with a story of adversity and decline. *Studs Lonigan* is a story of failure, made all the more tragic by the protagonist's limited ability to understand himself as either Irish or American, for unlike Stephen, Studs' Irishness is seen as a mark of difference in his environment with implications extending into categories of race and nationality.

Studs comes of age between World War I and the Great Depression and experiences the same pressures toward both cultural homogenization and ethnic authenticity as Amory Blaine; however, Studs grows up in an urban environment, which compounds his ethnic confusion with racial insecurity. Contemporary popular culture and pseudo-historic literature tend to minimize the early antagonism between Irish Americans and African Americans and the function of racism in the development of Irish-American identity, opting instead to posit a "romanticized narrative of shared oppression" between the two ethnic groups (Eagan 29). Farrell's work stands in stark contrast to later literature because it insists that, in this time and place, Irishness was largely defined by racial criteria. Studs stabilizes his ambiguous Irish identity by reinterpreting it as a brand of American whiteness. For him, membership in the South Side Irish community grants, above all other things, racial privilege and requires only that he defend the community from intrusions by racially undesirable groups. *Studs Lonigan* remains the most frank consideration of the racial construction of Irish-American identity in literature and offers an uncompromising perspective into an often ignored aspect of ethnic American history.

Studs became a symbol for a generation of Irish-American men who could identify with his ethnic anxieties and cultural confusions, even if they could not identify with his violent and immoral antics. In 1963, William V. Shannon remarked, "Few college educated Irish Catholics reach manhood without making [Studs'] acquaintance," and he went on to claim that the reading of Farrell's *Studs Lonigan*, along with Joyce's *Portrait*, was "part of a young Irishman's coming of age" (254). While Studs Lonigan might not hold the same currency in the Irish-American imagination as he once did, his story still proves a resonant narrative of ethnic transformation and functions as the pivotal Irish-American text between the stereotypes and sentimentalisms of the nineteenth-century and the later twentieth-century stories of ethnic reclamation.

Part of the declining popular interest in *Studs Lonigan* must be attributed to its critical, and sometimes scathing, depiction of Irish-American life. It is not a feel-good affirmation of Irish identity, and those who go into reading it with that expectation will be disappointed. Farrell had no interest in writing ethnic propaganda; he simply wanted to describe Irish America through the lens of literary realism. His Irish characters are far from any ideal and instead are bigoted, nervous people suspicious of social and economic reform and hostile to intellectual reason. They willingly submit to social and religious institutions that exploit them and suffer from a profound, culture-wide identity crisis. Daniel Shiffman argues that Farrell's novels do not celebrate diversity or affirm ethnic life, and due to this, they are largely ignored in the ethnic American canon. He adds,

> Farrell's portrayal of Irish-Americans suggests that ethnic experiences are not simply waiting for us to "celebrate" them . . . Learning to respond fully to the intolerance and self-delusion found in texts like *Studs Lonigan* is one of the biggest challenges in getting beyond a deliberately "celebratory"—and limited—multiculturalism. (77)

The intolerance and self-delusion that Shiffman mentions are in fact major components of Irish-American identity as understood by Farrell. *Studs Lonigan* describes a confusing and sometimes ugly moment in which the Irish-American community struggled to imagine itself in a rapidly modernizing American context, and it is the confusion and ugliness of this moment that define the Irishness of someone like Studs.

Born in Chicago in 1904, Farrell was the second of seven children in a lower-middle-class family of unambiguously Irish stock. All four of his grandparents were Irish-born immigrants who came to the U.S. in the wake of the Famine. Since 1830, when Irish immigrants arrived in Chicago to help build the Illinois and Michigan Canal, there had been a substantial Irish presence in the city; however, hostility from native Chicagoans kept the Irish in isolated communities (Landers 6). Farrell's parents were born in Chicago in the 1870s, around the same time as Frank Norris but on the opposite side of the city's Anglo–Irish divide. Though they were neither poor nor overburdened with children, Farell's parents sent him to be raised by his maternal grandparents who made their home in the South Side neighborhood described in *Studs Lonigan*. Critics have been at a loss to explain this apparently strange living arrangement of Farrell's youth; however, it seems likely that this was an example of Irish fosterage, a cultural tradition stretching back several centuries in which parents would give away a child to be raised and educated by another family member or close friend. Though uncommon in America, this was by no means uncommon in Ireland.[1]

Throughout his life, Farrell understood himself as both an American and an Irishman. He believed that the "effects and scars of immigration" were on his life, that the "past was dragging through [his] boyhood and adolescence," and that this past was defined by the "tragedy of his people" (Fanning 257). Unlike Fitzgerald's ethnic ambivalence, Farrell's ethnic certainty demonstrates a more confident and willing engagement with his history and heritage. Charles Fanning rightly identifies Farrell as a pioneer in reestablishing a self-consciously Irish voice in American fiction (258–60). This was possible largely because the Chicago community that Farrell grew up in was more self-consciously Irish than most.

Farrell describes the Chicago environment of his youth with what one critic calls "cartographic accuracy" (Carino 72). All of the settings of *Studs Lonigan* are based on real locations in and around 58th Street, near Washington Park. During the early twentieth century, Studs' neighborhood was an insular Irish enclave, though it was not, as many readers and critics assume, a stereotypical Irish tenement slum. Edgar M. Branch, a Chicago native who grew up during the same era only a few blocks from Farrell's neighborhood, remembers it like this:

> [A]n old, built-up district, plainer, more shopworn, less "modern" and less attractive than, for example, the expanding South Shore district, but nevertheless a respectable, mostly middle-middle class haven with a sprinkling of black residents. Generally speaking, the apartments and houses were well kept and pleasing. The streets were broad and clean. The stores of 58th Street, the central shopping strip for the neighborhood, were busy and served all the family needs of a striving, self-respecting community. (*Studs* 2)

Studs does not grow up in a ghetto overrun by gangs, filth, disease, and crime. He does not endure abject poverty or suffer conditions comparable to the ethnic neighborhoods described in the Chicago novels of Upton Sinclair, Richard Wright, or Theodore Dreiser. Unlike many other Chicago homes of the time, the house that Farrell grew up in had "steam heating, electricity, an indoor toilet, a telephone and even the services of a colored maid" (Landers 3). Likewise in Farrell's novel, the house that Studs grows up in is owned by the Lonigan family—a clear sign of their wealth and status. Farrell, who objected to the idea that his boyhood neighborhood was routinely characterized as "like, or akin to, a lower class Hell on the order of Dante's *Inferno*," did not want an imagined material poverty to overshadow the actual "pervasive spiritual poverty" of this working-class ethnic neighborhood (Branch, *Studs* 1; Shannon 254).

The real challenge of Farrell's South Side neighborhood was one of ethnic transformation. Just as Farrell reached manhood, the insular Irish community he grew up in was cracked wide open by a drop in Irish immigration and an increase in African-American migration to the Midwest. In less than a decade, the ethnic boundaries of Chicago were redefined in unprecedented fashion. Unlike the Irish of East Coast cities who were more accustomed to multi-ethnic environments, the Irish of Chicago had established themselves in well-defined neighborhoods and generally did not mix with other ethnicities, especially African Americans (Onkey 106). Farrell describes the South Side Irish community of 1916 as utterly unaware of the transformation that would change their lives in just under a decade: "[They] felt that they had become settled for life, and they did not realize that under their feet the growth of Chicago, the change of Chicago, was going on, and this whole neighborhood was going to change, and all that they felt secure was going to crumble" (*Reflections* 192–3).

Between 1916 (the year Farrell's novel begins) and 1918, 450,000 African Americans moved to Chicago. In 1920, only 15% of the population of the Washington Park neighborhood where *Studs Lonigan* is set was black, but that rises to 92% by 1930 (just a year before Studs dies) (Onkey 109). This radical and sudden shift in the ethnic composition of Chicago led to a series of race riots during the summer of 1919, as described in the second book of the *Studs Lonigan* trilogy. Farrell was not in the city during the riots, but he knew several boys who joined anti-black gangs in the wake of Chicago's "Red Summer" and later admitted that he shared their prejudices (Onkey 112).

Though *Studs Lonigan* is set in the time and place of Farrell's own childhood and populated with characters based on real persons he knew as a boy, Farrell stopped short of describing the book as autobiography. For starters, Studs Lonigan's story is not James T. Farrell's story. The Studs character was based on a boy that Farrell knew in his youth, William "Studs" Cunningham. Studs Cunningham had been a legendary street tough who, like his literary double, died young in pathetic circumstances right at the start of the Great Depression (Landers 82).[2] Farrell believed that Cunningham's limited aspirations and attitudes drove him toward social failure and an early death, but he also believed that those aspirations and attitudes were not uncommon, and that under slightly different circumstances, Cunningham's sad life could have been his own. Farrell wrote that *Studs Lonigan* was not an attempt to represent what life meant to him, but rather an attempt to "recreate a sense of what life meant" to Studs (Howland 22).

Nothing looms as large in Studs Lonigan's mind as his relationship to the insular society of his Irish Catholic community, and as a result his sense of what life means is largely determined by his social environment. Studs fundamentally understands himself within a group context and judges his successes and failures by his adherence to, or deviation from, communal values. To fully understand Farrell's urban tragedy, we must consider Studs' sense of his own place within his imagined community and his inability to sustain a functional Irish-American identity in relation to it.

If a community is distinguished, as Benedict Anderson suggests, by the style in which it is imagined, then what distinguishes Studs' neighborhood is the very privation of substantive imagining (6). The culture described in the books is opposed to creativity, free thought, and intellectualism, and it is suspicious of individuals who espouse notions of progress and reform. Boys like Danny O'Neill (Farrell's literary alter ego) who have ambitions for higher education and life beyond 58th Street are odd balls who single themselves out for mockery by other children. Studs knows that, in his community, boys who study music, read books, write poems, and paint pictures are "sissified" and "crazy" (101). Real men, men like Studs, do not think too much about things, because they are liable to have "goofy and fruity" thoughts about which they "hadn't better let anyone know" (99). Conforming to community expectations certainly means conforming to a kind of Irish masculinity that stands in opposition to Anglo gentility. Like McTeague, Sweeney, and Amory (during his "convalescence"), Studs associates his Irishness with his physical body and public behavior; however, the community also demands conformity of the mind, and so Studs learns to be Irish in both thought an action.

In 1948, Farrell wrote, "In *Studs Lonigan* you see boys, and also others, living in a world without ideas. The most wonderful instrument in this world is the human mind. The contempt for the mind, the contempt for reason and thought is implicit in the story of Studs" (qtd. in Branch, "Destiny" 103). Studs internalizes this contempt for the mind. Whenever he takes a moment to think about something, he criticizes himself and is ashamed. He considers his imagination dangerous because it makes him uncomfortable or leaves him depressed. It is when he indulges his imagination that he has "dirty thoughts" about his sister and concludes that he "must be a bastard" (58), or similarly, when he fantasizes about being a hero that he becomes "utterly miserable" (203). So he learns to avoid abstract thought and personal fantasy, and in effect, becomes a censor of his own mind.[3]

Though scholars almost always categorize Farrell as a practitioner of literary realism, his descriptions of Stud's fragmented identity and damaged psyche are thoroughly modernist and quite reminiscent of Fitzgerald's descriptions of Amory Blaine's collection of personas. In a moment of unusual self-awareness, Studs describes his own mind as "a compartment with many shutters in it, like a locker room," and behind these shutters he isolates aspects of his own identity that he cannot reconcile into a unified whole (36). He essentially understands his own mind as a site of surveillance and control for discrepancies with his external world. This has led scholars like Ann Douglas to conclude that Studs has no real inner life and that his thought patterns "constitute an external stream-of-consciousness" largely defined by his environment (494). Given the impossibility of Studs forging a consistent internally defined sense of self, it makes sense that he would fall back on his community for definition.

Studs' imagination never extends beyond his immediate context. For all practical purposes, there is no world beyond Washington Park for him. Even when he thinks of going to Europe to fight the Germans, he imagines that his company of marines will be comprised of "all the guys . . . from Fifty-eighth Street" (185). His sense of self is so grounded in his community that he can never imagine breaking away from it the way Tommy Mulligan and Huck Finn do. There is no frontier to which Studs can escape. He does not dream, like those earlier Irish-American boys, of independence and individual prosperity; rather, he dreams of conformity and the maintenance of the status quo.

Studs only understands himself in the context of a group, whether that be his family, his neighborhood, his ethnic community, or his country. He has no real individual identity or understanding of himself as an independent entity, only a sense (albeit a vague one) of what it means to be a Lonigan, or a 58th Street kid, or an Irish Catholic, or an American. He thinks of himself as a function within these communities, as an expression of their ideals, and as a paragon of their values. His greatest ambition is to be noticed, accepted, and admired by others in these communities, as demonstrated in his euphoria after defeating Weary Reilly in a street fight:

> [H]e was going to be an important guy, and all the punks would look up to him and brag to other punks that they knew him; and he would be . . . well, in the limelight. Maybe it would set things happening as he always knew they would; and he would keep on getting more and more important. (78)

The act of defeating Weary Reilly in his childhood becomes the defining moment of Studs' life because it creates the character of Studs Lonigan that he would perform for the rest of his life. Over a decade later, on the verge of death, he still believes that the "fundamental Studs" (to borrow Amory Blaine's rhetoric) is "the champ fighter of the block" (79).

Studs goes through his life as if he is the lead actor in the movie version of Studs Lonigan's life or as if he is trying to do an imitation of himself. Douglas describes him as, "in rehearsal for a fantasied on-stage performance" (494). At the start of the novel, Studs is in the bathroom mugging in front of the mirror and trying to perfect his persona: "He was Studs Lonigan, a guy who didn't have mushy feelings! He was a hard-boiled egg that they had left in the pot a couple of hours too long . . . He stuck the fag back in his mouth and looked like Studs Lonigan was supposed to look" (10). While still a child, Studs believes that his essential character is already predefined and waiting for him to embody it. All he needs to do is look and act like the character he imagines he is supposed to be. When Studs thinks of himself, it is in the third person. This, more than anything else, highlights the profound dislocation within his identity. He only understands himself as a character in the narrative of his community, and he thinks of himself in purely superficial terms that fluctuate with his rising or falling status in the neighborhood. In good times, he thinks of himself as "Young Lonigan, the Chicago sensation" or "The Great Studs Lonigan, the battler" (61, 251); when he feels abandoned he is "Lonewolf Lonigan . . . a man alone forced to fight by himself, an enemy of society, a burglar and robber" (228–9); in moments of misery or depravity, he is "Pig Lonigan" the drunk, or "Slob Lonigan" who cannot get himself a "decent girl" (363, 528). Such character titles simplify his identity and give him the illusion of knowing himself, but all he has really done is borrow identities from popular culture. His various personas are imitations of notable Irish-American celebrities like Gentleman Jim Corbett, the scientific boxer; Jimmy Cagney, the consummate tough guy actor; Rube Wadell, baseball's eccentric southpaw pitcher; and Bugs Moran, the notorious Chicago gangster. Douglas describes Studs' mind as "a collage of accepted clichés" (494). Indeed, Studs spends his short life slipping in and out of simplistic, ready-made identities, never for a moment imagining that there could be a Studs Lonigan independent of his reputation in the South Side of Chicago.

Studs describes having a persistent feeling of alienation, what he calls his "old not-belonging feeling," which is obviously a problem for a boy who defines himself solely by his status within his community (35). It seems odd that he would feel like an outcast given that he enjoys the privileges of being a favored son in an urban Irish enclave, that he worships along with a unified Irish Catholic parish, that his father's immigration confers on him an immediate sense of ancestry, and that he himself is seen by other children as having a face in which "all the Irish race" is personified (159). Studs should be able to use Irishness as the organizing principle of his identity, but all of his attempts to do so fail.

Studs is a brilliantly realized ethnic character in that he viscerally embodies the conflict between self-conscious identification and ancestral association. He is as confident in his Irish identity as Ned Harrigan's Dan Mulligan or Harold Frederic's Father Forbes, but nonetheless is as clueless about his Irish identity as Fitzgerald's Amory Blaine. For Studs, being Irish means adhering to a very thin set of behaviors circulating in popular culture. He knows almost nothing about Irish history and culture other than what he learns from movies and popular songs, and he largely remains unaware of Irish-American life beyond 58th Street. As for literature, Studs knows his father reads and enjoys Mr. Dooley's columns in the newspaper, but does not understand the humor or wisdom of the barroom philosopher.[4] Although many of the characters in the book think of Studs as authentically Irish and although many readers have looked at him as an essentially Irish boy, the actual Irish "stuff" of his persona is paper thin. Farrell thus presents an Irish-American icon whose Irish identity is weirdly contradictory. Yet, it is this apparent contradiction between simultaneous confidence in one's ethnic identity and confusion about the substantive qualities of that ethnic identity that Farrell describes as defining the Irish-American experience of Studs' generation.

Irishness, for Studs, is a local phenomenon. He has no understanding of a deeper Irish-American story in which he could exist or participate. His neighborhood is, as Farrell describes it, a "world without ideas," and so it becomes a hollowed-out cultural space that works like an echo chamber to amplify stereotypes, social clichés, and empty ethnic posturing—which is not to say that there is no substantive Irish-American narrative in the community, it is just that Studs has no access to it.

The Irish-American narrative offered to Studs is a story of immigrant suffering and sacrifice, a story that belongs, according to Farrell, to "the sons and daughters, the grandsons and granddaughters of the disinherited of the earth" (*Reflections* 10). It presupposes that Ireland is a lost paradise and that the Irish in America are exiles who left behind their hearts in a sweeter world, and it also frames the story of the Irish in America as primarily one of social and economic hardship. Farrell describes the established Irish-American narrative in a later essay as one of Old World persecution and New World perseverance: "They came from the shores of that island whose history is one of the most bitter of all nations. Most of them were poor immigrants. Some of them could not read or write. They belonged at the bottom of the American social and economic ladder" (qtd. in Shaughnessy 49). The narrative offered to Studs requires that he understand himself as engaged in a multi-generational climb up that ladder. His role in the Irish-American community is proscribed; he must lead a life that makes all of the earlier generation's sacrifices and sufferings worthwhile. He and his friends must finally lift the Irish community out of its period of misery into an era of prosperity.

Yet, this story does not resonate with Studs. He does not share his parents' nostalgia for the old country or dream, as his father does, that he will be able to "take a trip to the old sod . . . and look up all his relatives" (19). He does not go about singing John McCormack songs like his old man, nor does he find his father's descriptions of "those ragged days" of pauperism even remotely romantic (14). Irish history bores Studs, and it is unlikely he could even locate Ireland on a map. He hears some of the Irish around him discussing politics and Ireland's independence, but is ignorant of the issues and not interested in such topics. Riding the train in Chicago, he expresses contempt for Irish Americans who show interest and allegiance to Irish causes: "A monkey-faced mick blubbered tears, whining that Padraic Pearse was dead, whoever that guy was" (206). In short, there is no continuity between the Irish past and Studs' American present.

Yet, the older generation repeatedly tries to envision Studs and his friends as the legacy of impoverished immigrants. At graduation, Father Gilhooley evokes Famine-era imagery when he tells Studs and his classmates that their education has been a "journey across the stormy and wave-tossed sea of life" made possible only by parents who "suffered and worried and fretted, sacrificed, stinted" (28). Studs' father similarly chastises his boy by evoking the narrative of generational responsibility: "We worked hard for you, and we don't want to feel that we done it all for nothing. You owe us something in return" (226). Studs feels little obligation to what is to him an archaic past he faintly can imagine. He chafes at the insinuation that he is beholden to anyone and informs his father, "I'm my own boss" (226). Studs is a young man of the here and now, and his father's appeals to shared history and heritage mean almost nothing at all.

The old Irish narrative does not even make sense to Studs. The Irish in his community seem proud of the poverty of their past and wear the suffering they experienced in the old country like a badge of pride, but they also are critical of the so-called shanty Irish and "pig-in-the-parlor micks" who still live among them (311). Similarly, but at the other end of the spectrum, the older generation expresses a general commitment to education and financial development and a hope that their boys will grow up to be priests or prominent businessmen or politicians, but they regard "highbrow, lace curtain Irish" as undesirably effete (54). Pat Lonigan even tells his son that, though he needs to find a high-paying job, he is "better off without an education" because it might turn him into a "high-hat snob" (225). Studs does not know how to respond to an ethnic narrative that routinely undercuts its own ideals.

Similarly, he is unsure how to respond when that narrative grossly misrepresents the actual world he lives in. Farrell repeatedly emphasizes the discontinuity between the community's idealized narrative of their children's lives and the reality experienced by those same children. He juxtaposes Father Gilhooley's flattering description of Studs and his classmates as "sturdy, well-behaved, beloved, and, yes, handsome children" with scenes of those same boys cursing, smoking, and feeling-up girls at the graduation party (28). Later, Farrell offers an even more jarring example of the local narrative discrepancy in a short passage about Mrs. Lonigan and Mrs. Reilly. The two mothers brag to each other about how wholesome and wonderful their sons are, but this exchange sits right in the middle of descriptions of Studs and Weary drinking, fighting, whoring, and (in Weary's case) raping a young woman. Neither woman, even when presented with the evidence of her son's behavior, can relinquish the vision of her child as an essentially wholesome Irish Catholic boy.

Mary Lonigan wants her son to be a paragon of Irish Catholic virtue, and Pat Lonigan wants his son to grow up to be a "real Lonigan," but Studs does not know what any of this means (347). He knows that both ideas are rooted in a heritage that he nominally shares with his parents, but on the surface the ideas seem vague, ineffectual, and often contradictory. The Lonigans conceive of Irish America and their family's story in a way that does not speak to Studs' immediate circumstances. Shannon argues that one of the main difficulties for children of immigrants is an inability to understand "their often ambiguous relationship to the past of their own families," which is certainly the case with Studs (250). He does not see how his parents' nostalgia for Ireland or their love of Irish culture can help him find a job, or win Lucy Scanlan's heart, or beat Weary Reilly in a fight, or ensure his reputation on the street.

Complicating Studs' discomfort with his ethnic identity is his desire to claim a legitimate American identity. He experiences local pressure to be demonstrably Irish concurrent with a more global pressure to assert his Americanness, and the two do not always go hand in hand. Full assimilation proves problematic for Studs because even within his small Irish community there is a cultural history of unease with Anglo dominance. Irish identity in America still implied, to some degree, an anti-Anglo identity. Writers like Fitzgerald and T. S. Eliot interpreted this aspect of Irishness as evidence of commonality and vulgarity; however, other writers, including Margaret Mitchell, saw the anti-Anglo aspect of Irish identity as a sign of vitality and strength. In *Studs Lonigan*, Farrell shows the Irish community valorizing and rewarding the non-gentile, anti-Anglo qualities as well. The community wants their boys to be tough workingmen, with slightly rough edges and no pretensions. Studs embraces this fully and becomes the roughest, toughest boy in the neighborhood. The very qualities that make McTeague and Sweeney seem like monsters in an Anglo world make Studs seem like a champ in the Irish world. In his immediate context, Studs knows that he needs to be masculine, strong, unemotional, and sexually experienced. Yet, he also wants to assimilate and experiences discomfort similar to Huck Finn's when trying to fit in. As a result, his performance of Americanism becomes a grotesque parody.

Studs lives during a period in which American nationalism reached a fever pitch, and he understandably responds to the patriotic passion leading up to World War I with the requisite amount of fervor. He even offers up the greatest sign of loyalty a person can give to an imagined community; Farrell writes that Studs "was prepared to fight, and, if necessary die for his country," but he also hints at the boy's conflicted motives when he then has Studs lapse into a selfish fantasy of being a "brave and gallant soldier" that everyone recognizes and admires (182–3). Studs believes that his patriotism offers him tangible benefits in his world and entitles him to opportunities not available to ethnic others. He imagines that the act of espousing pride in America can ground his own unstable identity and give shape to his character. Shiffman describes Studs as having "an intense, even grotesque, faith in the American Dream" (70). This hyper-Americanism exists in relation to his hypo-Hibernianism as a more immediate, practical, and enticing prospect for his devotion.

Of course, Studs understands America in a woefully underdeveloped manner. He has no real sense of the country, its history, its politics, or its place in the world, and instead he clings to, in Shiffman's words, a "confused, idealized notion of a true, 'white' America" (73). Being American to Studs means something vaguely like being tough, respected, good, and superior. All he needs to do is show more pride than anyone else around him and he will be the most American of them all. He sees no irony or conflict in ideology when he steals a small flag from a little girl during a parade in order to demonstrate his own patriotism, or when he mutilates the pledge of allegiance in a moment of solemn tribute to Old Glory, or when he denies that people of foreign descent can be American (211, 182). Studs' brand of patriotism is mostly parroting of jingoistic slogans. "America is America," he proclaims, "and it should be for Americans" (821). In Studs' mind, blacks, Greeks, Italians, Jews, Poles, Eastern Europeans, and Bolsheviks of any national background have no claim to American identity, but he of course leaves room for the Irish, even though he is aware that others question his kind too.

In a brief scene in *The Young Manhood*, several boys taunt the Irish kids of Washington Park by questioning whether the Irish are "hundred-percent Americans." One boy says, "No, because they believe in the Pope," and another suggests that the Ku Klux Klan should "come around looking for the Irish some night" (267). Despite Studs' faith that he is as American as one can be, there are still some lingering notions in his country that the Irish are a foreign population. Nativism persists in 1920s Chicago and forces Studs to consider how the Irish are any different from all of the other immigrant communities that he himself despises.

For Studs, being Irish makes being American somewhat difficult because Irish identity still had a lingering symbolic connotation of inauthenticity. The Irish were almost, but not quite, fully American. There is still a vague whiff of the Old World in Studs' neighborhood, something vaguely foreign of which he remains suspicious. On some levels, he is eligible, if not entitled, to an American identity, but on others, he finds opportunity blocked by an ethnic narrative that runs counter to the national narrative. As has been observed by numerous scholars, U.S. history has largely been written within a context of Anglo-Saxon ambition and ideals. From its inception, the American narrative was fundamentally a narrative of white, Anglo-Saxon progress. Yet, Studs finds himself pulled back into an ethnic narrative that historically has been at odds with Anglo-Saxon culture and at times a victim of Anglo-American ideals. He cannot see his own life as coincidental with American history if he clings to an ethnic identity that casts him as the traditional counterpoint to the culture that defines that history. Whereas Amory Blaine suspected that being Irish was "somewhat common," Studs suspects it might be worse than that. Yet, it is not like he can just stop being Irish or the child of Irish parents or the young hero of the Irish block. The old Irish narrative that buffers and sustains his parents and their generation simply does not work for him, but that does not mean he cannot create a new Irish narrative.

Studs re-imagines Irishness as a fundamentally racial identity. He reconstructs his ethnic boundaries by asserting racial privilege, which appears to him the only useful and practical aspect of his Irish-American heritage. Membership in his community presupposes that he is Irish, but Studs has no real sense of what Irishness is, only what it is not. So, he spends the better part of the novel defining his own Irishness as a counterpoint to other ethnicities. He is Irish because he is not black or Jewish or Polish or Hungarian. Studs believes he lives in a "white man's neighborhood" near a "white man's park" inside of a "white man's country" (366, 221, 478). As other ethnic groups begin to encroach on his domain, he asks, "[W]here ull a white man go to?" which effectively re-imagines the dissolution of the urban Irish community as a narrative of racial conflict (124).

On the surface, Studs' attitudes toward African Americans might seem to be a repetition of Irish-American beliefs about race and whiteness from the nineteenth century. His racist rhetoric does not seem all that far removed from Pap Finn's ranting about freed black men or Dan Mulligan's call to arms against the black residents of the Five Points. Yet, Studs' racism works toward different ends. Noel Ignatiev's and David R. Roediger's studies of Irish whiteness focus almost exclusively on the nineteenth century and the early relations between Irish immigrants and freed blacks, but Studs lives in an era several generations removed from this. He is not an immigrant primarily concerned about labor competition with former slaves or about the "pleasures of whiteness" that provide an extra wage for his work (Roediger 13). In *Studs Lonigan*, the Irish community does not view the black newcomers as obstacles to economic success, but rather as invaders threatening the stability and purity of their community and, by extension, that of the nation. Studs' racism emerges from a primarily nationalist origin, not a financial one, and he mobilizes the energy of his prejudices toward clarifying Irishness as a brand of Americanness. He does not use his hatred primarily as socio-economic leverage, but as patriotic affirmation. In order to normalize Irish identity, he claims that the un-Irish is also un-American.

Studs' racism is not founded on a hierarchy of racial superiority/inferiority, but on an ideology of difference. Walter Benn Michaels links this shift in American thinking on ethnic difference to the "essentialized racism" of the 1920s Cultural Pluralism movement (*Our America* 64).[5] Michaels argues that the pluralist commitment to difference intensified racism by suggesting that all ethnic differences were part of "an unmeasurable and hence incomparable racial essence" (66). In such a system, the differences between a black man and a white man are not "of degree," but "of kind"; in other words, it was not that members from two races exhibited varying amounts of the same qualities, but instead they exhibited "essential" qualities and fundamental differences unique to their group (*Our America* 66). This pluralist type of racism that Michaels sees throughout modernist literature is very evident in *Studs Lonigan*. Unlike Pap Finn and Dan Mulligan, who believe in a hierarchy of races and struggle to show the Irish to be superior to blacks, Studs espouses a belief in the essential difference between the Irish and blacks. He does not want to merely claim to be better than a black man; he wants to show the black man to be fundamentally incomparable to the Irish. Studs believes that blacks have no claim to American identity because America is fundamentally a "white man's country." By asserting a pluralist definition of ethnicity, Studs aligns Irish identity with American identity on the grounds that both Irishness and Americanness are essentially different than blackness.

What Studs has in common with Pap Finn and Dan Mulligan is that an African-American presence gives him an opportunity to prove himself to mainstream America. Studs' essentialist racism not only affirms his status as a white man, but also asserts a claim to inclusion in the national community. The black man becomes, in Studs' imagination, a racial scapegoat who takes up the burden of difference and becomes fundamentally non-American so that the Irish can become fully and essentially American.

Studs is not alone in his pluralist racism. The expression of racial and ethnic differences is the primary means of self-definition for the entire South Side Irish community. In practical terms, to be Irish in Studs' neighborhood means giving voice to and sometimes acting on a range of prejudices. Studs and his neighbors construct their communal identity through inversion, through a racialized logic of deduction, and imagine themselves to be a desirable counterpoint to the African-American community. Their whiteness, which helps define their privilege and citizenship, is manufactured through their contact with a non-white community. In reading through the novels that constitute the trilogy, it is easier to assemble a list of what the Irish are not than what they are. A persistent nervousness exists in the neighborhood that compels the Irish characters to repeatedly affirm that they are not black or Jewish or Polish or Italian. The worst insults the boys lob at each other are racial; a degenerate Irish kid is a "nigger" or "hebe" (82). Adults describe noble Irish behavior and sportsmanship in contrast to that of "dagoes and wops and sheenies" (88). Studs himself gives in to this racial nervousness and obsesses throughout his life about having a very un-Irish "sheeny's nose" (5). This construction of ethnicity through inversion results in Irish-American identity becoming a kind of hollowed-out space with boundaries defined, not by the presence of Irish qualities, but by the rejection of foreign ones.

Shiffman suggests that "racism and ethnic chauvinism are rather desperate means of self-definition and entitlement" in Studs' neighborhood (68). In truth, at least for Studs' generation, they are the only means of definition. The Irish community makes itself more desirable to dominant American culture by affirming and emphasizing the undesirability of African Americans and other minority groups. By participating in a rhetoric that defines these groups as quintessentially un-American, Irish Americans imply their own status as part of mainstream America. For Studs and his friends, racism is the primary attribute of their American identity.

Though the black presence in the novel is persistent, it is vaguely defined. Notably, there are no realized black characters in *Studs Lonigan*. They mostly lurk at the margins of the story as faceless and motiveless figures that have no individual features or ambitions. As a result, the Irish community's response to the demographic threat is generalized, not specific. They do not hate a specific family or target an individual for punishment; instead, they detest an abstract, amorphous sense of blackness. Studs' racist rhetoric exhibits these generic qualities. Though passionate about his prejudices, he never actually expresses any specific reason why he hates blacks. They are different, and that is all that matters to him.

Since the Irish community's understanding of black identity is generalized, Studs' attempts to define himself in contrast to this identity results in an equally generalized persona; he is passionately, but generically, white and American. His attempts to construct a racialized account of Irish-American life similarly develop into a generic narrative of fear. To Studs, being Irish means being constantly under assault by non-white races. Lauren Onkey observes that the encroaching African-American community had a "potent—perhaps pathological—hold" on the Irish-American imagination, constantly reminding them of "the fragility of their position" (106, 108). However, while this fear was indeed "potent" enough to result in the dissolution of the 58th Street Irish community, it was largely a fear constructed in their own minds. The actual threat posed by the incoming black community bears little resemblance to the narrative of ethnic invasion that Studs and his neighbors communally imagine.

Studs' main complaint about the black community is that they are in his space. They do not appear to be a hostile presence, but they evoke Studs' anger by just being there. He complains about their presence at the beach, the park, the community center, and the church, never acknowledging that these specific places are environments where communities come together and where these newcomers are likely trying to acclimate and introduce themselves to their new neighbors, not engage in violence or mischief. Yet, Studs persists in seeing an invasion and imagines all kinds of dangers. He imagines that black men want to rape the good Irish girls of the neighborhood and that black women want to seduce and ruin Irish boys. He imagines black villains waiting to ambush him around every corner. And when black families start attending mass at the new St. Patrick's Church, he imagines the racial conflict rising to a whole new level. Studs remarks, "[I]t was a goddamn beautiful church, and what was it for now—a handful of black bastards" (521). He, of course, does not see the problem with taking the Lord's name in vain while praising the church; he only sees evidence that the Irish are under siege even in their most sacred spaces.

Onkey believes that "[o]nce African Americans enter the neighborhood, the Irish Americans feel that they have lost their distinctiveness" (115). However, it seems more accurate to say that the entrance of the black community actually shores up Irish distinctiveness. Onkey's statement suggests that Studs and his neighbors were in danger of losing their unique ethnic identity, when in fact they had already largely lost it. Especially among second-generation Irish Americans like Studs, Irishness had come to have few distinguishing features. The arrival of a new ethnic group does not endanger Studs' ethnic status—it finally gives him an opportunity (albeit a crude one) to be Irish. In *Studs Lonigan*, the perceived invasion by blacks gives the Irish (especially the ambivalently Irish second generation) the opportunity to perform their ethnic difference and to demonstrate the ways in which they are more eligible for American citizenship. The Irish community's racism (including the race riots described in *The Young Manhood*) and their eventual choice to abandon Washington Park and move elsewhere are the methods they choose to make Irishness an acceptably white, American identity.

The Irish community in *Studs Lonigan* confronts the demographic changes in the neighborhood by constructing a new narrative of ethnic invasion. In this narrative, the Irish are transformed into an innocent group besieged by savage aggressors and are the victims of cultural assault. They fear that wave upon wave of Jews and blacks are "gonna overrun the south side" (124). They even express their fear by adopting nativist rhetoric; the Irish claim that other minorities do not have "any right" to be in a white, American neighborhood (221). They of course do not see the irony in adopting the logic of those who objected to Irish immigration in the nineteenth century on the same grounds.

When the Irish families move out of the 58th Street neighborhood, they give up their insular ethnic community, scatter themselves throughout Chicago, and create a new urban Irish diaspora. Studs' father even describes the Irish community's forced exile from the South Side as equivalent to the Famine emigrants' exile from Ireland. After moving away, Pat Lonigan tells his son that he feels about 58th Street "the same way I feel about Ireland," as if he has lost his home all over again (510). As is the case with Gerald O'Hara (discussed in the next section), Pat Lonigan views his entire life through the filter of Anglo–Irish relations. He clings to a model of reality that ultimately does not work. He equates being forced out of his South Side home by another minority group with being driven out of Ireland by the British ruling class. His tendency to view both African Americans and British as the same kind of villain oversimplifies and misrepresents the actual issues. Such sentiment combines Irish and American narratives and conflates the defining tragedy of modern Irish identity with the ethnic transformation of Chicago.

Fanning argues that the *Studs Lonigan* trilogy criticizes one of Irish culture's most important symbols—home ownership—by showing its "ironic transformation" into something of diminished respectability: "The Irish immigrant's quest for safe shelter becomes racist flight from a new, black migration to the city" (267). Fanning is correct in calling attention to the importance of this aspect of Farrell's text. Some of the most disturbing and uncomfortable moments in the book occur when the Chicago Irish attempt to make sense of their current racial conflict through a lens of Irish cultural history. Farrell encourages readers to recognize that his characters' "white flight" is nothing like the history of Irish being driven from their homes by the British, and in this realization, readers perhaps can appreciate the depth of Studs' ethnic confusion. Studs knows that being Irish means you protect your home against invaders, but does not really know why. This is simply another truism of Irish identity that he accepts and attempts to enact in his character. Yet, having been cut off from his cultural history and the knowledge of why home ownership became an Irish cultural value, Studs fails to see the irony in his own prejudicial behavior. Without historical context, his attitude becomes empty ethnic posturing with possibly dangerous ramifications.

Studs' belief in a new Irish-American narrative founded on racial essentialism and the presence of non-white/non-American invaders fails to sustain him, but he refuses to abandon it. He clings to his racist posture because he believes whiteness is tangible and unchanging and that it confers on him a "primacy of identity" (Michaels, *Our America* 140). Studs believes in his essential Irishness. With such a belief, he cannot abandon his ethnic heritage the way Amory Blaine does by simply giving up certain beliefs and dissociating himself from Irish influences, nor can he abandon it by slipping past the nets of Irish culture like Stephen Dedalus. Instead, he must futilely try to maintain the ethnic boundaries in his world. He must continually assert the racial difference of Irish America even in the face of evidence that those differences are vanishing. Studs tries to maintain his position even as the South Side Irish community dissolves, as his sister marries a Jewish man, as Irish-American political activists call for Irish–black unity, and as Irish-Catholic congregations incorporate new non-Irish parishioners. Shiffman argues that Studs' downfall is attributable to his inability to clearly define "social and cultural boundaries" (67). Onkey goes as far as to suggest that Studs' racism sickens and eventually kills him (107–10). Yet, even after all of his failures and when approaching death, Studs never abandons his faith in the racialized narrative of Irish-American whiteness. As Studs dies, he imagines he sees "streaks of white light filtered weakly and recessively" through an "all-increasing blackness" (961). This very last image in his mind reduces the entirety of his life—the entirety of his personal narrative—to a fear of his fundamental ethnic difference being snuffed out by an "all-encompassing blackness" (961).

Farrell subtly undermines the entire foundation of Studs' racist sense of identity in the closing chapter of *The Young Manhood*. The narrative point of view shifts to a fourteen-year-old black boy named Stephen Lewis who now lives in Studs' old neighborhood. As Stephen walks down 58th Street, he fantasizes about winning the affections of a pretty neighborhood girl by becoming the hero of the block. This young black kid, who Studs would claim is essentially different than him, is actually exactly like him. The ethnic narrative comes full circle. Stephen, we can imagine, will repeat Studs' mistakes and likely doom himself to the same fate. Ultimately, Studs' ethnic anxieties and his identity crises are not unique. As Farrell states, *Studs Lonigan* was not conceived as exclusively an Irish-American tale, but "as the story of an American destiny in our time" (Shaughnessy 48).

Farrell uses a quotation from Frank Norris as an epigraph to *Studs Lonigan*: "A literature that cannot be vulgarized is no literature at all and will perish." This quotation comes from an essay in which Norris argues that literature must be "understandable to the common minds" (*Responsibilities* 281). Farrell's intent to "vulgarize" the story of Studs is evidence of a desire to de-mystify ethnic American identity. Farrell makes mundane an otherwise sensationalist narrative of racial and ethnic prejudice. He did not see Studs as unique; instead, he believed Studs was a fairly conventional "American boy" (*Reflections* 190). Studs' desire to find a stable ethnic identity and a functioning cultural narrative resonated with American readers through the mid-century. His failed attempts to reclaim his heritage and subsequent efforts to remake his ethnic identity into a racial identity exemplify a pervasive, and potentially dangerous, desperation in American society. Studs feels a need for an ethnic narrative that no longer exists, so he understandably refashions one from the materials available to him. His attempts to recreate Irish-American identity and to rewrite the Irish narrative in America predict the similar agendas of Irish-American characters searching for functional identities in the literature of the following decades. Faced with a dislocation between their ethnic past and their American present, they too would try to reconstruct Irishness as a fundamental component of an American identity.

A WILD IRISH (SOUTHERN) GIRL: MARGARET MITCHELL'S *GONE WITH THE WIND*

In 1939, F. Scott Fitzgerald was hired as the latest screenwriter to attempt to adapt Margaret Mitchell's *Gone With the Wind* for film. Fitzgerald had not read the book before being hired, but soon did so and wrote about his reaction to it in a letter to his daughter:

> [It is] not very original, in fact leaning heavily on *The Old Wives' Tale*, *Vanity Fair*, and all that has been written on the Civil War. There are no new characters, new techniques, new observations—none of the elements that make literature—especially no new examination into human emotions. But on the other hand it is interesting, surprisingly honest, consistent and workmanlike throughout, and I felt no contempt for it but only a certain pity for those who consider it the supreme achievement of the human mind. (qtd. in Pyron 386)

Fitzgerald's response, like that of many others, was decidedly mixed. He recognized Mitchell's book as quite surprisingly "a good novel" and understood the enthusiasm that readers had for it, but at the same time he found it disappointing that such a derivative work was being lauded as the great American novel (Pyron 386). In Fitzgerald's brief comments to his daughter, we can see in miniature the response of many readers who have categorized the book as non-serious popular literature, but who nonetheless sense an underappreciated complexity in Mitchell's work.

One area of complexity that has gone overlooked is Mitchell's treatment of Irish-American identity, perhaps because more people are familiar with the de-ethnicized film adaptation than the novel.[6] Mitchell's original vision of *Gone With the Wind* radiates with ethnic significance. In *Strange Kin: Ireland and the American South* (2005), Kieran Quinlan argues that the characterization and "central terms" of Mitchell's story are Irish and that "there seems no debating the Irish character of the South's best-known work of fiction" (123–4). Yet, many scholars never consider the O'Haras as an Irish-American family. As a result, studies have oversimplified the racial and ethnic dimensions of the novel, and as has been the case with *Huckleberry Finn*, they often emphasize an erroneous black–white binary despite evidence of something far more complex and interesting in the text. *Gone With the Wind* needs more attention not only because it proves to be a far more complicated work than it is usually given credit for, but also because it is one of the most significant and popular works by an Irish-American woman. Not surprisingly, Irish-American literature prior to the 1930s was dominated by male authors and male protagonists, but Mitchell offered a unique female voice and created a female character that appealed to Irish-American women in a way that a character like Studs Lonigan never could.

Everyone around Scarlett O'Hara informs her that she is essentially Irish: her father, Gerald, tells her that "[t]here's no getting away" from her "Irish blood" (39); Rhett Butler describes her as "a delicately nurtured Southern belle with her Irish up" (195); her neighbors call her a "highflying, bogtrotting Irish" (528); and the members of Georgia's high society constantly remind her that in her veins runs "the shrewd, earthy blood of an Irish peasant" (89). For the most part, Scarlett accepts these identifications of her ethnic heritage as true, even though she is not completely sure what such identification means. Yes, she is Gerald O'Hara's daughter, but her sense of her own Irishness is not the same as her father's. As an immigrant, her father's Irishness is rooted in Irish history and culture in a way that Scarlett's Irishness never can be. His life is an extension of an Irish narrative to which Scarlett has little access. Yet, neither does Scarlett's ethnicity seem easily comparable to that of the Irish-American laborers rebuilding Atlanta after the war. Despite knowing that the Irish workingmen are "as Irish as she," Scarlett cannot fully accept the socio-economic implications of the comparison (944). In addition, she will not allow herself to imagine common ethnic ground with the former Irish soldiers who fought for the Union Army and were now settling in Georgia or with the Yankee carpetbaggers of Irish heritage now preying on the carcass of the Old South. In her mind, Yankee Irish and Southern Irish are just not the same thing.

Gone With the Wind presents one of the most variable and convoluted descriptions of Irish-American character in the twentieth century and at times appears a bizarre conglomeration of both positive and negative Irish stereotypes. There is no monolithic sense of Irishness in the book, but rather, as Quinlan observes, "several Irishnesses" (129). Mitchell's metaphorical Irishwoman borrows heavily from the same pool of ethnic imagery and cultural associations of which every other writer in this study partakes. In Scarlett there are recognizable traces of Conn the Shaughraun, Dan Mulligan, Huck Finn, Celia Madden, McTeague, Sweeney, Amory Blaine, and Studs Lonigan. Scarlett's Irish identity is a bit of a patchwork made up of the full range of Irish-American clichés and supposed ethnic truisms. As a result, the book exhibits vacillating attitudes toward Irishness, and Scarlett's individual ethnic identity appears unstable, at best, and contradictory, at worst. Yet, these very uncertainties and instabilities accurately represent the ambiguous and shifting nature of Irish-American identity in the 1930s.

Gone With the Wind was one of the most commercially successful books of the twentieth century, but also one of the most harshly criticized. Floyd C. Watkins, in an essay typical of academic responses to the book, accuses *Gone With the Wind* of being "false to historical fact" and "false to the human heart," and concludes that, despite its popularity, it is "a bad novel" (200). Mitchell believed that the critical negativity toward her book after World War II was the result of Communist influences, America's shift toward the political left, and racial liberalism (Pyron 455–6). Mitchell biographer Darden Asbury Pyron thinks it had more to do with the advent of New Criticism, which prized "the difficulty and obscurity of art" and which viewed popularity as "*prima facie* evidence of failure" (459). Ultimately, it does not matter why critics turned against Mitchell, nor does it matter whether the book is good or bad. *Gone With the Wind*'s popularity ensured that more people were exposed to Mitchell's vision of Irish-American identity than that of almost any other writer. Scarlett O'Hara is an American icon. The only Irish-American character more familiar to American audiences is Huck Finn. The relative literary merits of Mitchell's novel do not change the fact that it had a tremendous impact on the literary characterization of Irish America, and any study of Irish-American literature that ignores the importance of *Gone With the Wind* is missing one of the biggest pieces of the puzzle. As Quinlan notes, "Mitchell throws light where she herself didn't intend to, or didn't see clearly enough to do so," but this gives us an opportunity nonetheless (127). Crude or not, the novel shaped popular perceptions on ethnic identity. In rewriting the story of Irish America, Mitchell established one of the most enduring myths of post-immigrant Irish identity.

Mitchell, like Scarlett, came from a family of mixed Old Southern and Irish heritage. The Mitchell family had been influential in Southern society since the seventeenth century and had lived in Atlanta since before it was called Atlanta (Pyron 10). In the nineteenth century, two Irish-born men (Philip Fitzgerald and John Stephens) married into Mitchell's family on the maternal side (Pyron 17–9). Pyron argues that the presence of these two men in Mitchell's family history profoundly impacted her sense of self:

> [T]heir Irishness added a new peculiarity to the family legacy. It set them apart from the Southern norm, but it also exaggerated the family's clannish self-consciousness, sense of its own distinction, and the feeling of being at odds with the world. These two Irishmen helped shape the most fundamental stuff of Margaret Mitchell's imagination. (17)

Mitchell was keenly aware that she was part Irish, and, according to Pyron, her ancestors "dominated" her life as "conduits of tradition" (10). Though Mitchell never specifically identified the sources for the characters in *Gone With the Wind*, it is hard not to see the influences that her own family history must have had.

Yet, the depiction of Irish-American life in *Gone With the Wind* is anachronistic and seems more like a genealogical fantasy than historical fact. Gerald O'Hara's status in the planter class and his rapid and overwhelming social and financial success would have been anomalies in the real antebellum South. The Irish of this era, including Mitchell's own ancestors, did not enjoy such easy lives. Pyron observes,

> While numerous Irish lived in the South, few resided in the interior, fewer planted cotton, and fewer still owned slaves or qualified as planters. They remained mostly in the large coastal cities like Charleston and Savannah; they lived mostly as single men rather than with families; and they came as close to representing a regional underclass as any category in the entire population.[7] (250)

Of course, this does not mean we need to reject the novel, as many early critics do, because it is "false"; rather, we need to approach it as a story about life in the 1930s couched in an imaginative facsimile of the 1860s. Mitchell used the Old South to explore the problems of the New South, and she used an imagined antebellum Irish identity as a metaphor for contemporary ethnic confusion. This re-imagining of Irishness is important because, in the novel's anachronisms and slippages, we can see evidence of a continuing effort by twentieth-century authors to rewrite an ethnic past in order to make it more compatible with the American present.

Before turning to Mitchell's revision of Irish-American identity in her novel, it is important to consider her use of Irish character stereotypes, because it is her varying acceptance and rejection of these stereotypes that eventually gives shape to the new Irish narrative at the end of the novel. *Gone With the Wind*, despite being the most contemporary work in this study, makes use of some of the oldest conventions and tropes. Scarlett is the child of a cliché, and in order to understand the development of her Irish identity, we must first start with her father's Irish identity, because as was the case with Huck and Pap Finn, the parent predicts what the child might become.

Gerald O'Hara was born into a peasant family in Ireland and came to America "hastily" because he murdered an absentee landlord's rent agent (44). The first pieces of information we learn about his character are familiar: he is impoverished, impulsive, violent, and hateful. We also learn in short order that he is a compulsive gambler with a taste for alcohol. Mitchell's physical description of Gerald further reinforces the character's debt to classic stereotype: "His face was as Irish a face as could be found . . . round, high colored, short nosed, wide mouthed and belligerent" (32). What Mitchell describes here are the same prognathic qualities and animal-like features that informed the descriptions of McTeague and Sweeney. Despite Gerald's living in America for ten years, a "brisk brogue clung to his tongue" and he still exhibited the "truculent manner" and "shrewdness" of an Irishman (47, 52). Mitchell explicitly evokes Gerald's Irish ethnicity and stereotypical appearance and behavior nearly every time he appears in the novel. The narrator of *Gone With the Wind* always describes him in ethnic terms (i.e., "the bandy-legged little Irishman," "the little Irishman from up country") and ascribes his passions and desires to Irish origins (44, 56). At virtually every stage of his life, his motivations emerge from his Irishness: he wants to own land because he is Irish (50); he rides horses because he has an "Irishman's passion" for the animals (90); he pursues a wife from a higher social class than he because he has an Irishman's unwillingness to admit inferiority (55); and he joins the Confederate Army because he comes from a long line of Irish rebels and warriors (45). There really is nothing to distinguish Gerald from the stereotypical Paddy figure, except that he had the good fortune to win a plantation and a slave in a game of cards, and his new wealth is often enough to make others overlook his faulty ethnicity.

Mitchell also repeatedly describes Scarlett as fundamentally Irish. Scarlett's appearance, except for her green eyes, are attributed to her mother's French ancestry, but her disposition and passions are attributed to her father's "forthright Irish blood" (117). All of Scarlett's most important decisions and actions are informed by, often even dictated by, her ethnicity. She does what she does because she shares Gerald's "easily stirred passions," his "Irish temper," his "shrewd practicality," his "hard-headed Irish sense," and even his "rage" that drove him to murder (62, 218, 335, 172, 120). Gerald tells his daughter that her Irish blood predisposes her to certain attitudes and behaviors (39). Just as McTeague and Amory Blaine came to accept that their fundamental personalities were largely defined by their paternal inheritance, Scarlett too comes to accept "simply and without question" that she is Irish like her father (428). She believes that her Irishness compels her to throw off artificial manners, to challenge her society, to fight for her land, and even to murder those who wish her family harm.

Mitchell is clearly not ignorant of the potential for insult within the stereotypes she uses and often acknowledges such through the character of Rhett. Rhett frequently compares Scarlett to the stereotype, sometimes teasingly, sometimes maliciously: he suggests that she should be more like a typical Irishman and not think so much before she speaks (236); he suggests she might prefer to kiss a pig because he had "always heard the Irish were partial to pigs" (304); he tells her that she cannot lie because "Irish are the poorest liars in the world" (616); and, in anger, he accuses her of lacking courage even though he has "never known an Irishman to be a coward" (920). While *Gone With the Wind* is full of potentially derogatory stereotypes and other unflattering depictions of Irish identity, Mitchell is not trying to vilify the Irish. Instead, she is trying to invert the stereotype, as Dion Boucicault and Edward Harrigan did, to show previously derided Irish qualities to be beneficial and valorous attributes. Gerald might embody many classically unappealing ethnic features and qualities, but Mitchell wants readers to acknowledge that these qualities actually give him a "brisk and restless vitality" that sets him above "indolent gentle-folk" (47). Readers are to believe that Gerald's bull-headedness, impulsiveness, and Irish passions facilitate his success in the Old South. Similarly, Mitchell credits Irish heritage for Scarlett's courage and perseverance through the war and its aftermath. Lauren S. Cardon suggests that Mitchell intended her Irish characters to have a positive, invigorating effect on Southern society: "As the daughter of an Irish immigrant, Scarlett, from a breeder's perspective, might bring some new energy into an increasingly washed-out bloodline" (61). Cardon further adds that Mitchell believed such incorporation of Irish qualities "necessary for Americans to survive the modern world" (62). This is the same argument that Harold Frederic makes through the voice of Father Forbes in *The Damnation of Theron Ware*. Yet, whereas Frederic saw potential for "a new type of humanity" in the progressive aspects of Irish identity, Mitchell appeals to the recessive aspects (Frederic 222). This is an odd choice, which ultimately does not work.

While both Boucicault and Harrigan achieved great success in transforming the stage Irish stereotype into a positive character, Mitchell does not. During the mid to late nineteenth century, such a transformation was subversive and appealed to audiences eager to see slanderous portrayals of Irish identity replaced with something empowering. Yet, writing in the 1930s, Mitchell fails to recognize the incongruity of such a strategy in a modern context. Instead of inverting a stereotype, she more or less reintroduces a stereotype that had been dormant for decades. Other writers, including Fitzgerald and Farrell, refer to classic Irish stereotypes in their works, but always in an effort to differentiate the modern Irishman from his past. They use humor to establish an ironic distance between their characters and the classic Paddy figure. In Mitchell, there is no irony in the use of Irish stereotypes, and this more than anything else is the problem. She suggests that Gerald's greatest qualities are his ability to out-drink, out-gamble, and out-bluster everyone around him, and further attributes these qualities to inherent traits. Though Monsignor Darcy and Pat Lonigan both make claims to authentic Irishness, both Fitzgerald and Farrell clearly show that each man's Irishness is a performative identity learned from sentimental songs and romanticized cultural assumptions. Mitchell, on the other hand, describes Gerald as exhibiting characteristics that emerge from a true Irish essence. In doing so, she reinforces an erroneous (and potentially dangerous) notion about ethnic authenticity. Mitchell assumes that biology defines ethnicity and that Irish qualities emerge from physical traits. By claiming that Irish identity originates in the blood rather than the mind, Mitchell establishes heredity as the foundation on which all Irish-American narratives must be written and lays the groundwork for the racialization of ethnic identity evident in the later portions of the novel.

Mitchell's assertion that Scarlett inherits her Irishness presupposes that the character is fundamentally and essentially Irish. Her heredity dictates her identity and proves an inescapable determinant in her life. According to the rules of ethnicity to which Mitchell ascribes, Scarlett can never choose to stop being Irish the way Amory Blaine can. For Scarlett, Irishness is not just a theoretical orientation or a set of political and social biases, as it was for Amory. Instead, Irishness is biological inheritance. As Scarlett searches for an Irish-American narrative, this belief in biological authenticity informs, and sometimes undercuts, her attempts to situate herself within an increasingly modern narrative.

Since Scarlett cannot simply give up her Irish identity in order to become fully American, she must find a way to make her Irishness part of her Americanness. Her strategy throughout the novel is to find a way to make an Irish narrative compatible with an American one, which for the first half of the novel means a specifically Confederate American narrative. This is no easy task for her, because, unlike Studs who had access to an Irish community while growing up, Scarlett only has access to one example of Irishness—her father, Gerald. She never comes to understand herself as part of an Irish community, but instead imagines herself as part of a history of individual struggle and survival.

Gerald's own understanding of being Irish in America establishes a powerful model for his daughter, because through him she sees the fusing of disparate histories and distinct national loyalties into a new, ideal Southern identity. In comparison with *Gone With the Wind*'s Anglo gentry, Gerald appears rough and undignified, but Mitchell suggests that his immigrant struggles have better prepared him for American life. Gerald may be quintessentially Irish, but he also believes he is unambiguously American.

When Gerald leaves Ireland, his father's parting admonition is, "Remember who ye are and don't be taking nothing off no man" (45). This single piece of advice gives structure to Gerald's future as an Irish American, prompting him to never forget his heritage and to never accept the insinuation that he is inferior. He arrives in the U.S. impoverished but idealistic. He can imagine nothing that might impede his success in his new country. This is a very different kind of Irish immigrant story than most. Mitchell suggests that America "had been kind to the Irish" and goes on to claim that "even the most ignorant of bogtrotters" could make his fortune here (46). This claim for the most part is historically false, but it nonetheless establishes an uncommon state of mind for Gerald that likely resonated with twentieth-century Irish Americans.[8] Gerald arrives in the country without the overwhelming alienation or dislocation more typical of nineteenth-century immigrants and does not acknowledge any fundamental difference between himself and the Anglo population. He does not even seem to consider himself an immigrant once he steps off the boat and believes himself already American.

It takes Gerald ten years to "arrive" in Southern society, but he is not aware of this. Mitchell writes, "[I]t never occurred to him that his neighbors had eyed him askance . . . there had never been any doubt that he belonged" (53). Gerald is utterly ignorant of ethnic boundaries and the status of immigrants in his new community, and so he proceeds with his life as if no discriminatory obstacles exist. His great pride in himself, his confidence, and his father's admonition give him the attitude needed to enter into a society that many thought he had no right to enter.

In a letter from 1937, Mitchell writes that the "Southern Irish became more Southern than the Southerners," and this is certainly how she portrays Gerald (Cardon 66). In merging with the society and culture of the South, Gerald surpasses any reasonable measure of assimilative success. He fully gives in to his cultural transformation: "There was much about the South—and Southerners—that he would never comprehend; but, with the wholeheartedness that was his nature, he adopted its ideas and customs, as he understood them, for his own" (47). He does what he believes is expected of a good Southern gentleman: he marries a woman of aristocratic blood, he joins the planter class, he grows cotton, he buys slaves, he participates in local society, and when the time comes he joins the Confederate Army. No one in the novel displays greater pride in his plantation or patriotism for the Confederacy than Gerald. He has passed through a gauntlet to become an exemplar of Southern identity.

Gerald's story of assimilation is unusual, but again, it likely appealed to twentieth-century readers who saw in it affirmation that such a process was possible and even easy. Within ten years, Gerald advances from abject poverty to astonishing wealth and from social outcast to social insider. Mitchell unapologetically presents him as a realization of the American Dream, a rare type of character with both immigrant credibility and American integrity who through his own hard-headedness and perseverance achieves success. Mitchell condenses several generations of Irish character stories into the body of one man. Wrapped up in Gerald's composite character are the narrative histories of the Irish peasant, the Irish rebel, the unwilling emigrant, the struggling urban immigrant, the ethnic minority social climber, the lace curtain gentleman, and the fully assimilated patriot. Mitchell works very hard to create in Gerald an Irish immigrant character whose challenges and concerns better reflect the 1930s (largely non-immigrant) Irish-American culture than the mid-nineteenth century culture to which he ostensibly belongs. While Gerald seems one of the most unusual and unrealistic Irish Americans in literature, such a bizarre character uniquely personifies the presence of ethnic history that imposed itself on twentieth-century Irish America.

To facilitate his assimilation, Gerald constructs an Irish-American narrative that will allow him to access both an ethnic and national legacy. There is no real precedent for Gerald, no other Irish-American stories he can model his own story on, and so he simply combines Ireland and America in his imagination. He merges their physical features, their histories, and their politics into a single imaginative construct. With uncompromising determination, he imagines the South as a New Ireland in which "the O'Haras would rise again" (50).

The first step in Gerald's project is to literally reconstruct an image of Ireland and Irish society in Georgia's interior. Mitchell explicitly connects Gerald's American ambitions with his Irish past:

> With the deep hunger of an Irishman who has been a tenant on the lands his people once had owned and hunted, he wanted to see his own acres stretching green before his eyes. With a ruthless singleness of purpose, he desired his own house, his own plantation, his own horse, his own slaves. And here in this new country, safe from the twin perils of the land he had left—taxation that ate up crops and barns and the ever-present threat of sudden confiscation—he intended to have them. (48)

This passage makes clear Gerald's desire to invert the dynamic he experienced in Ireland by placing himself and his family in a position of power. He does not want to abandon the system of land ownership and privilege, just renegotiate it so that he is on top. America, then, is not so much a chance for a new life as it is a chance to rewrite his old life.

After winning land in a poker game, Gerald builds what at first appears to be a traditional Southern plantation house and calls it Tara. Some critics have assumed that this is simply Gerald's first major step toward joining the Southern planter class and that Tara is a reference to "terra" or earth (McGraw 125); however, in Gerald's mind, he is building a replica of an Irish Big House, the residence from which the Anglo-Irish ascendancy controlled their land possessions in Ireland. He calls it Tara not in reference to the Latin term for earth, but in reference to Ireland's Hill of Tara, the ancient seat of Irish kings, located near Gerald's birthplace in County Meath near the River Boyne. The slaves that Gerald purchases to work at

Tara take to speaking with an Irish brogue in honor of their new master, and Gerald takes up the habits and pastimes of the Anglo-Irish landlords that his family had fought against for generations (49). Of course, Gerald's Big House is presided over by a Catholic Irishman, not an Anglo Irishman, which paradoxically allows him to live out the fantasy of an Irishman's reclaiming of his ancestral land while also making a claim to membership in Georgia's Anglo planter society.

The ownership of land proves to be the element that links white Southern identity and Irish identity during the era of *Gone With the Wind*. For Southerners and the Irish, possession of land determines an individual's relative freedom; if you own land, you are by definition a freeperson of high social status and cultural entitlement, but if you work on land you do not own then you are not free, not entitled, and (potentially) not white. In *Fenians, Freedmen, and Southern Whites* (2007), Mitchell Snay argues that both the Irish and Southern white planters used land ownership "to define the meaning and limits of freedom" (85). In both Irish and Southern narratives, the land functions as a metaphor for the most central aspects of personal identity under siege by the forces of English and Yankee aggression. Mitchell repeatedly emphasizes Gerald's obsession with land ownership. Early in the novel, he tells Scarlett that "[l]and is the only thing in the world that amounts to anything," and he later adds, that for an Irishman, "the land they live on is like their mother . . . 'Tis the only thing worth working for, fighting for, dying for" (38, 428). While Gerald's instructions to Scarlett emerge from what he himself identifies as Irish origins, they obviously have practical relevance to the Civil War era South. Gerald is trying to explain to his daughter the need for the O'Haras to defend Tara and Georgia from Yankee aggressors, and he achieves success by mixing contemporary circumstances with an ancestral, ethnic rationale. Mitchell does question this Irish obsession with the land, once again using Rhett to voice her skepticism: "The Irish . . . are the damnedest race. They put so much emphasis on so many wrong things. Land, for instance. And every bit of earth is just like every other bit" (574). Rhett's criticism insinuates that after the war, Gerald's brand of sentimental attachment to the land will not help Scarlett survive in the New South. Such imagined connections between individual identity and the land prove harder, if not impossible, to maintain. Given the radical changes to property ownership after the war and the implosion of Southern social hierarchies and economies, Scarlett will need to find some other way to affirm her Irish and Southern identities.

In addition to blending Irish and American land metaphors in his narrative, Gerald also mixes together Irish and American history and politics. Unfortunately, Gerald has an imperfect understanding of history and is only familiar with "the manifold wrongs of Ireland" (46). In constructing his Irish-American identity narrative, he uses his understanding of Ireland's history of conflict and struggle as a model to understand events in America, and he goes as far as to re-imagine Americans in Irish roles. He equates the

Civil War with the Battle of the Boyne (a conflict in which his family had proudly fought), the Union Army with Orangemen, and the Confederacy with Irish nationalists.[9] He frequently, almost as if senile, confuses Irish history with his American present: he accuses his neighbors, the Scots-Irish MacIntoshs, of being both Orangemen and abolitionists, which positions them as enemies of both Ireland and the Confederacy (51); to celebrate going to war with the Yankees, he sings "Irish ditties" including "The Wearing of the Green" and a lament for Robert Emmet (84); and he equates those soldiers that die for the Confederacy with those men in Ireland "who died on scant acres, fighting to the end rather than leave the homes where they had lived, plowed, loved, begotten sons" (404). Gerald never displays any true understanding of the politics of the South nor the causes of the war; he simply imagines that history is repeating itself.

After the war, Gerald equates the South's loss with Ireland's and considers Southern rebels (including the Ku Klux Klan) to be the equivalent of Ireland's militant nationalist groups. Snay suggests that this was not an uncommon comparison in the South and points to a Reconstruction era speech in which Senator James Chesnut, Jr., argued that the KKK, like Ireland's militant organizations, arose because of despotic governments (13).[10] Gerald's allegiance to the South is an extension of his loyalty to Ireland. Like Dan Mulligan, his American patriotism is informed by his Irish patriotism to such an extent that he celebrates his new home with the traditions and customs of his old home.

Like Farrell's Pat Lonigan, Gerald views his world through a somewhat distorted lens of Irish history and politics. As much as he wants to believe that Southerners are like the Irish and Northerners like the English, the comparison is inaccurate and cannot be sustained. Gerald struggles to maintain his fantasy through willful ignorance. He tries not to think too much about the large number of Irishmen fighting for the Union or about the similarities between slavery in the South and British colonial policies in Ireland, and he never once acknowledges that he has remade himself in the image of an Anglo-Irish landlord—a fact that would undercut so many of his ideals and invalidate his early life as a rebel who killed a rent agent in Ireland. To avoid potentially crippling self-contradictions, Gerald retreats further and further into his fantasy as the novel progresses, but his increasing unease with his surroundings and his mental instability after the war suggest that Scarlett will not be able to pursue the same course. In his imagination, Gerald creates a powerful model of Irishness to which his daughter can aspire, but what worked for Gerald in the Old South will not work for Scarlett in the New South.

As was the case with Studs, Scarlett has limited access to her father's narrative of Irish-American identity, though she does try to embrace it at first. Since her babyhood, she had "listened half-bored, impatient and but partly comprehending" to Gerald's stories of her Irish ancestors (414). As an adult woman, she tries to find inspiration in the ambiguous "shadowy folks whose blood flowed in her veins," but she only receives vague "wordless encouragement" from them (414). She does not perceive her ancestors the way Gerald does, as figures persistently "crowding behind" her and driving her forward, but instead she experiences them as immaterial dreams whose presence and meaning are unclear (404). Even though she knows that both her first and last names signify a connection to ancestors who fought at the Battle of the Boyne, her link to her ancestors is tenuous at best and increasingly irrelevant in the later portion of the novel.[11]

Similarly, Scarlett proves unable to blend Irish and American history and politics the way her father did. Her attempts to do so reveal an ignorance of Irish history greater than Gerald's. When Rhett informs her of Sherman's upcoming siege on Atlanta, she unsuccessfully tries to equate it to Cromwell's siege at Drogheda (303). Rhett once again chastises Scarlett, mocks her fear, ridicules the many historical errors in her comparison (including her belief that Cromwell's invasion of Ireland was a recent event), and concludes by emphasizing that "Sherman isn't Cromwell" (303). This is the first, but sharpest, slap in the face that Scarlett receives for trying to imagine the South like Ireland. Rhett's challenge to her shakes her allegiance to her father's habit of analogizing Irish and American stories and forces her to acknowledge that the events of her life are not merely a repeat of vaguely remembered events from her ancestral past. Half recollected, half imagined events from Irish history cannot sustain Scarlett in her American present.

Neither can Scarlett equate her enemies in America with the enemies of her ancestors. Like her father, she hates the neighboring MacIntoshs, though not because they are historically linked with the Scots-Irish Orangemen who fought against her family in the past, but because they are Union sympathizers who profit at the expense of former Confederates in the present. Scarlett, like her father, is also aware that large numbers of Irishmen fought with the Union Army. Yet, whereas Gerald took this as a personal insult and considered these Irishmen traitors and blackguards seduced by Yankee money, Scarlett sees nothing unusual in the allegiance of some Irishmen to the Union (202). She does not conflate Irish patriotism and American patriotism like her father, nor does she imagine herself essentially connected to the North's "wild Irishmen who talk Gaelic" in a way that might wound her ethnic pride (272).

Scarlett's New South context requires her to develop a very different narrative of Irish-American identity than that of her father, something more genteel and modern. Gerald built his narrative in order to allow him access into a new society, but Scarlett needs a narrative that will help her survive the collapse of that society. Her situation is not all that different from Irish Americans of the 1930s experiencing a social and economic upheaval of their own while uncertain how their ethnic heritage might help or hinder their ambitions. As Charles Rowan Beye observes, at the time of *Gone With the Wind*'s publication, "vast numbers of people were devastated by hunger, homelessness, and joblessness," but at the same time women and immigrant groups were "freed from middle class gentility" and had new social opportunities (380). Being a second-generation Irish American, Scarlett, like Studs and millions of others, needs a different narrative than the one that served the previous generation. James P. Cantrell argues that Scarlett's difficulties in the novel emerge from her "tragic perception that her life has been false in cultural terms" (12). Certainly, blindly accepting her father's version of Irishness would be false, and so Scarlett must redefine the terms of her own ethnic identity. While several critics have observed that Scarlett's identity crisis seems analogous to the South's identity crisis of the 1930s, it also seems to speak directly to the specifically Irish-American identity crisis of the same period.

Like Studs, Scarlett arrives at a belief that Irishness, more than anything else, is a signifier of racial status. It is the term through which she can negotiate her whiteness, and while she is very aware that her father's Irish blood complicates her claim to white racial identity and privilege, she also is confident that "Irish" is definitively not "black." Scarlett's move toward embracing a racialized narrative of Irish-American identity appears responsive to the social and cultural dynamics of 1930s America, and like Studs' efforts to transform his Irishness into an affirmation of whiteness, Scarlett's re-imagining of her ethnicity speaks directly to the ambiguous and anxious dimensions of the status of Irish Americans during the Great Depression. Yet, whereas Farrell's novel reflected modernist nativism's shift toward racist theories of difference, Mitchell's book tries to reassemble a classic hierarchy of racial superiority. In the process, Mitchell tries to renegotiate the position of the Irish in that hierarchy by arguing that the qualities that made them inferior in the past now make them superior in the present. Such a project is filled with problems that undercut its own goals. As Eliza Russi Lowen McGraw suggests, Mitchell disputes the traditional narrative that divides the South into black and white by offering "a more complex matrix" of ethnicities (124). For this, Mitchell should be credited with progressing the consideration of Southern racial dynamics past simplistic precedents; however, simplistic and erroneous elements still remain in her own formulation.

It had been easier for Scarlett's father to assert whiteness than it was for her to do so. Gerald was very conscious of the importance of whiteness to Southern identity and made every effort, even before Scarlett was born, to establish his family as unquestionably white. He believes "coastal Georgians" to be a "pleasant race" distinct from the Irish, but he also believes that their racial borders, like their social borders, are permeable enough to allow an Irishman entrance (47). He makes his first claim to whiteness in the simplest and most direct way he knows how: he acquires slaves. He thinks that the definition of a white man involves the owning of black men. Cardon argues that the "unquestioned loyalty" of Gerald's slaves "helps to 'whiten' the Irish immigrant" and makes him eligible for inclusion in Southern society (66). Unfortunately for Scarlett, owning slaves is no longer an available method for acquiring whiteness in the New South, and so she must pursue other means of advantageously racializing her ethnic identity.

As the old social structures collapse in the South, so too do certain racial hierarchies that previously sustained Irish whiteness. It is not until after the abolition of slavery that Scarlett realizes that many people see little difference between the Irish and freed blacks. In the past, slavery had so clearly defined the difference; the Irish were never eligible to be bought and sold as property, and so they existed at a slightly elevated status above blacks. Yet, with that difference eliminated, Scarlett witnesses those around her questioning if there are any real distinctions to be made between the two groups. A former Southern gentleman of French descent, who now delivers pies, dreams that in the future, Southerners "weel own ze Irish slaves instead of ze darky slaves" and predicts that Scarlett will "milk ze cow, peek ze cotton" (595). Such a suggestion horrifies Scarlett, who still understands racial differences in largely economic terms. Milking cows and picking cotton, while no longer slave work, were still, in Scarlett's mind, black work. The Irish (which in her limited experience includes only Gerald and herself) do not lower themselves to such a level.

Scarlett is even more startled to realize the attitudes that Northerners have toward the Irish. The wife of a former Union officer who is settling in Georgia asks Scarlett where she can find a nurse for her children. Scarlett assures her that black women from the country make for the best nursemaids. The Northern woman is offended by such a suggestion: "Do you think I'd trust my babies to a black nigger? . . . I want a good Irish girl." Scarlett becomes "sick with rage" at the suggestion and tells her that the Irish do not work as servants in the South. She then further explains herself by conflating Irishness and whiteness: "Personally, I've never seen a white servant and I shouldn't care to have one in my house" (662–3). Scarlett is completely ignorant of Northern attitudes and prejudices toward the Irish and is unaware that in the North, Irish men and women regularly engage in work she would consider non-white. For the first time in her life, she is forced to defend her racial status, which she had always assumed was clearly distinct from a black person's. Prior to the war, race trumped ethnicity, but in the novel's New South (which is more reflective of the attitudes of the 1930s than the 1860s), race and ethnicity become overlapping categories.

Though Scarlett has never had to directly address her racial status before, she has always known that she was different from other Southern girls. She knows that, hereditarily speaking, she is not as attractive to men as someone of so called pure blood like Melanie Hamilton or India Wilkes, who tells her, "[Y]ou aren't one of us and you have never been" (787). Despite possessing the "magnolia-white skin . . . so prized by Southern women" (an inheritance from her mother), she remains a marginal member of society because of her father's Irish blood (5). Though no one considers her black, many do not consider her fully white either. Scarlett tries to dress like and act the part of a good Southern daughter, but her green eyes and Irish temper reveal her as a poseur. McGraw suggests that Scarlett's story is akin to the tragic mullata narrative, and that *Gone With the Wind* describes its heroine's attempts at "racial passing":

> The question of pretending, or passing, haunts the South, where racial identity stood as the primary identifier of station, and although Scarlett's Irishness is something she may try to repress, she cannot contain it . . . She tries to pass as a lady, subduing her "Irishness" . . . [she] aspires toward the whitest part of her lineage, desiring at times to be like her mother. (129)

In the Old South of *Gone With the Wind*, an acceptable social identity is equated with a white racial identity. As a result, Scarlett's desire to be a true Southern lady admired by those of good breeding is best facilitated by her attempts to assert her whiteness. In Scarlett's world, social desirability and racial desirability are the same thing.

McGraw further argues that "Irishness prevents Scarlett from entirely representing the Southern belle figure" (126). Despite Scarlett having become an icon for that figure in contemporary society, *Gone With the Wind* repeatedly emphasizes her deviance from that identity. She rejects the submissiveness and passiveness implicit in the character; she ignores its social positioning by engaging in unladylike work and behavior; and she eventually foregoes the graces of her mother's lineage in favor of the practicality offered by her father's heritage. Her refusal to adhere to conventions further complicates Scarlett's claim to a white identity. In rebelling against the expectations of her society, she risks becoming an other.

Yet, Mitchell suggests a certain degree of otherness is needed to survive in the New South. Scarlett's challenge, then, is to assert Irishness as a variant whiteness, different enough from the inbred and weak whiteness of the former aristocracy to allow survival in the New South, but not so different as to be confused with a black identity. McGraw describes Scarlett's ethnic identity as a "revision of Southerness" that strengthens "southern whiteness" with "other-tainted strength" (124, 130). Mitchell suggests that Irishness is a safe racial alternative and an acceptably different ethnic identity. While not as purely white as most daughters of the Old South, Scarlett embodies an alternative whiteness that offers a more sustainable identity and a better defense against the shifting racial politics brought about by the South's defeat in the war and the abolition of slavery.

Scarlett's revision of her Irish identity starts to gain traction when she realizes that her ethnic difference, which had handicapped her in the Old South, was now a strength in the New South. Throwing aside old conventions and customs, she takes charge of the family and their property, she starts a new lumber business and begins to lift the family out of their post-war poverty, she forms relations and friendships with working-class Georgians and even some Northerners, and she is the only character more interested in building a future than trying to recover a past. While some of her former neighbors refuse to accept the change to their lives, Scarlett finds a way to thrive. Mitchell suggests that the weaker women of the Old South like Melanie wilt and wither unable to adapt to their new environment and the prideful but defeated men either die or try to continue the fight in secret. Scarlett is the only one who immediately tries to carve out a future for herself in the New South. The lives of her friends and neighbors had always depended so much on categories of "us" and "them," but because Scarlett had always been a little bit of both, she finds a way to move forward when no one else can. Her sense of ethnic individualism prepares her to support herself even when nearly all of the apparatus of social privilege collapses under her. In effect, Scarlett's Irishness allows her to bridge the gap between life in the Old South and life in the New South.

The key to life in the New South is not land ownership, as it had been for Gerald, but versatile whiteness. In *Gone With the Wind*, those who cling to the narrow racial categories of the past fail to assimilate to the new racial categories of the present. Whiteness could no longer mean ownership of slaves, economic privilege, cultural entitlement, and a life of leisure. Those who fail to accept this fact are doomed to lives of frustration. Mitchell's New South needed a new definition of whiteness, which still maintained the racial hierarchy, but which did not depend on the criteria of the past. Mitchell presents Scarlett as the new white ideal. Her Irishness is, in Diane Negra's terms, a form of "enriched whiteness" (1). It grants her the privileges and advantages of white identity without the weaknesses. Scarlett's whiteness is made of sterner stuff than Melanie's or Ahsley's or any other Southerner's. It allows her to form connections across previously impassable economic, geographic, and social boundaries. In the New South, Scarlett forges relationships with the working class, with Northerners, and with a more diverse white ethnic population than she had ever known.

Mitchell cements Scarlett's status as a new variant of essential whiteness by making her the recipient of Ku Klux Klan protection. While traveling through the woods near Shantytown, Scarlett is assaulted by a black man and experiences "terror and revulsion such as she had never known" (780). When the community learns of the assault, members of the KKK (including Ashley Wilkes and Scarlett's husband Frank) ride out to Shantytown, find the man involved and his accomplice, and lynch them both. This episode in the novel confirms Scarlett's racial identity by emphasizing that an attack on her body is an attack on whiteness. The KKK responds to what they perceive as a black man's assault against a white woman, and their actions are the clearest indicator in the novel that, despite her differences, Scarlett is considered white by her community.

Critics, including Ruth Elizabeth Burks, have found Mitchell's valorization of the KKK disturbing and note similarities between her work and D. W. Griffith's *Birth of a Nation* (1915).[12] Burks writes that both *Gone With the Wind* and *Birth of a Nation* "present members of the Ku Klux Klan as

honorable men who put their lives on the line in such desperate times to protect white womanhood and to restore white (need I say male?) supremacy"
(54). What is unusual about Mitchell's portrayal of the KKK, and is yet
another example of historical anachronism, is that an Irish Catholic would
be the object of defense rather than the target of hostility for the KKK.
During the 1860s, the racial status of the Irish was generally not clear and
the KKK saw Roman Catholics, along with blacks, Jews, and other minorities, as dangers to America.[13] Farrell acknowledges the potential for tension
between the Irish and the KKK as late as the 1920s in *Studs Lonigan*, but
Mitchell glosses over the issue and presumes that Scarlett's Irishness poses
no real obstacle for her categorical whiteness. While Studs consistently
asserts his whiteness and gives voice to racist sentiments, Farrell undercuts
his character, shows the flaws in the boy's argument, and clearly intends
for readers to see Studs as hobbled by (if not killed by) his racism. Mitchell
does not try to point out any irony or problems with Scarlett's claim to
a white identity, nor does she seem to object to the character's agenda of
remaking Irishness into a new kind of whiteness. Mitchell presents Scarlett
as embodying hope for the future, but behind such promise lurks a renewed
commitment to a racial hierarchy. *Gone With the Wind* uses Irishness to
revise the model of white American identity, and in the process, it repri-
oritizes the terms of Irish-American identity to favor racial inheritance.
Though both Farrell and Mitchell acknowledge the importance of racial
criteria in twentieth-century Irish-American identity, it is very clear that
they disagreed about whether such criteria were beneficial or harmful.

Scarlett survives, and that is the key attribute of her new Irish narrative.
Stripping away the superstitions and stories of her father and putting aside
her imagined obligations to her ancestry, Scarlett is left with a belief that
Irishness is the source of her vitality and endurance. It no longer provides
her with a historical context, a cultural reference point, or a sense of lineage, but with physical and emotional power. Her ethnicity becomes her
biology and behavior. Scarlett never gives up her belief in Irish heredity—
she thinks her daughter's "Irish blue eyes" and recklessness come from
Gerald—but she does become more selective about what traits are passed
down through her Irish blood (979). What she inherited from Gerald and
what she passes on to her own children are, she believes, the essential racial
strengths and passions of the Irish.

In the New South of *Gone With the Wind*, everyone is a kind of immigrant. Southerners unwillingly have been forced out of their old life and
into a new one. They are ill prepared for the requirements of their new
world and experience culture shock. They find themselves marginal members of the post-war national community, second-class citizens who suffer
socially and economically for their differences. Their allegiance to their old
way of life hampers their assimilation into a new community, and their nostalgia for an unrecoverable past further alienates them in the present. They
are immigrants, not from another country, but from another time, and like

all immigrants, they desperately struggle with the terms of their identity. In post-war America, Southerners find themselves in the same position that Gerald found himself on his arrival from Ireland: they are viewed as suspicious, potentially dangerous, others. Scarlett outperforms most Southerners because she is a generation ahead of them; she is already post-immigrant. Her Irish identity has already enabled her to move past the anxieties and challenges of the cultural newcomer and prepared her for life beyond the myths of her past. If she can put aside Gerald's stories and the weight of her Irish ancestry while redefining her ethnic identity, she certainly can put aside any obstacle in the way of developing her new Southern identity. At the end of *Gone With the Wind*, Mitchell presents a racial fantasy in which the Irish, because of their dynamic whiteness and proven assimilability, become the heralds of a new identity for Southerners in America.

Afterword
Huck Finn's People

"Who are Huck Finn's people?"

That was the question my high school English teacher asked us. We had just finished Twain's novel, and after covering some of the usual topics (the river as symbolic mother, individual vs. communal morality), we arrived at our discussion of the racial themes of the book. Our choice of words sometimes revealed how unfamiliar it was for us to talk publically about these issues. No one seemed quite sure what we could say or even which words we could use. We knew the language of the book itself was inappropriate but were not sure what terms and ideas were acceptable or politically correct. We were as tactful as teenagers could be.

Instead of referring to "blacks" or "African Americans," the students in my class started talking about "Jim's people." It seemed we had arrived at safe and productive terminology. We were being vague and euphemistic, but no one felt they were going to get in trouble.

Then our teacher wanted to know whether Huck had people, too.

We had no idea what she meant.

Our teacher pointed out that Huck did not seem to belong to any group, that nobody seemed to want to really include him, and that in the end, he leaves everyone, including Tom and Jim, behind and goes off by himself. She argued that we as a class had been very quick to read Jim as representative of a people, but slow to read Huck the same way.

As was often the case in high school, the bell rang and the subject was dropped, but every time I encountered Huck after that class I always remembered the question. I have had different answers to it at different times. Sometimes Huck's people have seemed racially defined to me, other times age defined, and still at other points regionally defined. I first started thinking of Huck as Irish when watching a very young Mickey Rooney portray the character in the 1939 film adaptation of the book. Yet, even after coming to the conclusion that Huck Finn's people are Irish, I still did not feel like I had really answered the question. So what if his people are Irish? What does it mean? What does his belonging to that ethnic group signify? Why do so many people seem to not know or care that he is Irish?

I conclude this study knowing that there is a certain irony in its central premise. Huck Finn is a novel that valorizes the individual over the community and repeatedly describes its hero's escapes from society. Yet, this study tries to establish Huck's place in the imagined community of Irish America and puts him in the context of a group identity.

Despite being the loneliest character in literature, Huck seems the most connected. Over the past century, he has become part of an impressive lineage of Irish-American characters. The Maddens, the McTeagues, the Blaines, the Lonigans, and the O'Haras are all Huck Finn's people, of course, but his legacy also includes those Irish-American characters who came later: Elwood P. Dowd, Dean Moriarty, Sebastian Dangerfield, Frank Skeffington, James Tyrone, Randle McMurphy, Ignatius J. Reilly, Francis Phelan, and many more.

Of course, Huck is not just a part of Irish-American literary history, but also of broader American cultural history. His story has become a kind of foundational myth of American individualism, humanism, and social conscience. He is now an icon for all Americans, irrespective of race, ethnicity, class, gender, or age. Huck Finn's people are Irish, but they are also non-Irish. This overlap in Huck's status, his role as a formative figure in both the American and the Irish-American literary imaginations, points to a need for better understanding the relationship between our ethnic literatures and our common culture. In books like *Huck Finn*, the Irish-American story has become the American story. Discovering how and why this happened can give us all a greater sense of the relationship between our ethnic and national identities.

My inquiry into Irish-American literary characters began with an attempt to understand Huck's choice to leave civilization. Throughout this study, I have argued that other Irish-American characters have faced similar choices. It seems appropriate then to come back to that moment in Twain's novel and consider its cultural ramifications and ethnic significance.

Huck lights out for the Territory and in the process chooses the promise of an unknown future over the limitations of a stifling past. In ending the book with the character in motion toward opportunity and satisfaction, Mark Twain offers a very inspiring literary vision that establishes an American mythology of heroes running just ahead of the tide of modern progress. The conclusion of Twain's novel became the quintessential American literary ending, with writers throughout the twentieth century echoing it. On the last page of numerous American novels, characters make a familiar choice to break away from their pasts and run toward their futures, chasing after Huck.

How disappointing, then, that Huck did not make it very far in Twain's imagination.

Twain wrote several sequels to *Huck Finn*, almost all of which are generally considered failures by readers and critics. Among the disappointments in these later texts is Twain's bizarre choice to rescind the progress Huck makes in the earlier novel. In *Huck Finn and Tom Sawyer Among the Indians*, Huck forgets about going west and agrees to go back home to be civilized, and having forgotten his falling out with Tom, he once again reverts to being the other boy's sidekick. In *Tom Sawyer's Conspiracy*, Huck even participates in another one of Tom's disturbing and painful racist pranks and helps his friend pretend to sell Jim back into slavery.

The maturity and wisdom that Huck gained while traveling the Mississippi River with Jim seem to have completely vanished in the later books. His self-determination and independence are gone too as he once again shambles after Tom, constantly deferring to the other boy's authority. He tells Tom, "Whatever your plan is, it'll suit me; I'll do whatever you say. Go on" (*Among the Indians* 49). He follows Tom around the world, narrating their adventures, never quite recapturing the excitement he felt at the end of his own story. In the concluding moments of *Tom Sawyer Abroad*, Huck says, "So then we shoved for home—and not feeling very gay, neither" (190). This ending, in which Huck miserably sets out for home, stands in stark contrast to the ending in which he joyfully planned his escape from that same home.

Huck's plan to go west never quite comes true. According to the later books, he fails to escape the assimilation readers assume he breaks away from at the end of *Huck Finn*. While this does not necessarily change how we read and appreciate the earlier novel or diminish the sense of hope found in that book (many readers are likely inclined to view these later stories, especially the ones not published during Twain's lifetime, as apocryphal), it does suggest that Twain was more interested in the way he could use Huck's status as an ethnic outsider to comment on mainstream American identity (i.e., Tom's identity) than he was in exploring the further development of Huck's individualism. As a literary figure and as a cultural metaphor, Huck describes the attractiveness of the other. His value to Twain was in his promise for change, but not necessarily in the realization of change. Because Huck remains a perpetual outsider he can remain a perpetual critic whose Irishness is useful primarily for contrast.

The works discussed in this study display the same trend. Like Huck, all of the characters considered here offer America a way to see itself from the vantage point of the other. These are stories about pioneers of Americanization, told from the point-of-view of individuals whose ambiguous status on the fringes of culture and society allow them to better see the contours of the country. In their efforts to become American, and in society's reciprocal efforts to assimilate or eliminate their differences, we can see the building blocks of a national mythology. Though the writers considered in this study display varying and contradictory attitudes, they agree on one point: by speaking from the margins, the Irish-American character can impact the defining features of the nation. It is precisely because the Irish in America lived on the boundary—between civility and savagery, between white and black, between foreigner and patriot, between poverty and success—that they could function metaphorically as transformational figures. Irish-American characters could be reminders of a simpler and better past in one instance and harbingers of modern progress in the next; they could represent the worst in humanity in one novel while being held up as the ideal in another; and they could be characterized as foreign threats by one writer even as another writer could describe them as fully American.

Explorations of Irish identity in American literature almost always function as methods to forecast danger and opportunity for the country at large with Irish-American characters existing on the boundaries, experiencing turbulence and transformation ahead of the rest. They are the canaries in the coalmine, warning of cultural, national, and racial dangers. Over the past century and a half, Irish-American characters have plotted the course toward Americanization, and as they learned to become American, so too did everyone else. Irish-American characters uniquely have belonged to both the in-group and the out-group; they have stood with one foot in the white mainstream and one foot in the ethnic margins, and because of this, Irish-American stories have laid the groundwork for narratives of both mainstream inclusion and ethnic exclusion. The histories of both canonical literature and ethnic literature in the U.S. owe a great deal to stories of the Irish in America, especially the formative story of a boy from Missouri who refused to assimilate.

Now in the twenty-first century, it would seem that, with assimilation long behind them, Irish Americans have been all but subsumed by a more homogenous American culture. Yet, recent studies of contemporary representations of Irish-American identity in popular culture by scholars like Diane Negra show that this is not the case. According to Negra, an Irish identification in the U.S. has come to be seen as a "platform for discursive legitimacy" (6). In other words, after spending more than a century trying to fit into mainstream America, Irish Americans are reasserting their ethnic heritage in an effort to claim cultural authenticity and ethnic uniqueness in an era when ethnic difference has become desirable. Like Huck, many Irish Americans seem to be questioning the benefits of total assimilation, and our literature has once again begun to evoke the Irish character as a figuration of difference in the U.S.

No other ethnic character has been used so variably and pervasively in American literature as the Irish American. From the end of the Civil War through the Great Depression, Irishness served as a vehicle for national debate as the hopes and fears of the country were played out on the bodies of Irish-American characters, and though Irishness became an increasingly invisible ethnicity throughout the twentieth century, it remains, in the imagination of the American community, a marker of dynamic Americanism.

Notes

NOTES TO THE INTRODUCTION

1. Most notably, Toni Morrison in *Playing in the Dark* (1992).
2. Anderson points out that Gellner presupposes that there are "true" communities that are more desirable than the "falsity" of nations (6). A similar presupposition can be found in the influential study *The Invention of Tradition* edited by Eric Hobsbawm and Terrence Ranger and published in the same year as both Gellner's and Anderson's works (1983). Several of the contributors equate "invention" with "falsity," though Hobsbawm himself does not make this assertion in his introduction.
3. The OED traces the origin of the word "ethnic" to John Hardyng's *Chronicle* (c. 1470) and notes that this definition persisted through the nineteenth century.
4. Theorist George Lakoff studies the process of categorization in *Women, Fire, and Dangerous Things* (1987) and suggests that all categories (including stereotypes) display the kind of asymmetry and radial relations that I describe here.

NOTES TO CHAPTER 1

1. British and Irish plays with stage Irish characters that proved popular in America include David Garrick's *The Irish Widow* (1772); Richard Brinsley Sheridan's *St. Patrick's Day, or The Scheming Lieutenant* (1775); William Macready's *The Irishman in London* (1792); John O'Keefe's *The Poor Soldier* (1783), *Love in a Camp, or Patrick in Prussia* (1791), and *The Irish Mimic* (1795); Alicia LeFanu's *Sons of Erin* (1812); Richard Butler's *The Irish Tutor* (1822); Samuel Lover's *Rory O'More* (1837); Tyrone Power's *St. Patrick's Eve, or The Order of the Day* (1837); and John Baldwin Buckstone's *The Irish Lion* (1838) (Bischoff 62; Murphy 22–3).
2. Boucicault's Irish plays prior to *The Shaughraun* include *The Colleen Bawn* (1860), *Arrah-na-Pogue* (1865), *The Rapparee* (1870), and *Daddy O'Dowd* (1873). Subsequent to *The Shaughraun* are two others, though neither would achieve the acclaim of his previous works: *The Amadan* (1883) and *Robert Emmet* (1884).
3. The Abbey would acquit him of this charge during their 1968 revival of the play, though a review of the time notes that Boucicault "has always been mistrusted" in Ireland (Wardle 54). The Abbey revived *The Shaughraun* again in 2004 as the centerpiece in their centenary celebration. It was directed by John McGolgan of *Riverdance* fame and proved largely successful, despite

some criticism. One critic argues that the play reinforces stereotypes rather than subverts them and suggests that "this glossy, *Riverdance*-inflected (lots of dancing) and unashamedly 'Oirish' production missed the point" (O'Brien 138).

4. Despite questioning his artistic talents, theater historians credit Boucicault with revolutionizing copyright law, formalizing theater insurance, improving the safety of set designs, standardizing the fireproofing of theaters, and introducing new payment contracts more favorable to writers and actors.

5. There is some disagreement on Boucicault's birth date, with some arguing that he was born in 1822. Richard Fawkes offers strong evidence for the earlier date (3–4).

6. Fawkes believes that Boucicault's application for citizenship was motivated partly out of a love for America, but also because it gave him certain business advantages. Boucicault would, of course, continue to travel internationally throughout his career, but always returned to New York. His final residence, with third wife Louise, was at 105 W. 55 Street in New York, and he is buried in the Mount Hope Cemetery in Hastings-on-the-Hudson in New York (Fawkes 238, 243).

7. This autobiographical fragment held at the Special Collections Department, University of South Florida Tampa Library presents itself as the reminiscences of Charles Lamb Kenney regarding his friend Dion Boucicault. However, the work is clearly by Boucicault himself and is in his handwriting (a fact verified by a notation from his wife L. Thorndyke/Boucicault-Cheney on the manuscript). Richard Fawkes has confirmed that Boucicault published under his friend's name after Kenney's death (222). This audacious and clever approach to autobiography predicts similar approaches taken by Henry Adams, Gertrude Stein, Sean O'Casey, and others in the following decades.

8. Synge saw key similarities between himself and Boucicault and thought that *The Shaughraun* realized the goals of the Celtic Revival (Harrington, "Rude" 92). Declan Kiberd suggests that early Irish-American audiences accepted the mask of the stage Irishman because they, at first, had no other "ready-made urban identity" (24).

9. Boucicault likely borrows from a long tradition of Molineux-like characters, that is, disoriented Englishman with presuppositions about Ireland who soon fall in love with a beautiful Irish girl. Lady Morgan's *The Wild Irish Girl* (1806) features a similar character.

10. All quotations from *The Shaughraun* reference *Selected Plays of Dion Boucicault* (1987).

11. Due to the audience's overwhelming approval of the Fenian themes of *The Shaughraun*, Boucicault was able to write a letter on their behalf to Benjamin Disraeli, the British Prime Minister, demanding the release of Fenian prisoners in England and Australia (Fawkes 196).

12. Krause is not the only one who believes there to be a relationship between Conn the Shaughraun and Huckleberry Finn. Hogan claims that Conn has "a very endearing Huckleberry Finn quality" (92).

13. The sequels to *The Mulligan Guard Ball*, all of which were extremely successful, are *The Mulligan Guard Chowder* (1879), *The Mulligan Guards' Christmas* (1879), *The Mulligan Guards' Surprise* (1880), *The Mulligan Guard Nominee* (1880), *The Mulligans' Silver Wedding* (1881), *Cordelia's Aspirations* (1883), and *Dan's Tribulations* (1884). Harrigan also revisited the characters in a later novel, *The Mulligans* (1901).

14. Harrigan also lived and worked for a time in San Francisco. William H. A. Williams suggests that San Francisco's cultural pluralism and lack of

ghettoization allowed Harrigan to develop a "satiric distance" and "sense of ethnic confidence" regarding the Irish (158).

15. For the purposes of this study, I refer to the text available in *Nineteenth Century American Musical Theater*, Volume 10, edited by Katherine K. Preston (1994). This is the longest and most complete version of the play available and comprises photographic reproductions of the original typescript and manuscript materials. There is a significantly shorter version of the play, with some substantial differences, available in Richard Moody's *Dramas from the American Theatre* (1966).

16. In his script, Harrigan did not write anything in Irish, but instead wrote it in English with a notation that it should be translated into Irish in performance. (This is a different approach than Boucicault, who usually wrote out Irish language passages phonetically in his scripts).

17. In fact, Dan runs for public office in one of the sequels to *The Mulligan Guard Ball*.

NOTES TO CHAPTER 2

1. A notable objection to Howe's remarks comes from Jonathan Arac, who writes, "If Huck is representative, it can't be in the sense of average or typical, or 'it was just like that.' If most Americans before the Civil War had felt about slavery the way Huck does about Jim, there would have been no war" (3).

2. See early critic Charles Miner Thompson, who lauds Huck's "essential honesty, his strong and struggling moral nature" as "so notably Anglo-Saxon" (446); or Leslie Fiedler, who despite having a famously unorthodox reading of the novel, still suggests that Huck's whiteness is counterpoint to Jim's blackness.

3. Christopher Gair believes that there is a black–white polarity in the novel, with Pap Finn being somehow "whiter-than-white" (188). Carl F. Wieck similarly describes Pap Finn as "negative white" (109).

4. See Shelley Fisher Fishkin's *Was Huck Black?* (1993).

5. In various other interviews and correspondence, Twain states that the real-life inspiration for Huck Finn was Tom Blankenship. At other times, he claims it was Bence Blankenship, Tom's older brother. It seems likely that Huck is a composite character. Nonetheless, it is noteworthy that, no matter who inspired Huck's antics, Twain saw fit to give him an Irish label.

6. However, Kemble's model for Huck Finn was an Irish-American boy named Cort Morris.

7. Twain ascribed to a complex understanding of heredity that J. Harold Smith calls "evolutionary determinism" (386). Unlike Frank Norris, who argues for biological roots to criminality, Twain believed that environmental factors played a large part in determining behavior.

8. It is Thomas Sergeant Perry who labels Pap a "worthless father" in the first major American review of Huck Finn (335). This sentiment has dominated thinking on the book, though more recent scholarship has suggested that Pap is not the demon he is often made out to be. See Scott Donaldson, "Pap Finn's Boy" (1971).

9. For an excellent interpretation of Pap's rant about the black man from Ohio and how it relates to his working class whiteness, see Eric Lott's *Love & Theft* (1993) (31–6).

10. For a consideration of "bad boys" in late nineteenth-century American fiction, including the works of Twain, see John Hinz, "Huck and Pluck" (1952).

11. For examinations of the end of Tom and Huck's friendship see Eric Sundquist's *To Wake the Nations* (1993) and Scott Donaldson's "Pap Finn's Boy" (1971).

12. It has been widely debated whether this titling discrepancy was accidental or intentional on Frederic's part. In an 1898 article in the *Utica Sunday Journal*, shortly after Frederic's death, Florence Hayward says she asked Frederic about the titles once, and whether he intended to convey that Illumination and Damnation "were one and the same" (1). Frederic told her no, that the mismatched titles were indeed a printing accident, and that Illumination was the title he had settled on in the end.

13. The series of stories includes "In the Shadow of Gabriel," "The Path of Murtogh," "The Truce of the Bishop," and "The Wooing of Teige." Frederic intended to write seven to eight stories in the series, but likely never completed this project (H. J. Smith 99).

14. See Carrie Tirado Bramen, "The Americanization of Theron Ware" (1997), as well as Robert M. Myers, "Antimodern Protest in *The Damnation of Theron Ware*" (1994).

15. A review printed on the front page of Frederic's hometown paper, *The Utica Observer*, on October 19, 1896, seems to recognize and acknowledge the difficult ending. The reviewer implies a wish for a sequel to Theron Ware that will clarify his redemption/salvation: "We surmise that we have not heard the last of Ware. He had a bad fall, but he was not of the kind of men who die of it."

16. In *The Descent of Love* (1996), Bert Bender argues that Frederic saw the Irish as having hereditary physical weakness that left them deteriorating in America. He points to Celia's sickly father and brothers as examples of how the author showed the Irish dying off in America. Frederic's interest in cultural intermingling can be seen, in part, as a way of strengthening the Irish stock. In Chapter 4, I consider the opposite belief—that Irish blood was needed to strengthen weakening Anglo-American bloodlines.

17. Christopher DenTandt explores the "naturalist appropriation of Darwinian discourse" in *McTeague* and further argues than the novel is a "genealogical narrative," but does not consider that McTeague's genealogy is specifically Irish (130–3). Similarly, William B. Dillingham unpacks the origins of Norris' racism and notes that a belief in "Anglo-Saxon superiority was an article of faith—even to uneducated Americans," yet he does not examine how McTeague's Irishness reinforces this prejudice (56). Other critics avoid issues of heredity all together. Richard Chase argues that McTeague is "an innocent animal-like man who falls victim to the corrupt ways of city life" (341). This misreading of the novel ignores completely that Norris specifically blames McTeague's bad blood for his evil deeds. It is difficult to imagine McTeague as an innocent corrupted by the city, when he is the source of corruption.

18. Modern historians agree that San Francisco was unusually receptive to the Irish: J. J. Lee looks at the economic and social opportunities for the Irish in the west and calls the San Francisco of this era "the polar opposite of Boston" (12); Timothy Meagher goes as far as to describe San Francisco as "one of the most hospitable places on earth" for the Irish (*Columbia* 85). San Francisco's reputation as an Irish city did not persist through the twentieth century. It peaked around the time of Éamon de Valera's visit to the city in 1919. According to Sarbaugh, after 1920, "the Irish of San Francisco were only religiously Irish, and today even this last vestige of their group identity appears to be vanishing" (174).

19. For a detailed account regarding the influence of the Collins murder on Norris, see Donald Pizer, "The Genesis of McTeague" (1997).

20. Charles W. Eliot, president of Harvard during Norris' time there, was a vocal critic of papal doctrine and Catholicism. Dennis P. Ryan documents the ways in which Harvard professors of this time distorted history and sociology classes with an anti-Irish slant (74–5).

21. Importantly, the Sieppes are an immigrant family as well and are of Swiss-German heritage. Norris plays on some Swiss-German stereotypes, mostly for comedic effect, but generally shows the family to be more successfully assimilated than most other ethnic groups in the novel, possibly because he saw their ancestry as more closely aligned with that of Anglo-Saxons.

22. For a study of this phenomenon, see Michael Neill's "Broken English and Broken Irish" (1994).

23. McTeague does not even understand that sex leads to children. When he and Trina receive a box of toys as a wedding gift, he has no comprehension of the implication (92). Later in the novel, when he does imagine becoming a father, his dream is described as only one of the "very vague, very confused ideas of something better" which he "for the most part borrowed from Trina" (109).

24. Several historians suggest that what some viewed in the late nineteenth century as an Irish resistance to family formation was actually a strategy for surviving economic hardship learned during the Famine years. Kevin Kenny observes that in the aftermath of the Great Famine "early marriage came to be regarded as reckless" and young men with no prospect for inheriting land had little incentive to marry since they could barely support themselves, let alone a wife and children (*American* 135). Initially, the early Famine immigrants to America returned to pre-Famine patterns and began marrying young and building families, but as economic conditions worsened near the end of the century, they readopted the old strategy of "increasingly delaying, then even avoiding, family formation" (Doyle 237). Kenny even suggests that the fraternizing among men and heavy drinking, which many thought was the cause of poor domestic structures among the Irish, was actually a coping mechanism for men with few prospects for marriage and a way to sublimate their sexual desires (136).

25. For more on Irish-American domesticity, see Patrick O'Sullivan (ed.), *Irish Women and Irish Migration* (1995), as well as Robert E. Kennedy, Jr., *The Irish: Emigration, Marriage, and Fertility* (1973), and for an excellent study of the link between immigration and sexuality, see Eithne Luibhéid, *Entry Denied* (2002).

26. For an analysis of the Biddy stereotype, see Margaret Lynch-Brennan's "Ubiquitous Bridget" (2006).

NOTES TO CHAPTER 3

1. Of course, these accusations were largely unfounded. The Irish-American community overwhelmingly rallied to America's cause on the declaration of war in 1917, and many served in the military. Shannon also points out that critics of Irish nationalism in America failed to recognize that Irish Americans saw their support for a free Ireland as the wishing of American ideals on Ireland, which they considered a demonstration of their commitment to the American national spirit (132).

2. Some critics even see proto-Sweeney figures in several other poems. J. C. C. Mays argues that the satyr figure hiding in the shrubbery of "Mr. Apollinax," the hippo of "Hippopotamus," and Bleistein in "Burbank with a Baedeker: Bleistein with a Cigar" are all proto-Sweeney figures (14). Kinley Roby

sees Sweeney-like figures in "Preludes" and "The Love Song of J. Alfred Prufrock" (5).

3. Jonathan Morse's "Sweeney, the Sties of the Irish, and *The Waste Land*" (1985) is the most notable exception.

4. I consider Eliot primarily in his American context, mostly because his formative encounters with Irishness occurred in the U.S. While Eliot's fascination with Anglo culture and identity (even prior to his 1927 conversion to Anglicanism and his becoming a British subject) certainly influenced his thinking on Irish issues, Sweeney is the product of an essentially American debate regarding Irish compatibility with American socio-cultural principles. An American context for the Sweeney material is also emphasized by John Perryman, who notes that Eliot started writing the Sweeney poems while rereading American literature in preparation for a series of lectures (251).

5. Eliot's notable ancestors and relations include (among many others) two U.S. presidents (John Adams and John Quincy Adams) and such literary icons as John Greenleaf Whittier, Noah Webster, Herman Melville, Louisa May Alcott, Henry Adams, and Nathaniel Hawthorne (Gordon 14–6).

6. Most notably, Christopher Ricks' *T.S. Eliot and Prejudice* (1988), Anthony Julius' *T.S. Eliot, Anti-Semitism, and Literary Form* (1995), and Donald J. Childs' *Modernism and Eugenics* (2001).

7. For a study of the possible connections between Eliot's character and Mad King Sweeney, see Herbert Knust's article "Sweeney Among the Birds and Brutes" (1985).

8. For a consideration of Joel Walker Sweeney's influence, see David E. Chinitz's *T.S. Eliot and the Cultural Divide* (2003) (105–6).

9. When Eliot met James Joyce for the first time, he found the Irishman "burdensome" and "arrogant" (J. Miller 341); however, he eventually came to believe they were kindred artists. There is nothing to suggest that Eliot held Joyce's Irish ethnicity against him, nor did he share Virginia Woolf's disdain for *Ulysses*, but there is some indication that Eliot may have been trying to separate Joyce from an Irish context in his mind. He met Joyce when they were both expatriates and may have seen Joyce's life in Paris as a rejection of Irishness. He once wrote that he found Joyce "more protestant than Catholic," and he oddly never mentions the Irish or Ireland in his critical writings on *Ulysses* (J. Miller 341).

10. Eliot's understanding of English identity has been questioned by scholars. Donald Davie says that Eliot "knew England and the English very imperfectly" and believed England was "to all intents and purposes London." Davie goes on to explain that, in Eliot's mind, the terms "English" and "British" had exactly the same meaning—a notion that marginalizes the Scots, Welsh, and Irish citizens of the United Kingdom (182).

11. Roby calls Sweeney a "pilgrim figure" and reads *Sweeney Agonistes* as the culmination of a spiritual journey in which the character struggles to explain what he has learned (13). Carol H. Smith similarly describes Sweeney as a "spiritual exile in an alien world" (73).

12. Sweeney attributes this story to a man he knew who used to come visit him and have a drink; however, many scholars read this, as I do, as a slightly veiled story of Sweeney's own actions.

13. Sears Jayne reads Sweeney as a "poet-philosopher" not unlike Eliot himself, who has experienced a glimpse of truth and is frustrated in his attempts to share that truth with others (112).

14. The original typescript carried the title *He Do the Police in Different Voices*. Valerie Eliot published the typescript in 1971 (complete with Eliot's and Ezra Pound's notations) in *The Waste Land: A Facsimile and Transcript*.

My references to the original opening of the poem are found on page 5 of this collection.

15. Which Cohan wrote in honor of Ned Harrigan.

16. Eliot and Fitzgerald only vaguely knew each other, but generally admired each other's work. Fitzgerald considered Eliot the "greatest living poet in any language" (*Letters* 199). Eliot, in turn, considered Fitzgerald's work the "first step forward in the American novel since Henry James" (*Letters* 237). Fitzgerald met Eliot in person in 1933 and described him as "very broken and sad & shrunk inside" (Meyers 226).

17. Fitzgerald was named after Francis Scott Key, the author of the National Anthem, who was a distant cousin.

18. Fitzgerald's paternal grandfather, Michael Fitzgerald, was also Irish, but virtually nothing is known about him. His paternal Irish ancestors seem not to have been Famine immigrants, and Fitzgerald did not consider the Fitzgeralds to have "the immediacy of the Irish connection" that his mother's family had (Rhodes 32).

19. All of the Fitzgerald biographies examine the relationship between Fitzgerald and Monsignor Fay, but for a specific consideration of the Catholic context of their relationship, see Joan M. Allen's *Candles and Carnival Lights* (1978).

20. In the same letter, Fitzgerald says that he is "nearly sure" he will follow in Fay's footsteps and join the priesthood; however, he would instead marry Zelda the next year.

21. The only individual that seemed capable of greatness was Amory's friend Dick Humbird, whose unexpected death in a car accident prior to the war only reinforces Amory's feelings that his generation's potential was undermined from the beginning. Humbird's ghost haunts Amory throughout the rest of the novel, constantly reminding him of what had been lost and what could have been; in effect, Amory is literally haunted by his generation's lost potential.

22. Amory never tries to use his paternal heritage in the same way. "Blaine" is a traditionally Scottish surname, but Amory shows no interest in his father, his paternal ancestors, or the other half of his ethnic heritage.

23. Several critics believe that Fitzgerald increasingly put aside his class prejudices and accepted his Irish identity in a way that Amory does not. Rhodes sees a progression in Fitzgerald's novels, which though still focusing on class issues, clearly position the Irish as victims of unscrupulous wealthy predators (45–6). Similarly, Shannon sees this Irish class sympathy in Fitzgerald's work as a major influence on his stories about "men of no social background" struggling with "women of high social status" (235).

24. This is a largely autobiographical element of *This Side of Paradise*. Shane Leslie believed that had Monsignor Fay lived, Fitzgerald would have tried harder to remain a Catholic himself (Allen 59).

25. When Fitzgerald read James Joyce's *Ulysses*, he found the descriptions of bourgeois Irish life uncomfortable and remarked that they made him feel "appallingly naked" and gave him a "hollow, cheerless pain" (Allen 22).

26. Irish songs from Tin Pan Alley included nationalist laments ("Remember the Boys of '98," "Savourneen Deelish"), love songs ("Bedelia," "My Irish Molly O"), and nostalgic odes to Ireland ("Remember Boy, You're Irish," "Mother Machree"). See William H. A. Williams' *'Twas Only an Irishman's Dream* (1996) for more on popular Irish-American songs from Tin Pan Alley.

27. Many of the Irish phrases have a conventional meaning of "alas," though I have offered more specific translations. Standard spellings of the Irish phrases in the poem: Ochone=Ochón; Awirra strhue=A Mhuire, is trua; Aveelia Vrone=A mhile bhrón; Mavrone go Gudyo=Mo bhrón go deo; A Vich Deelish=A mhic dhílis; Jia du Vaha Alanav=Dia do bheatha a leanbh; Och Ochone=Och Ochón.

28. This is reflective of Fitzgerald's attitude about his own military career. He was "one of the first officers discharged from his unit" and remarked that he seemed "unusually dispensable" (Meyers 47).

29. There is perhaps another level to Darcy's interest in Amory's biological inheritance. Fitzgerald makes a few insinuations that Darcy, who had an affair with Beatrice many years before, might actually be Amory's biological father. This might explain Darcy's belief that Amory is so much like him as to be almost a reincarnation.

30. *This Side of Paradise*'s Eleanor Savage seems a direct borrowing of *The Damnation of Theron Ware*'s Celia Madden. Eleanor's self-awareness, witty observations, and criticisms of the church are strikingly similar to Celia's.

NOTES TO CHAPTER 4

1. Farrell was the only one of his parents' children sent away to live with the grandparents. Robert K. Landers, Farrell's most recent biographer, disproves the long-held belief that it was a decision made because of the family's poverty, but does not offer a clear counter-explanation (11).

2. Farrell believed that Studs Cunningham saved his life when they were younger, and he was distraught on learning that Cunningham had died in 1929 (Landers 52). After the publication of *Studs Lonigan*, the Cunningham family was "quite sore" at what they perceived as Farrell's exploitation of their family's story for financial motive (Landers 163).

3. It is only on his deathbed that Studs relinquishes control of his imagination. In a fevered state, he cannot control his thoughts anymore, and thirty years of pent-up fantasies burst forth in one disturbing hallucination. All of the major figures in his life appear and reenact moments from his past in perverse and horrifying fashion (897–900).

4. Mr. Dooley was the fictional persona of Finley Peter Dunne, a syndicated writer based in Chicago.

5. Michaels points to Lothrop Stoddard as the definitive voice of Cultural Pluralism during this period. According to Stoddard, America needed to abandon "theoretical questions of 'superiority' or 'inferiority' . . . and get down to the bedrock of *difference*." Michaels believes that the substitution of culture for race, which on the surface seems to replace essentialist racial criteria with performative criteria, still presupposes essentialist group identities (*Our America* 14–5).

6. Though Scarlett is still Irish in the film, her ethnic characterization is significantly less important than in the novel. Many moments of ethnic significance were cut when adapting the novel into a screenplay, and much of Mitchell's sense of Irish-American identity does not come through in the finished film. Nonetheless, the movie studio played up actress Vivien Leigh's Irish heritage while marketing the film, which demonstrates a desire to establish the character as ethnically different even if that difference is not explored in detail (Quinlan 122).

7. Some critics have challenged Pyron's claims about the Irish in the South; however, Kieran Quinlan's *Strange Kin: Ireland and the American South* (2005) argues that Pyron's assertion is "in its broad outline" accurate (125). Quinlan's study, while showing the Irish experience in the South to be more complex and varied than usually assumed, also acknowledges that the Irish were not cultural insiders in Southern society and not at all "part of the story of the South" as it was traditionally conceived (3).

8. Mitchell mischaracterizes and idealizes Irish immigration in the early part of the century. A large number of the early nineteenth-century Irish immigrants would have been (according to modern ethnic categories) Scots-Irish Presbyterians and not Irish Catholics like Gerald O'Hara. In addition, these new arrivals generally were manual laborers who existed at the bottom of America's economic and social hierarchy. By 1860, only 84,000 Irish born immigrants lived in the South and they were, according to Dennis Clark, "alienated from the small plantation stratum" (qtd. in McGraw 126). For a detailed analysis of pre-Famine Irish in America, see David Noel Doyle's "The Irish in North America, 1776–1845" (2006).

9. Gerald was not alone in conflating the Civil War with Ireland's struggle against British oppression. In an 1882 interview in New Orleans, Oscar Wilde proclaimed, "The case of the South in the civil war was to my mind much like that of Ireland today" (qtd. in Quinlan). Kieran Quinlan observes that "numerous defeated peoples" including the Irish have identified with the American South (2).

10. Snay also notes that there were many who disagreed with the analogy between the South's struggles and Ireland's troubles. He quotes Michael Scanlon from Chicago's *Irish Republic*: "Let us hear no more of Ireland and the South. The South drew the sword for the maintenance of the vilest kind of slavery; Ireland draws the sword for Liberty" (14).

11. Her first name comes from Gerald's mother's people—the Scarletts—who fought alongside the O'Haras.

12. Mitchell's papers and letters reveal that she had great admiration for the novels of Thomas Dixon, including *The Leopard's Spots* (1902) and the other books in his Ku Klux Klan trilogy, which were the basis of *Birth of a Nation*. She corresponded with Dixon and expressed her appreciation for his work, and in turn, he had planned to write a book-length study of *Gone With the Wind* before his death (Burks 55).

13. In the twentieth century, some Irish Americans began to identify with Aryan organizations and confusingly tried to express white supremacy through a combination of Irish national and Ulster loyalist symbolism. This more modern and "contradictory" Irish "ideology of whiteness" is explored in Natasha Casey's "'The Best Kept Secret in Retail': Selling Irishness in Contemporary America" (2006).

Bibliography

Aesop. "The Donkey and the Pet Dog." Trans. Laura Gibbs. *Aesopica: Aesop's Fables in English, Latin & Greek.* Oxford UP, 2002. Web. 12 December 2007. <http://www.mythfolklore.net/aesopica/oxford/338.htm>

Alba, Richard D. *Ethnic Identity: The Transformation of White America.* New Haven: Yale UP, 1990.

Allen, Joan M. *Candles and Carnival Lights: The Catholic Sensibility of F. Scott Fitzgerald.* New York: New York UP, 1978.

Almeida, Linda Dowling. "Irish America 1940–2000." *Making the Irish American: History and Heritage of the Irish in the United States.* Ed. J. J. Lee and Marion R. Casey. New York: New York UP, 2006. 548–73.

"Amusements." *New York Times* 31 March 1860: 5.

"Amusements." *New York Times* 7 April 1860: 5.

"Amusements." *New York Times* 15 November 1874: 7.

"Amusements." *New York Times* 16 November 1874: 5.

Anderson, Benedict. *Imagined Communities.* London: Verso, 2003.

Arac, Jonathan. *Huckleberry Finn as Idol and Target.* Madison: U of Wisconsin P, 1997.

Atkins, Anselm. "Mr. Eliot's Sunday Morning Parody." *Critical Essays on T.S. Eliot: The Sweeney Motif.* Ed. Kinley E. Roby. Boston: G.K. Hall & Co., 1985. 31–3.

Barth, Frederik. *Ethnic Groups and Boundaries: The Social Organization of Culture Difference.* Long Grove: Waveland, 1998.

Bender, Bert. *The Descent of Love: Darwin and the Theory of Sexual Selection in American Fiction, 1871–9126.* Philadelphia: U of Pennsylvania P, 1996.

Bennett, Bridget. *The Damnation of Harold Frederic: His Lives and Works.* Syracuse, NY: Syracuse UP, 1997. 174–97.

Beye, Charles Rowan. "Gone With the Wind and Good Riddance." *Southwest Review* 78.3 (1993): 366–80.

Bhabha, Homi. *The Location of Culture.* London: Routledge, 2006.

Bischoff, Peter, and Peter Noçon. "The Image of the Irish in Nineteenth-Century American Popular Culture." *Literary Interrelations: England, Ireland, and the World, Vol. 3: National Images and Stereotypes.* Ed. Wolfgang Zach and Heinz Kosok. Tübingen, Narr, 1987. 61–75.

Blum, Edward J. *Reforging the White Republic: Race, Religion, and American Nationalism, 1865–1898.* Baton Rouge: Louisiana State UP, 2005.

Booth, Michael R. "Irish Landscape in the Victorian Theatre." *Place, Personality, and the Irish Writer.* Ed. Andrew Carpenter and Lorna Reynolds. New York: Barnes & Noble, 1977. 159–72.

Boucicault, Dion. "A Bit of Autobiography of Dion Boucicault in His Own Hand-writing." Special Collections Department, University of South Florida Tampa Library.

———. "Leaves From a Dramatist's Diary." *North American Review* 149 (1889): 228–36.

———. *Selected Plays of Dion Boucicault*. Washington, DC: Catholic U of America P, 1987.

Bower, Stephanie. "Dangerous Liaisons: Prostitution, Disease, and Race in Frank Norris's Fiction." *Modern Fiction Studies* 42.1 (1996): 31–60.

Brace, Charles Loring. *The Dangerous Classes of New York, & Twenty Years' Work Among Them*. Washington: National Association of Social Workers, 1973.

Brackenridge, Hugh Henry. *Modern Chivalry*. Lanham: Rowman & Littlefield, 2003.

Bramen, Carrie Tirado. "The Americanization of Theron Ware." *Novel: A Forum on Fiction* 31.1. (1997): 63–86.

Branch, Edgar M. "Destiny, Culture, and Technique." *University of Kansas City Review* 29 (1962): 103–13.

———. *Studs Lonigan's Neighborhood and the Making of James T. Farrell*. Newton: Arts End Books, 1996.

Burks, Ruth Elizabeth. "*Gone With the Wind*: Black and White in Technicolor." *Quarterly Review of Film and Video* 21 (2004): 53–73.

Camfield, Gregg. *The Oxford Companion to Mark Twain*. Oxford: Oxford UP, 2003.

Cantrell, James P. "Irish Culture and the War Between the States: Paddy McGann and Gone With the Wind." *Eire-Ireland* 27.2 (1992): 7–15.

Cardon, Lauren S. "'Good Breeding': Margaret Mitchell's Multi-Ethnic South." *Southern Quarterly* 44.4 (2007): 61–82.

Carino, Peter. "Chicago in *Studs Lonigan*." *Midamerica* 15 (1988): 72–83.

Casey, Daniel J., and Robert E. Rhodes. "The Tradition of Irish-American Writers: The Twentieth Century." *Making the Irish American: History and Heritage of the Irish in the United States*. Ed. J. J. Lee and Marion R. Casey. New York: New York UP, 2006. 649–61.

Casey, Natasha. "'The Best Kept Secret in Retail': Selling Irishness in Contemporary America." *The Irish in US*. Ed. Diane Negra. Durham, NC: Duke UP, 2006. 84–109.

Cave, Richard Allen. "The Presentation of English and Irish Characters in Boucicault's Irish Melodramas." *Literary Interrelations: Ireland, England, and the World, Vol. 3*. Ed. Wolfgang Zach. Tübingen: Narr, 1987. 115–23.

———. "Staging the Irishman." *Acts of Supremacy: The British Empire and the Stage 1790–1930*. Ed. Jacqueline S. Bratton. Manchester: Manchester UP, 1991. 62–128.

Chase, Richard. "*McTeague*." *McTeague: An Authoritative Text Backgrounds and Sources Criticism*. Ed. Donald Pizer. New York: W.W. Norton & Co., 1977. 341–4.

Childs, Donald J. *Modernism and Eugenics*. Cambridge: Cambridge UP, 2001.

Chinitz, David E. *T.S. Eliot and the Cultural Divide*. Chicago: U of Chicago P, 2003.

Coghill, Nevill. "Sweeney Agonistes (An Anecdote or Two)." *Critical Essays on T.S. Eliot: The Sweeney Motif*. Ed. Kinley E. Roby. Boston: G.K. Hall & Co., 1985. 115–9.

"Collins Arrested." *Evening Bulletin* [San Francisco] 10 October 1893: 4.

Colwell, James L. "Huckleberries and Humans: On the Naming of Huckleberry Finn." *PMLA* 86.1 (1971): 70–6.

Conners, Margaret E. "Historical and Fictional Stereotypes of the Irish." *Irish American Fiction: Essays in Criticism.* Ed. Daniel J. Casey and Robert E. Rhodes. New York: AMS, 1979.

Crawford, Robert. *The Savage and the City in the Work of T.S. Eliot.* Oxford: Clarendon Press, 1987.

"Criticising *The Shaughraun.*" *New York Times* 4 May 1884: 5.

Curtis, L. Perry, Jr. *Anglo-Saxons and Celts: A Study of Anti-Irish Prejudice in Victorian England.* Bridgeport: U of Bridgeport, 1968.

Dalton, Van Broadus, D.D.S. *The Genesis of Dental Education in the United States.* Cincinnati: Spahr & Glenn, 1946.

David, Beverly R. "The Pictorial Huck Finn: Mark Twain and His Illustrator, E.W. Kemble." *American Quarterly* 26.4 (1974): 331–51.

Davie, Donald. "Anglican Eliot." *Eliot in His Time.* Ed. A. Walton Litz. Princeton, NJ: Princeton UP, 1973. 181–96.

Dawson, Hugh J. "The Ethnicity of Huck Finn—and the Difference It Makes." *American Literary Realism* 30.2 (1998): 1–16.

———. "McTeague as Ethnic Stereotype." *American Literary Realism* 20 (1987): 34–44.

DenTandt, Christopher. *The Urban Sublime in American Literary Naturalism.* Chicago: U of Illinois P, 1998.

Dickens, Charles. *American Notes.* 1842. *Project Gutenberg.* 2006. Web. 6 June 2008. <http://www.gutenberg.org/etext/675>

Dillingham, Thomas F. "Origen and Sweeney: The Problem of Christianity For T.S. Eliot." *Christianity and Literature* 30.4 (1981): 37–51.

Dillingham, William B. *Frank Norris: Instinct and Art.* Lincoln: U of Nebraska P, 1969.

Donaldson, Scott. "Pap Finn's Boy." *South Atlantic Bulletin* 36.3 (1971): 32–7.

Dormon, James H. "Ethnic Cultures of the Mind: The Harrigan-Hart Mosaic." *American Studies* 33.2 (1992): 21–40.

Douglas, Ann. "Studs Lonigan and the Failure of History in Mass Society: A Study in Claustrophobia." *American Quarterly* 29.5 (1977): 487–505.

Doyle, David Noel. "The Irish in North America, 1776–1845." *Making the Irish American: History and Heritage of the Irish in the United States.* Ed. J. J. Lee and Marion R. Casey. New York: New York UP, 2006. 171–212.

———. "The Remaking of Irish America, 1845–1880." *Making the Irish American: History and Heritage of the Irish in the United States.* Ed. J. J. Lee and Marion R. Casey. New York: New York UP, 2006. 213–52.

Duggan, G. C. *The Stage Irishman: A History of the Irish Play and Stage Characters From the Earliest Times.* New York: Benjamin Blom, 1969.

Eagan, Catherine M. "Still 'Black' and 'Proud': Irish American and the Racial Politics of Hibernophilia." *The Irish in US.* Ed. Diane Negra. Durham, NC: Duke UP, 2006. 20–63.

Ebest, Ron. *Private Histories: The Writing of Irish Americans, 1900–1935.* Notre Dame, IN: U of Notre Dame P, 2005.

Eby, Clare. "Of Gold Molars and Golden Girls: Fitzgerald's Reading of Norris." *American Literary Realism* 35.2 (2003): 130–58.

Eliot, T. S. *After Strange Gods: A Primer of Modern Heresy.* New York: Harcourt Brace, 1934.

———. "Introduction to *Adventures of Huckleberry Finn.*" *Adventures of Huckleberry Finn.* 3rd ed. Ed. Thomas Cooley. New York: W.W. Norton, 1999. 348–54.

———. *Letters of T.S. Eliot, Vol. 1: 1898–1922.* Ed. Valerie Eliot. San Diego: Harcourt Brace, 1988.

———. "Sweeney Agonistes: Fragments of an Aristophanic Melodrama." *Collected Poems 1909–1935.* New York: Harcourt Brace, 1952. 74–85.

———. "Ulysses, Order, and Myth." *The Dial* 75.5 (1923): 480–3.

———. *The Waste Land: A Facsimile and Transcript of the Original Drafts Including the Annotations of Ezra Pound.* Ed. Valerie Eliot. New York: Harvest, 1971.

———. *The Waste Land and Other Poems.* Ed. Frank Kermode. New York: Penguin, 1998.

Ellison, Ralph. "What America Would Be Like Without Blacks." *Time* 6 April 1970: n.p. Web. 16 September 2008. < http://www.time.com>

Fanning, Charles. *The Irish Voice in America: 250 Years of Irish-American Fiction.* 2nd ed. Lexington: UP of Kentucky, 2000.

Farrell, James T. *Reflections at Fifty.* New York: Vanguard, 1954.

———. *Studs Lonigan: A Trilogy.* Ed. Pete Hamill. New York: Library of America, 2004.

Fawkes, Richard. *Dion Boucicault: A Biography.* London: Quartet, 1979.

Ferraro, Thomas J. "Of 'Lascivious Mysticism' and Other Hibernian Matters." *U.S. Catholic Historian* 23 (2005): 1–17.

Fetterley, Judith. "The Sanctioned Rebel." *The Adventures of Tom Sawyer.* Ed. Beverly Lyon Clark. New York: W.W. Norton, 2007. 279–90.

Fiedler, Leslie. "Come Back to the Raft Ag'in, Huck Honey." *Leslie Fiedler and American Culture.* Ed. Steven G. Kellman and Irving Malin. Newark: U of Delaware P, 1999. 26–34.

Fishkin, Shelley Fisher. *Was Huck Black? Mark Twain and African-American Voices.* New York: Oxford UP, 1993.

Fitzgerald, F. Scott. *In His Own Time: A Miscellany.* Ed. Matthew J. Bruccoli and Jackson R. Bryer. Kent: Kent State UP, 1971.

———. *Letters of F. Scott Fitzgerald.* Ed. Andrew Turnbull. New York: Scribner, 1963.

———. *This Side of Paradise.* New York: Scribner, 2003.

Frederic, Harold. *The Damnation of Theron Ware.* Amherst: Prometheus, 1997.

Funchion, Michael F. *Chicago's Irish Nationalists 1881–1890.* New York: Arno, 1976.

Gair, Christopher. "Whitewashed Exteriors: Mark Twain's Imitation Whites." *Journal of American Studies* 39.2 (2005): 187–205.

Garner, Stanton. "Some Notes on Harold Frederic in Ireland." *American Literature* 39.1 (1967): 60–74.

Gellner, Ernest. *Nations and Nationalism.* Ithaca, NY: Cornell UP, 1983.

Gordon, Lyndall. *T.S. Eliot: An Imperfect Life.* New York: Norton, 2000.

Gordon, Milton M. *Assimilation in American Life: The Role of Race, Religion, and Natural Origins.* New York: Oxford UP, 1964.

Grant, Madison. *The Passing of the Great Race or The Racial Basis of European History.* New York: Scribners, 1918.

Graves, R. B. "The Stage Irishman Among the Irish." *Theatre History Studies* 1 (1981): 29–38.

Grene, Nicholas. *The Politics of Irish Drama.* Cambridge: Cambridge UP, 1999.

Hallissy, Margaret. *Reading Irish-American Fiction: The Hyphenated Self.* New York: Palgrave, 2006.

Harrigan, Edward. "Holding the Mirror Up to Nature." *Pearson's Magazine* 10 (November 1903): 499–506.

———. "The Mulligan Guard Ball." In *Nineteenth Century American Musical Theater, Vol. 10: Irish American Theater.* Ed. Katherine K. Preston. New York: Garland, 1994.

Harrington, John P. *The Irish Play on the New York Stage, 1874–1966.* Lexington: UP of Kentucky, 1997.

——— (ed.). *Irish Theater in America: Essays on Irish Theatrical Diaspora.* Syracuse, NY: Syracuse UP, 2009.

———. "'Rude Involvement': Boucicault, Dramatic Tradition, and Contemporary Politics." *Eire-Ireland* 30.2 (1995): 89–103.

Hayward, Florence. "Harold Frederic." *Utica Sunday Journal* 20 November 1898: 1.

"He Was Born For the Rope." *Examiner* [San Francisco] 14 October 1893: 8. Rpt. in *McTeague: Authoritative Text Contexts Criticism.* 2nd ed. Ed. Donald Pizer. New York: W.W. Norton, 1997. 253–7.

Hinz, John. "Huck and Pluck: 'Bad' Boys in American Fiction." *South Atlantic Quarterly* 51 (1952): 120–9.

Hobsbawm, Eric and Terence Ranger (ed.). *The Invention of Tradition.* Cambridge: Cambridge UP, 2006.

Hochman, Barbara. *The Art of Frank Norris, Storyteller.* Columbia: U of Missouri P, 1988.

Hogan, Robert. *Dion Boucicault.* New York: Twayne, 1969.

Horner, Harlan Hoyt. *Dental Education Today.* Chicago: U of Chicago P, 1947.

Howard, June. *Form and History in American Literary Naturalism.* Chapel Hill: U of North Carolina P, 1985.

Howe, Lawrence. "Will Huck Now Be Sold Down the Mississippi?" *New York Times* 25 July 1992: 20.

Howells, William Dean. "Editor's Study." *Harper's Monthly* July 1886: 315–7.

———. "Editor's Study." *Harper's Monthly* July 1889: 314–9.

———. "My Favorite Novelist and His Best Book." *Munsey's Magazine* 17 (1897): 28. Rpt. in *William Dean Howells as Critic.* Ed. Edwin H. Cady. London: Routledge, 1973. 268–80.

———. "Review." *Adventures of Tom Sawyer.* ed. Beverly Lyon Clark. New York: W.W. Norton, 2007. 265–6.

Howland, Bette. "James T. Farrell's Studs Lonigan." *Literary Review* 27 (1983): 22–5.

Ignatiev, Noel. *How the Irish Became White.* New York: Routledge, 1995.

"Ireland As It Is." *New York Times* 12 June 1886: 8.

James, Henry. *The American Scene.* New York: Penguin, 1994.

———. "Some Notes on the Theatre." *The American Theatre as Seen by its Critics 1752–1934.* Ed. Montrose J. Moses and John Mason Brown. New York: Norton, 1967. 122–6.

James, Pearl. "History and Masculinity in F. Scott Fitzgerald's *This Side of Paradise.*" *Modern Fiction Studies* 51.1 (2005): 1–33.

Jayne, Sears. "Mr. Eliot's Agon." *Critical Essays on T.S. Eliot: The Sweeney Motif.* Ed. Kinley E. Roby. Boston: G.K. Hall & Co., 1985. 100–15.

Joyce, James. *A Portrait of the Artist as a Young Man.* New York: Signet, 1991.

Julius, Anthony. *T.S. Eliot, Anti-Semitism, and Literary Form.* Cambridge: Cambridge UP, 1995.

Kahn, E.J., Jr. *The Merry Partners: The Age and Stage of Harrigan and Hart.* New York: Random House, 1955.

Kennedy, Robert E. Jr. *The Irish: Emigration, Marriage, and Fertility.* Berkeley: U of California P, 1973.

Kenny, Kevin. *The American Irish: A History.* Harlow: Longman, 2000.

———. "American-Irish Nationalism." *Making the Irish American: History and Heritage of the Irish in the United States.* Ed. J. J. Lee and Marion R. Casey. New York: New York UP, 2006. 289–301.

———. "Race, Violence, and Anti-Irish Sentiment in the Nineteenth Century." *Making the Irish American: History and Heritage of the Irish in the United States.* Ed. J. J. Lee and Marion R. Casey. New York: New York UP, 2006. 364–78.

Kiberd, Declan. *The Irish Writer and the World*. Cambridge: Cambridge UP, 2005.

Knobel, Dale T. "A Vocabulary of Ethnic Perception: Content Analysis of the American Stage Irishman, 1820–1860." *Journal of American Studies* 15.1 (1981): 45–71.

Knust, Herbert. "Sweeney Among the Birds and Brutes." *Critical Essays on T.S. Eliot: The Sweeney Motif.* Ed. Kinley E. Roby. Boston: G.K. Hall & Co., 1985. 196–209.

Kosok, Heinz. "Dion Boucicault's 'American' Plays: Considerations on Defining National Literatures in English." *Literature and the Art of Creation*. Ed. Robert Welch. Totowa: Barnes & Noble, 1988. 81–97.

Krause, David. *The Profane Book of Irish Comedy*. Ithaca, NY: Cornell UP, 1982.

Lacker, Lionel. "Redemption and *The Damnation of Theron Ware*." *South Atlantic Review* 55.1 (1990): 81–91.

Lakoff, George. *Women, Fire, and Dangerous Things: What Categories Reveal About the Mind*. Chicago: U of Chicago P, 1987.

Landers, Robert K. *An Honest Writer: The Life and Times of James T. Farrell*. San Francisco: Encounter, 2004.

Lee, J. J. "Introduction: Interpreting Irish America." *Making the Irish American: History and Heritage of the Irish in the United States*. Ed. J. J. Lee and Marion R. Casey. New York: New York UP, 2006. 1–60.

Leerssen, Joep. *Mere Irish and Fíor-Ghael*. Notre Dame, IN: U of Notre Dame P, 1997.

Leslie, Shane. "This Side of Paradise." *Dublin Review* 167 (1920): 286–93.

Lott, Eric. *Love & Theft: Blackface, Minstrelsy, and the American Working Class*. New York: Oxford UP, 1993.

Luibhéid, Eithne. *Entry Denied: Controlling Sexuality at the Border*. Minneapolis: U of Minnesota P, 2002.

Lynch-Brennan, Margaret. "Ubiquitous Bridget: Irish Immigrant Women in Domestic Service." *Making the Irish American: History and Heritage of the Irish in the United States*. Ed. J. J. Lee and Marion R. Casey. New York: New York UP, 2006. 332–53.

Maguire, John Francis. *Irish in America*. New York: D. & J. Sadlier, 1868.

Matthews, Brander. "Review: *Adventures of Huckleberry Finn*." *Adventures of Huckleberry Finn*. 3rd ed. Ed. Thomas Cooley. New York: W.W. Norton, 1999. 330–3.

Mays, J. C. C. "Early poems: from 'Prufrock' to 'Gerontion.'" *The Cambridge Companion to T.S. Eliot*. Ed. A. David Moody. Cambridge: Cambridge UP, 1994: 108–20.

McCaffrey, Lawrence J. "The Irish-American Dimension." *The Irish in Chicago*. Ed. Lawrence J. McCaffrey. Urbana: U of Illinois P, 1987.

McConachie, Bruce A. *Melodramatic Formations: American Theatre and Society, 1820–1870*. Iowa City: U of Iowa P, 1992.

McElrath, Joseph R. Jr. and Jesse S. Crisler. *Frank Norris: A Life*. Urbana: U of Chicago P, 2006.

McFeely, Deirdre. "Between Two Worlds: Boucicault's *The Shaughraun* and Its New York Audience." *Irish Theater in America: Essays on Irish Theatrical Diaspora*. Ed. John P. Harrington. Syracuse, NY: Syracuse UP, 2009. 54–65.

McGraw, Eliza Russi Lowen. "A 'Southern Belle with Her Irish Up': Scarlett O'Hara and Ethnic Identity." *South Atlantic Review* 65.1 (2000): 123–31.

Meagher, Timothy. *The Columbia Guide to Irish American History*. New York: Columbia UP, 2005.

———. "The Fireman on the Stairs: Communal Loyalties in the Making of Irish America." *Making the Irish American: History and Heritage of the Irish in the*

United States. Ed. J. J. Lee and Marion R. Casey. New York: New York UP, 2006. 609–48.

———. *Inventing Irish-America: Generation, Class, and Ethnic Identity in a New England City, 1880–1928*. Notre Dame, IN: U of Notre Dame P, 2002.

Meer, Sarah. "Dion Boucicault, the 'Political Shaughraun': Transatlantic Irishness and an International Theatre." *Symbiosis* 10.2 (2006): 147–66.

Melville, Herman. *The Encantadas and Other Stories*. Mineola: Dover, 2005.

Mensh, Elaine and Harry Mensh. *Black, White, and Huckleberry Finn*. Tuscaloosa: U of Alabama P, 2000.

Meyers, Jeffrey. *Scott Fitzgerald*. New York: Harper Collins, 1994.

Michaels, Walter Benn. *The Gold Standard and the Logic of Naturalism*. Berkeley: U of California P, 1987.

———. *Our America: Nativism, Modernism, and Pluralism*. Durham, NC: Duke UP, 2002.

Miller, James Edwin. *T.S. Eliot: The Making of an American Poet, 1888–1922*. University Park: Pennsylvania State UP, 2005.

Miller, Kerby A. *Emigrants and Exiles: Ireland and the Irish Exodus to North America*. New York: Oxford UP, 1985.

Mitchell, Margaret. *Gone With the Wind*. New York: Warner Books, 1993.

Moloney, Mick. "Harrigan, Hart, and Braham: Irish America and the Birth of the American Musical." *Irish Theater In American: Essays on Irish Theatrical Diaspora*. Ed. John P. Harrington. Syracuse, NY: Syracuse UP, 2009. 1–18.

Moody, Richard. *Dramas from the American Theatre 1762–1909*. New York: Houghton Mifflin, 1966.

———. *Ned Harrigan: From Corlear's Hook to Herald Square*. Chicago: Nelson-Hall, 1980.

Morrison, Toni. *Playing in the Dark*. New York: Vintage, 1992.

Morse, Jonathan. "Sweeney, the Sties of the Irish, and *The Waste Land*." *Critical Essays on T.S. Eliot: The Sweeney Motif*. Ed. Kinley E. Roby. Boston: G.K. Hall & Co., 1985. 135–46.

"The Mulligan Guards Again." *New York Times* 29 November 1892: 4.

Murphy, Maureen. "From Scapegrace to Grásta: Popular Attitudes and Stereotypes in Irish American Drama." *Irish Theater In American: Essays on Irish Theatrical Diaspora*. Ed. John P. Harrington. Syracuse, NY: Syracuse UP, 2009. 19–37.

Myers, Robert M. "Antimodern Protest in *The Damnation of Theron Ware*." *American Literary Realism* 26.3 (1994): 52–64.

Negra, Diane. "The Irish in Us: Irishness, Performativity, and Popular Culture." *The Irish in US*. Ed. Diane Negra. Durham, NC: Duke UP, 2006. 1–19.

Neill, Michael. "Broken English and Broken Irish: Nation, Language, and the Optic of Power in Shakespeare's Histories." *Shakespeare Quarterly* 45 (1994): 1–32.

Norris, Frank. *McTeague: Authoritative Text Contexts Criticism*. 2nd ed. Ed. Donald Pizer. New York: W.W. Norton, 1997.

———. *Responsibilities of the Novelist*. New York: Doubleday, 1903.

O'Brien, Diarmuid. "Flight of the Centenary: Irish Theater in 2004." *New Hibernian Review* 9.3 (2005): 137–43.

O'Connor, Thomas H. *The Boston Irish: A Political History*. Boston: Northeastern UP, 1995.

O'Grady, Joseph P. *How the Irish Became Americans*. New York: Twayne, 1973.

O'Sullivan, Patrick (ed.). *Irish Women and Irish Immigration*. London: Leicester UP, 1995.

Onkey, Lauren. "James Farrell's *Studs Lonigan* Trilogy and the Anxieties of Race." *Éire-Ireland* 40 (2005): 104–18.

———. "'A Melee and a Curtain': Black-Irish Relations in Ned Harrigan's *The Mulligan Guard Ball.*" *Jouvert* 4.1 (2000): n.p. Web. 4 December 2009. <http://social.chass.ncsu.edu/ jouvert/v4i1/con41.htm>

Orel, Gwen. "Reporting the Stage Irishman: Dion Boucicault in the Irish Press." *Irish Theater in America: Essays on Irish Theatrical Diaspora.* Ed. John P. Harrington. Syracuse, NY: Syracuse UP, 2009. 66–77.

Ostendorf, Berndt. *Black Literature in White America.* Sussex: Harvester, 1982.

Ower, John. "Pattern and Value in 'Sweeney Among the Nightingales'." *Critical Essays on T.S. Eliot: The Sweeney Motif.* Ed. Kinley E. Roby. Boston: G.K. Hall & Co., 1985. 67–75.

"Perfect Brute, A." *Morning Call* [San Francisco] 12 October 1893: 4.

Perry, Thomas Sergeant. "The First Major American Review." *Adventures of Huckleberry Finn.* 3rd ed. Ed. Thomas Cooley. New York: W.W. Norton, 1999. 334–6.

Perryman, John. "Back to The Bay Psalm Book: T.S. Eliot's Identity Crisis and 'Sweeney Erect.'" Midwest Quarterly 47 (2006): 244–61.

Piacentino, Edward J. "The Significance of Pap's Drunken Diatribe Against the Government in Huckleberry Finn." *Mark Twain Journal* 19.4 (1979): 19–21.

Pizer, Donald. "The Biological Determinism of McTeague in Our Time." *American Literary Realism* 29.2 (1997): 27–32.

———. "The Genesis of *McTeague.*" *McTeague: Authoritative Text Contexts Criticism.* 2nd ed. Ed. Donald Pizer. New York: W.W. Norton, 1997. 288–97.

———. *The Novels of Frank Norris.* New York: Haskell House, 1973.

Podhoretz, Norman. "The Literary Adventures of Huck Finn." *New York Times.* 6 December 1959: BR5+.

Potter, George. *To the Golden Door: The Story of the Irish in Ireland and America.* Westport, CT: Greenwood, 1960.

Pula, Cheryl A. "A Capital Road from Cork to Utica." *Ethnic Utica.* Ed. James S. Pula. Utica, NY: Ethnic Heritage Studies Center at Utica College, 2002.

Pyron, Darden Asbury. *Southern Daughter: The Life of Margaret Mitchell.* New York: Oxford UP, 1991.

Quinlan, Kieran. *Strange Kin: Ireland and the American South.* Baton Rouge: Louisiana State UP, 2005.

Raubicheck, Walter. "The Catholic Romanticism of *This Side of Paradise.*" *F. Scott Fitzgerald in the Twenty-first Century.* Ed. Jackson R. Bryer, Ruth Prigozy, and Milton R. Stern. Tuscaloosa: U of Alabama P, 2003. 54–65.

Rhodes, Robert E. "F. Scott Fitzgerald: 'All My Fathers'." *Irish-American Fiction: Essays in Criticism.* Ed. Daniel J. Casey and Robert E. Rhodes. New York: AMS, 1979. 29–51.

Ricks, Christopher. *T.S. Eliot and Prejudice.* Berkeley: U of California P, 1988.

Riis, Jacob A. *How the Other Half Lives.* New York: Penguin, 1997.

Roby, Kinley E. "Introduction." *Critical Essays on T.S. Eliot: The Sweeney Motif.* Ed. Kinley E. Roby. Boston: G.K. Hall & Co., 1985. 1–29.

Roediger, David R. *The Wages of Whiteness: Race and the Making of the American Working Class.* London: Verso, 2003.

Ryan, Dennis P. *Beyond the Ballot Box: A Social History of the Boston Irish, 1845–1917.* Rutherford, NJ: Fairleigh Dickinson UP, 1983.

Said, Edward. *Orientalism.* New York: Pantheon: 1978.

Salpeter, Harry. "'The Next Fifteen Years Will Show How Much Resistance There is in the American Race'." *F. Scott Fitzgerald In His Own Time: A Miscellany.* Ed. Matthew J. Bruccoli and Jackson R. Bryer. Kent: Kent State UP, 1971. 274–7.

Sarbaugh, Timothy. "Exiles of Confidence: The Irish American Community of San Francisco, 1880–1920." *From Paddy to Studs: Irish-American Communities in the Turn of the Century Era, 1880–1920.* Ed. Timothy J. Meagher. New York: Greenwood, 1986. 161–79.

"Serious British Topics." *New York Times* 7 January 1882: 2.

Shannon, William V. *The American Irish.* New York: Macmillan, 1964.

Shaughnessy, Edward L. "Oliver Alden and Studs Lonigan: Heirs to Spiritual Poverty." *Marham Review* 4 (1974): 48–52.

"The Shaughraun." *New York Herald* 7 March 1875: 5.

Shiffman, Daniel. "Ethnic Competitors in *Studs Lonigan.*" *MELUS* 24.3 (1999): 67–79.

Smith, Carol H. "An Alliance of Levity and Seriousness." *T.S. Eliot: Plays.* Ed. Arnold P. Hinchliffe. Houndmills: Macmillan, 1985. 73–6.

Smith, Henry Nash. *Virgin Land: The American West as Symbol and Myth.* Cambridge, MA: Harvard UP, 1970.

Smith, Herbert J. "Harold Frederic and the Irish." *Mid-Hudson Language Studies* 4 (1981): 95–118.

Smith, J. Harold. "The Expressed Opinions of Mark Twain on Heredity and Environment." Diss. U of Wisconsin, 1955.

Snay, Mitchell. *Fenians, Freedmen, and Southern Whites: Race and Nationality in the Era of Reconstruction.* Baton Rouge: Louisiana State UP, 2007.

Sollors, Werner. *Beyond Ethnicity: Consent and Descent in American Culture.* New York: Oxford UP, 1986.

———. "Invention of Ethnicity." *The Invention of Ethnicity.* Ed. Werner Sollors. New York: Oxford UP, 1989. ix–xx.

Sundquist, Eric. *To Wake the Nations: Race in the Making of American Literature.* Cambridge, MA: Harvard UP, 1993.

"Surly and Insulting." *Examiner* [San Francisco] 11 October 1893: 4.

Thompson, Charles Miner. "Mark Twain as an Interpreter of American Character." *Atlantic Monthly* 79.474 (1897): 443–50.

Turner, Frederick Jackson. *The Significance of the Frontier in American History.* March of America Facsimile Series Number 100. Ann Arbor: U of Michigan Microfilms, 1966.

Twain, Mark. *Adventures of Huckleberry Finn.* 3rd ed. Ed. Thomas Cooley. New York: W.W. Norton, 1999.

———. *Adventures of Tom Sawyer.* New York: W.W. Norton, 2006.

———. *Huck Finn and Tom Sawyer Among the Indians and Other Unfinished Stories.* Berkeley: U of California P, 1989.

———. *Tom Sawyer Abroad.* New York: Golden, 1967.

Utica Observer 19 October, 1896: 1.

Wardle, Irving. "London Applauds Victorian Play." *New York Times* 22 May 1968: 54.

Waters, Maureen. *The Comic Irishman.* Albany: State U of New York P, 1984.

Watkins, Floyd C. "Gone With the Wind as Vulgar Literature." *Gone With the Wind as Book and Film.* Ed. Richard Harwell. Columbia: U of South Carolina P, 1983. 198–210.

Wharton, Edith. *The Age of Innocence.* New York: Collier, 1993.

Wieck, Carl F. *Refiguring Huckleberry Finn.* Athens: U of Georgia P, 2000.

Williams, William H.A. *'Twas Only an Irishman's Dream: The Image of Ireland and the Irish in American Popular Song Lyrics, 1800–1920.* Urbana: U of Illinois P, 1996.

Wonham, Henry B. *Playing the Races: Ethnic Caricature and American Literary Realism.* New York: Oxford UP, 2004.

Wray, Matt. *Not Quite White: White Trash and the Boundaries of Whiteness.* Durham, NC: Duke UP, 2006.

Index